CULTURE, MODERNITY AND REVOLUTION

'It is ironic that at the moment that the post-communist East looks to the West for the model of modernization it is at last free to follow, the West displays the uncertainties of postmodernity. Zygmunt Bauman has long commented on West and East with an independence of mind that has won rare respect. It is thus fitting that Kilminster and Varcoe should have secured essays which really do honour him by addressing so perceptively life in our time.'

Chris Bryant, *University of Salford*

'Varcoe and Kilminster have put together an important set of essays on the central concerns of one of Europe's major social theorists, and have sandwiched these essays together between a very useful introduction and conclusion. Sociologists familiar with the work of Zygmunt Bauman will find much of value here and will feel that this collection does justice to the life's work of an important sociologist.'

Stephen K. Sanderson,
Indiana University of Pennsylvania

Culture, Modernity and Revolution is a remarkable sociological commentary on the problems facing East-Central Europe and, at the same time, an exposition of some of the key, hitherto neglected, features of the modern cultural universe.

The book has a unity of purpose: to honour Zygmunt Bauman. In no sense is it a development of Bauman's ideas by followers. Its editors retain a critical distance and seek to present the man and his ideas to a wide audience.

Contributors: Tom Bottomore, Lewis A. Coser, S. N. Eisenstadt, Agnes Heller, Krishan Kumar, Edmund Mokrzycki, Gianfranco Poggi and Jerzy J. Wiatr.

Richard Kilminster and **Ian Varcoe** are Lecturers in Sociology at the University of Leeds.

Zygmunt Bauman by Peter Hamilton, the Open University

CULTURE, MODERNITY AND REVOLUTION

Essays in Honour of Zygmunt Bauman

Edited by
*Richard Kilminster and
Ian Varcoe*

London and New York

First published 1996
by Routledge
11 New Fetter Lane, London EC4P 4EE

Simultaneously published in the USA and Canada
by Routledge
29 West 35th Street, New York, NY 10001

© 1996 Richard Kilminster and Ian Varcoe, selection and editorial
matter; individual chapters, the contributors.

Phototypeset in Times by Intype, London
Printed and bound in Great Britain by
Mackays of Chatham PLC, Chatham, Kent

British Library Cataloguing in Publication Data
A catalogue record for this book is available from the British Library

Library of Congress Cataloguing in Publication Data
A catalogue record for this book has been requested

ISBN 0–415–08266–8

CONTENTS

CONTENTS

NOTES ON CONTRIBUTORS

Tom Bottomore (1920–1992) Formerly Professor Emeritus of Sociology, University of Sussex; previously Lecturer/Reader in Sociology, London School of Economics, 1952–64, and Professor and Head of Department of Political Science, Sociology and Anthropology at the Simon Fraser University in Vancouver, 1965–7. President of the British Sociological Association, 1969–71, and President of the International Sociological Association, 1974–8. Author of numerous books, the most recent being: *The Socialist Economy: Theory and Practice*, 1990; *Classes in Modern Society*, second edition, 1991; *Between Marginalism and Marxism: The Economic Sociology of J. A. Schumpeter*, 1992; *Political Sociology*, second edition, 1992; *The Blackwell Dictionary of Twentieth-Century Social Thought* (ed. with William Outhwaite), 1993; *Élites and Society*, second edition, Routledge, 1993.

Lewis A. Coser Distinguished Professor Emeritus of Sociology at the State University of New York at Stony Brook and Adjunct Professor of Sociology at Boston College. He is a former President of the American Sociological Association and of the Eastern Sociological Society. Among his books are: *The Functions of Social Conflict*, 1956; *Masters of Sociological Thought*, second edition, 1977; *Sociological Theory: A Book of Readings* (ed. with Bernard Rosenberg), fifth edition, 1982; *Men of Ideas*, 1965; *Books: The Culture and Commerce of Publishing*, 1985 (with W. W. Powell and Charles Kadushin); and *Refugee Scholars in America*, 1984.

S. N. Eisenstadt Rose Isaacs Professor of Sociology at The Hebrew University, Jerusalem. Visiting Professor at numerous universities, including Chicago, Harvard, Zurich, Stanford, LSE, Manchester, Vienna and Alberta. Former President of the Israeli Sociological Association and recipient of several international social science prizes and awards, including the Balzan Prize in 1988. More recent books are *European Civilization in a Comparative Perspective*, 1987; *Japanese Models of Conflict Resolution* (ed. with E. Ben-Ari), 1990; *Jewish Civilization: The Jewish Historical Experience in a Comparative Perspective*, 1992; and *Martin Buber on Intersubjectivity and Cultural Creativity* (ed.), 1992.

Agnes Heller Hannah Arendt Professor of Philosophy, Graduate Faculty, New School for Social Research, New York. Formerly Reader in Sociology at La Trobe University, Melbourne. A doctoral student of Georg Lukács and assistant professor in his department in Budapest. Left Hungary for Australia in 1977. Member, editorial boards of *Praxis International, Aut Aut* (Milan), *Social Praxis* and *New German Critique*. Awarded Lessing Prize of the Free and Hanseatic City of Hamburg, 1981. Author of many books in a number of languages, including *The Theory of Needs in Marx*, 1976; *A Theory of Feelings*, 1979; *A Theory of History*, 1982; *Radical Philosophy*, 1984; *Everyday Life*, 1984; *Dictatorship Over Needs* (with F. Féher and G. Markus), 1983; *Hungary 1956 Revisited* (with F. Féher), 1983; *Reconstructing Aesthetics* (ed. with F. Féher), 1986; and *Can Modernity Survive?*, 1990.

Richard Kilminster Lecturer in Sociology, University of Leeds. Author of *Praxis and Method*, 1979; *The Sociology Spiral* (forthcoming, Routledge, 1996) and numerous articles on sociological theory, the sociology of knowledge and Norbert Elias. Member, Editorial Board of *Sociology*, 1985–8; Co-Convenor of the Sociological Theory Group of the British Sociological Association from 1983 to 1991. Associate Editor, *Theory, Culture & Society*; Corresponding Editor for the UK of 'Figurations', twice-yearly Newsletter of the Norbert Elias Foundation, Amsterdam.

Krishan Kumar Professor of Social and Political Thought, University of Kent at Canterbury. He has also been a BBC Talks Producer, a Visiting Fellow at Harvard University and a Visiting Professor of Sociology at the University of Colorado at Boulder. Among his writings are *Prophecy and Progress: The Sociology of*

Industrial and Post-Industrial Society, 1978; *Utopia and Anti-Utopia in Modern Times*, 1987; *The Rise of Modern Society*, 1988; and *Utopianism*, 1991.

Edmund Mokrzycki Professor of Sociology and Chair of the Theoretical Sociology Unit at the Polish Academy of Sciences. His other current affiliations include the Central European University and the College of Europe. His latest books are: *Sociology in Philosophical Context* (in Polish, 1990); *Modes of Thought and Rationality* (ed. in Polish, 1992); *The New Great Transformation?* (ed. with Christopher Bryant, Routledge, 1994); and *Democracy in Context* (ed. with Christopher Bryant, forthcoming). His main research interests include theoretical sociology and the theory of post-communist societies.

Gianfranco Poggi William Kenan Jr Professor of Sociology, University of Virginia, Charlottesville. Previous to moving there in 1986 he was Professor of Sociology at the University of Edinburgh. He writes on the history of social theory (*Images of Society: Essays on the Sociological Theories of Tocqueville, Marx and Durkheim*, 1972; *Calvinism and the Capitalist Spirit: Max Weber's Protestant Ethic*, 1983; *Money and the Modern Mind: Georg Simmel's Philosophy of Money*, 1993) and on the sociology and history of political institutions (*The Development of the Modern State: A Sociological Perspective*, 1976; *The State: Its Nature, Development and Prospects*, 1990).

Ian Varcoe Lecturer in Sociology, University of Leeds. Author of *Organizing for Science in Britain: A Case Study*, 1974, and (ed. with Maureen McNeil and Steven Yearley) *Deciphering Science and Technology: The Social Relations of Expertise*, 1990, and *The New Reproductive Technologies*, 1990, as well as articles on the history and social organization of science and technology. In addition to the sociology of science, he has research interests in sociological theory and comparative and historical sociology. He is a member of the Max Weber Study Group of the British Sociological Association.

Jerzy J. Wiatr Professor of Political Sociology in the Department of Sociology, University of Warsaw. He has served as President of the Polish Association of Political Sciences (1964–7 and 1976–9);

Vice-President of the International Political Science Association (1979–82); and Vice-President of the International Studies Association (1980–1). Member of the Editorial Board of the *International Political Science Review*. In his political career he has been a member of the national leadership of the Social Democracy of the Republic of Poland and (since 1991) a Member of Parliament. His most recent books include: *The Soldier and the Nation: The Role of the Military in Polish Politics, 1918–1985*, 1988, and *Four Essays on East European Democratic Transformation*, 1992.

ACKNOWLEDGEMENTS

We would like to thank Zygmunt Bauman for the part he has played in the genesis of this book. He kindly gave us a lengthy autobiographical interview in August 1990 (a shortened version of which appears as an Appendix to his book *Intimations of Postmodernity*, London: Routledge, 1992). In consultation with him we deliberately planned for a relatively small number of contributors. We wanted in-depth essays around a few themes, rather than a large number of small pieces, which would have made the contents of the volume rather disparate and hence less academically useful.

We owe a debt to the contributors, whom we thank for responding with goodwill and enthusiasm to our initial invitation and for dealing patiently with our editorial suggestions.

We also wish to thank the following people, each of whom helped in the conception or production of this book in different ways: Janina Bauman, Roy Boyne, Christopher Bryant, Anne Gee, Anthony Giddens, Anthea Kilminster, William Outhwaite, Chris Rojek, Ann Varcoe, Dennis Warwick, Julia Wassall, Terry Wassall and Victor Zaslavsky. We also benefited from the efficiency of both the Brotherton Library and Computer Services at Leeds. Finally, our thanks are due to the staff and students of the School of Sociology and Social Policy for their encouragement and support.

R.K. and I.V.
Leeds 1995

INTRODUCTION: INTELLECTUAL MIGRATION AND SOCIOLOGICAL INSIGHT

Richard Kilminster and Ian Varcoe

In honouring Zygmunt Bauman, who occupied the Chair of Sociology at the University of Leeds from 1971 to 1990 and whose seventieth birthday falls this year, this volume departs from the customary format of the *Festschrift*. It contains no lengthy homages to, or extensive personal recollections about, the man it honours. Despite his undoubted gifts and scholarly achievements, Zygmunt Bauman is a modest man with a low public profile and a book of that kind would have been an anathema to him. Neither are the contributions collected here those of pupils working within a particular paradigm founded by him. Although, as we show in the Addendum, there are thematic continuities in Bauman's writings, he is nevertheless not a system-builder and has never made any pretence at founding a school of sociology, as such.

For these reasons, we felt that the most appropriate way to honour him was via a working volume of studies by some of his friends, colleagues and admirers in areas to which he has devoted most of his own scholarly effort. The contributors were invited to write exploratory pieces in the fields of culture, the sociology of intellectuals, industrial society, socialism and socialist societies, the fate of modernity and revolutionary transformation. Together, the essays collected here discuss some of the fundamental features of modernity and the most bewildering changes and pressing problems of our time, appropriately, in view of Bauman's biography, from both Western and Eastern European viewpoints.

1

Bauman has experienced fascism, lived under communism and settled, after his expulsion from Poland in 1968, in capitalist Britain, the home of classical liberalism. He has, however, remained true to the calling of the independent intellectual. He has used the resources of sociological culture and the Western intellectual inheritance generally, to maintain a critical distance from all these systems. It is his ambivalent position and the richness of his experiences which are the source of his analytical edge and sociological insight.

In his period at Leeds, Bauman had a remarkable talent for creating a lively intellectual environment for imaginative research and bold discussion, particularly in the burgeoning graduate school. For him, the importance of sociology partly lay in its role as a form of active self-reflection on social life. He stimulated research on cultural themes as well as projects on the borderlines of sociology with social philosophy and the history of ideas and never recoiled from posing fundamental questions, even if they were uncomfortable. The Department acquired the justified reputation for being strong in what subsequently came to be called 'theory', although arguably we were only asking the same kinds of questions that sociologists have been asking for two centuries.

When Bauman arrived in Leeds in 1971 from Warsaw via Israel to take up the first Chair of Sociology, following the departure of the demographer Professor Eugene Grebenik, British sociology was deep in its conflict phase (Kilminster 1992). The 'orthodox consensus' (Giddens) consisting of the Anglo-American tradition of the structural-functionalism of Talcott Parsons and Robert K. Merton, which was committed to promoting sociology as a science, testing theories and building up empirical findings, was under fire. This was a highly politicized period, both inside and outside of sociology. Rival paradigm-communities, schools and factions (such as ethnomethodology, Althusserian Marxism, critical theory, structuralism, feminism, phenomenology, 'theorizing', existential sociology) competed fiercely to be heard in the sociological marketplace. The process whereby political and ideological conflict in the wider society expresses itself in complex ways inside sociology is a topic worthy of further investigation (Elias 1987: 224ff). One may also speculate that the competition between paradigm-communities at this time had something to do with the particular institutional situation of sociology in Britain.

Recently there had taken place a major, unprecedented expan-

2

sion of British higher education, following the Robbins Report (Halsey et al. 1961; Banks 1968: ch. 2; Edwards 1982). In the 1960s sociology benefited from this expansion. For the first time it entered the university in Britain as a significant discipline, on a par with the established ones. Sociologists were recruited in the newly founded universities in particular. (In Oxford and Cambridge sociologists, although still recruited, did not have the same scope to create 'single honours' degrees in sociology.) In the redbrick universities sociology was fitted more or less successfully into the structure of the already existing traditional disciplines, as a subject in its own right. But the overall expansion of sociology was phenomenal. According to data cited by Abrams (1981: 62), in the 1960s twenty-eight new university departments and thirty new chairs of sociology were established (with a parallel expansion in the former polytechnics and colleges of education). There was a 450 per cent increase in the output of sociology graduates between 1952 and 1966 (ibid.).

In these settings, 'the new sociologists', Abrams maintains, 'were to a quite remarkable degree left free to define sociology in any way they chose' (ibid.). But in this unusual context they also faced a comparatively novel problem: they had to explain to themselves and others what this burgeoning discipline was. The paramount way to do this seemed to be to deal with its epistemological foundations. (Writing histories of the discipline or exegetical works on classical sociologists also served a similar purpose.) This epistemological task had in any case become a pressing one with the simultaneous collapse of logical empiricism, both as a philosophy of science and in its application to the social sciences by philosophers such as Ernest Nagel.

In Britain, Marxism proved exceptionally vibrant and fashionable in the 1970s, partly because of the British cultural obsession with social class. But it was also because Marxists were able to present their paradigm as a serious contender for the social-scientific crown in the new situation of open theoretical competition. This had been created by, on the one hand, the exceptionally favourable institutional setting (an expanding discipline, popular with students, fashionable in a variety of cultural-intellectual circles) and, on the other, a pervasive uncertainty as to what this new 'science of society' (Marxism or something else) actually was.

Bauman came into the tail-end of the expansion. He was able

3

to benefit from the posts that his new department obtained and the large number of postgraduate research awards available. Without a professor of sociology it is doubtful whether sociology could have become established in Leeds. But such a national rate of growth could not be sustained and, as everyone knows, the expansion halted and times became very hard in the universities. By the early 1980s, intense competition had set in among the university disciplines to pass shrinkage and retrenchment on to 'someone else'. These conflicts were frequently fought out using arguments about what were 'core' university subjects and peripheral ones. Sometimes sociology lost out, as in the case of the University of Birmingham. Later, in the social sciences, in the 1980s, the criterion of disciplinary worth was to become policy-relevance, i.e. the marketability of research results.

On the purely intellectual front, by the early 1970s the older functionalist paradigm continued, but was beleaguered during the 'war of the schools', in Bryant's (1990) phrase. As part of this search for alternatives to the orthodox consensus, many manifestos appeared announcing sundry 'new directions' for the reorientation of sociology (e.g. Filmer et al. 1972; Pelz 1974; Thorns 1976). And for many sociologists, their searches and questionings took them into the arcane and very un-British works of European philosophers such as Hegel, Heidegger, Husserl, Merleau-Ponty, Nietzsche, Adorno, Lukács, Sartre and many more, without whose works no budding theoretical sociologist's bookshelf was complete. Doubts were expressed about previously hallowed principles regarding knowledge, truth and the basics of social science, and relativism became the order of the day. Debates were often heated and frequently expressed in highly charged, polarized either/or alternatives: positivism versus hermeneutics; humanist versus structuralist Marxism; ethnomethodology versus orthodox sociology; and feminist theory versus malestream sociology. The controversy of Marxism versus sociology was particularly prominent.

Responding to this situation, Bauman wrote a good deal in the 1970s in the areas of phenomenology, Marxist theory, structuralism, hermeneutics and ethnomethodology. Although he was *au fait* with Parsonian thinking and American political science, Bauman was from outside the Anglo-American tradition as such. He brought with him a refreshing agenda of issues, partly arising from the influence of his teachers, Julian Hochfeld and Stanisław

Ossowski, and partly posed by humanistic Marxists in the context of the Polish socialist experiment (Bauman 1972b; Kilminster and Varcoe 1992). Although he was, and to some extent has remained, an outsider to the British sociology establishment, he was a good deal better read in European philosophy and Western Marxism than many of them.

The result was that he had a breadth of vision and a perspective on the fashionable paradigms that few could match. For example, he lampooned the ethnomethodologists for their philosophical illiteracy and told them that for all their anti-positivism, their programme had essentially reproduced it (Bauman 1973b). He also saw very early on that the critique of positivistic scientism, so dominant at the time in just about all of the schools, was in danger of careering over into the 'distrust of all reason' which undermined its very existence (Bauman 1972b: 202–3). Bauman was an intriguing figure with obvious socialist sympathies and a radical sociological mission. The students were drawn to him. They would quote with delight a line from David Bowie's album *The Rise and Fall of Ziggy Stardust and the Spiders from Mars*, which was popular at the time: '[Ziggy] played it left hand ... became the special man, then we were Ziggy's band.'

THE REFUGEE SCHOLAR

More broadly, the reception of Bauman in British sociology is a case study which tells us a great deal about the effects of intellectual migration and the receptivity or not of British culture to such imports. Bauman is one in a long line of refugee intellectuals who have shaped, or tried to shape, British culture (Anderson 1968; Bailyn and Fleming 1969; Hughes 1975; Hirschfeld 1984; Hoch 1985). Bauman's style is very un-British – very 'continental', in fact. He prefers a high level of generality, is highly reflective and, for the most part, deploys empirical data only selectively and suggestively. He is relatively uninterested in methodology, or purely conceptual discussions or other technical matters of sociological investigation for their own sake. There are no lengthy preliminaries in his work on the basic definitions or conditions of the inquiry, which must be settled before we can begin. He is more interested in society than in the squabbles between different theorists of society. His work is problem-orientated and diagnostic rather than purely academic or professional in the narrower sense.

The cast of Bauman's work as a whole thus contrasts with that of one particularly dominant strand of the British tradition, namely Fabian, policy-orientated, ameliorative social science. To this, and other somewhat less influential strands, Bauman and other exiled sociologists who preceded him such as Karl Mannheim, Adolphe Löwe, Norbert Elias, Ilya Neustadt, Gi Baldamus and others have, in their very different ways, added broader concerns. They stimulated the courage to theorize about society as a whole in a culture which is dominated in large part by empiricism and pragmatism. They also encouraged putting the profounder questions of truth and morality more directly than they were on to the sociological agenda. And to undertake empirical research shaped by *sociological* as distinct from social-administrative concerns. These concerns were shaped by traumatic events and political oppression, of a kind which British sociologists have not experienced so intensely as have the citizens of some other European societies. As Bauman declared:

So I have seen morally inspired, noble and lofty ideals smashed to pieces by the merciless logic of the reality their bearers failed to assess. I was with those who took ... it upon themselves to re-define the world they lived in, to fill the world with a new, better, more human meaning, to deny its repulsive reality in the name of the untrammelled human potential. I was with them still when they saw their ambition shattered against the wall of the same stubborn reality they refused to admit, and the same moral squalor sprouting again from below the thin film of ideals. And then, fortunately, I saw the same, always young and vigorous, indomitable spirit of exploration and perfection rising again to challenge the ungratifying reality. There seemed, indeed, to be no end to the drama in which the meaning and the reality, the subjective and the objective, the free and the determined, merge continuously to mould our present into our future.

(1972b: 186)

The Polish experience up until 1968, when he was expelled along with several other prominent university teachers, led Bauman to a particular view of the nature and role of sociology in society and the function of intellectuals. For him, sociology was the product of the realization of the discrepancy between people's intended actions and the consequences of their actions, which then rebound upon their intentions. He described this duality in terms of various discrepancies: between 'Is' and 'Ought'; 'intractable human reality' and 'goal-oriented reason'; and the 'already-accomplished' reality and 'potential ... hankered after worlds' (1972b: 187; 1973a: 176–7). Sociology was therefore inherently ambiguous, having two inseparable faces: one descriptive and implicitly legitimatory, drawing on knowledge of the solidified, repetitive social reality; and the other restless and implicitly critical, questioning the established reality by relativizing it.

Bauman is interested in both sides: that is, in developing models of the way in which societies reproduce themselves; and in how visions of new worlds and new meanings develop out of the structuring capacity of human beings. These imaginary visions are then somehow to be ploughed into the accomplished social reality, thus shaping and reshaping it, as Gramsci, the intellectual love of Bauman's life, taught (Kilminster and Varcoe 1992: 206). This is why Bauman has always been interested in culture and why he was absorbed for some time in structuralism (ibid.: 211). (We discuss the main continuities in Bauman's ideas in the Addendum to this volume.)

But in his more programmatic statements (Bauman 1972b; 1973a: 157–78) he built up the maverick strand into an entire style of sociology, which pitted itself against established institutions, bureaucracies and their associated ideas and values, in the name of human potentials and possible futures. This would serve as bulwark against rulers and bureaucrats declaring that a particular social system was the best of all possible worlds, as he had seen in Poland. This side of his work could be termed a sociological version of 'negative dialectics'. Bauman has on his office wall one of Picasso's lithographs of Don Quixote tilting at windmills, which clearly symbolized one of his major identifications.

This view of the role of sociology fitted well into the structure of the former state socialist societies of Eastern Europe such as Poland. There, the all-pervasive communist state was more affected than the state in the West by expressions of intellectual dissent which challenged its legitimacy. The 'critical' kind of sociology probably presented itself as a model because social criticism does appear to have had a palpable effect, the state, owing to the suppression of civil society, being the automatic addressee of criticism. Furthermore, as Lewis A. Coser argues in his chapter

7

in this volume, in Eastern Europe intellectuals (whether sociologists or not) have always generally tended to have a high status, providing spiritual leadership and social criticism for the nation as a whole. (However, this may be changing: see the chapter by Edmund Mokrzycki.)

BRITISH SOCIOLOGY: HOW RECEPTIVE?

The question arises: is British soil a particularly fertile one for sociology in either the politically charged critical mode, or the mode granting comparatively free rein to the reasoning mind and to high-level social diagnosis, to which Bauman is particularly attached? And which has tended to be very closely linked to the kind of broad-ranging and imaginative sociological research carried out by the best continental, European sociologists, including the émigrés. For a short while in the more politicized late 1960s and early 1970s, it might have seemed that it was a fertile soil for sociology in the 'critical mode', as sociologists became enamoured of variants of this view in the work of the Frankfurt School, in particular. At that time, it did still seem to some people as if socialism, in some form, as carried by the labour movement, in particular, was an imminent prospect. And for this, many Marxists believed, it was essential to have a suitably flexible and humanistic theoretical instrument. Old-style Soviet Marxism, which was associated with Stalinism, certainly would not do. In the short term, a critical theory with teeth would serve to attack what was widely seen as the main obstacle: bourgeois ideology.

These hopes faded in the 1980s, as market-enhancing policies swept the board, together with broader changes in the structure of national and global economies. There is not much evidence that this kind of approach to sociology has many followers today. Nor is there much evidence that sociology in the classical continental mode, posing important questions (of the bases of order and change) in the context of a tradition of empirical research, has fared as well in Britain (notable exceptions aside) as it has elsewhere. This is partly because the political climate has changed dramatically, but there is also perhaps a deeper reason.

In the long run, perhaps the inertia of the British social development tends to foster the tradition of social policy-orientated social research to a greater degree than it does other strands, so that tradition reasserts itself. The current trend towards policy-relevant social research is partly explicable by sociologists responding to the demands of their paymasters, but it is arguably also simply British sociology reverting to type: a particular indigenous profile of concerns and research interests. As Geoffrey Hawthorn (1976) has pointed out, the nineteenth-century sociologists in the British tradition, unlike their German and French counterparts, were never preoccupied with the problem of defining society in relation to the state. Much continental sociology, on the other hand, in the classic age of the discipline, was born out of social crisis. In Britain, at this stage, its well-developed, long-established political institutions and relatively coherent social structure meant, among other things, that 'the force of society was so pervasive that it went largely unremarked' (ibid.: 112).

For many of the social scientists of the British tradition it seemed self-evident that it was just a question of gathering factual knowledge of the social conditions of underprivileged groups so as to aid improving those conditions through political institutions, which were taken for granted. Their origins, nature and potential fragility were never questioned. Nor was the moral value of social improvement or amelioration of the worst manifestations of inequality. Nor, because of widely shared assumptions about what useful information was, was the possibility of producing valid knowledge.

The larger questions – what is society? how does it hold together? how can we see through political ideologies? what should be our commitments, national allegiance and moral choices? how should the state and state action be understood? – were not posed in such a way that sociological categories required to be developed in order to answer them. Karl Mannheim perceived at first hand the peculiarity of British society and its consequences for intellectual life during his second experience of exile in London during the 1930s and 1940s. As he put it in a letter to Louis Wirth in 1936: 'The great security which reigns in this land has not revealed the problem of the sociological backgrounds of consciousness to even the clearest heads of the intelligentsia living here' (quoted in Woldring 1986: 404).

In other countries of Europe, with well-developed sociological traditions, particularly those from which the earlier migrant intellectuals came, it was a very different story and one repeated in many of its essentials later in the case of Poland and Bauman and his colleagues. In these countries one could not take democratic institutions entirely at face value nor take the integrity of the national social reality fully for granted, nor assume that objective truth in the social sphere was a relatively unproblematic matter. The British tradition, on the other hand, has been developed on the implicit acceptance, firstly, of the existence of responsive, established state institutions serving as a conduit for reform, and does not question their authority or legitimacy, as such; and, secondly, of a thoroughly industrialized, commercial society, managing to include all its members around a core of similar economic activities, which does not ask what a national community is.

Britain, in the formative years of social science (and more recently still), was a long-unified, long-established, stable nation-state which provided a considerable measure of security and self-evident predictability in social life. In this context, given the comparative responsiveness of the state, the 'critical', relativizing kind of sociology, pitted against domination and bureaucracy, will seem, to all but a few, incomprehensible and even irrational. For some people in the British reality neither will the theoretically self-conscious sociology in the classical manner, which is also so much part of Bauman's style, seem to be pointing sociology in a particularly fruitful direction, for the reasons we have outlined. Of course, the general question of intellectual migration will continue to be a fascinating research topic.

But, the particular case is what must concern us here. One can no longer talk about Britain as a separate, isolated society. Increasingly, our place in a global system is impinging more and more on our daily lives, producing unexpected and bewildering changes. These are the sort of fundamental changes discussed in this volume under the headings of culture and revolution, arguably comparable in scale to the previously mentioned upheavals in some European societies which fostered classical sociology. In this new situation, Bauman's reflective, diagnostic kind of sociology is able to pose the questions that people are having to ask themselves today, and for sociologists this is a matter of opening up new scenarios, suggesting analyses, posing new problems and proposing new research agendas.

MODERN CULTURE – EUROPEAN SOCIETIES

Common to the four chapters grouped together in Part I (those by Eisenstadt, Poggi, Varcoe and Heller) is their authors' conviction that the onset of modernity ushered in a historically unique form of society, which is crystallized in the diversity of modern culture. Modernity is inherently dynamic, enabling the human control of nature, the active transformation of social life and the peaceful management of conflicting interests via democratic politics. Modern Western political discourse assumes as a matter of course that tensions such as that between majoritarian decisions and the basic rights of minorities will be worked out in the political-constitutional arena. The phenomenal potential of modernity for the realization of human possibilities far exceeds that of any preceding civilization, but carries with it various challenges and dangers. In its own way, each chapter in Part I explicitly or implicitly acknowledges that paradox and warns of various negative consequences, be they intense social alienation dividing people from each other; a loss of the capacity of people to orientate themselves according to values; the erosion of politics by the spread of technocratic scientism; totalitarian potentialities; or nihilism and moral relativism.

S. N. Eisenstadt's chapter is a synoptic and metatheoretical exploration of the political dimension of modern culture, mapping out the cultural co-ordinates of modern political regimes, which he calls 'constitutional-democratic' regimes. These include the liberal capitalist, fascist, communist and post-communist variants. He delineates the political tensions that arise within them, which are played out in various ways in the constitutional arena. For him, the innovation of modernity was that the gap between the ideal and the real could now potentially be closed in practical politics. The potential mastery of both the natural world and the social destiny of humankind became basic premises of a new culture, the historically fragile 'cultural programme of modernity', which then became institutionalized in modern societies.

For Eisenstadt, events of political life and the chances of social stability in whatever modern regime are the result of the constant playing out of a series of tension-balances inherent in that cultural-political programme, in which all modern peoples ultimately participate. These include the antinomies of equality versus freedom, solidarity versus personal identity, good social order versus

11

narrow interests, community versus individual autonomy and the utopian versus procedural components of political life. All these antinomies presuppose the state/civil society relation. In the case of the former communist regimes, their downfall was partly attributable to this relationship becoming heavily unbalanced towards the state, at the expense of the development of civil society.

Gianfranco Poggi expounds three themes from Georg Simmel's *Philosophy of Money* and uses these as a vehicle for exploring the sociological problem of obtaining a nuanced understanding of the pluses and minuses of modernity. Poggi suggests that Simmel realized clearly that the social condition of modernity allowed the expression and cultivation of human potentialities which were repressed in pre-modern societies. For Simmel, it is the advanced money economy that largely shapes modern society, which is also prone to alienation. Money firstly intellectualizes social existence, shifting people's orientation towards *means*, in longer and longer means/goals chains characteristic of the colossal complex of the modern money economy. Secondly, it reinforces a quantitative orientation, inducing a proneness to calculation. And thirdly, the acceleration of the tempo of social life in modernity is connected with the capacity of money to transfer values because of its symbolic character, thereby assisting the speed and variety of exchanges.

Poggi draws out of Simmel his warning that whilst money increases personal freedom, it can also create an 'inner barrier between people' (quoted by Poggi, p. 55), brought about by the contrasting interests that develop between people involved in monetary transactions for goods and services. It can also contribute to the growth of materialistic attitudes and a consequent inability of people to attune themselves to transcendental beliefs and values. Money leads to the loss of the capacity for the discriminating appreciation of values and imparts more and more a sense of abstractness, artificiality and even unreality to modern life.

Ian Varcoe's chapter is an extensive exploration of the nature and consequences of technocratic thinking, which he distinguishes from other social outlooks by its intense commitment to means–ends rationality. He sees it as a permanent feature of modern societies. He insists that science and technology have to be understood as intertwined with structures of power, the centre–

periphery relationship between nations or between groups or regions within nations being particularly important. This affects the ways in which technocratic solutions are canvassed, diffused and received. In left- or right-wing variants, they have been increasingly invoked and can be seen as an expression of the failure of liberal political solutions to the economic, political and cultural crises of the twentieth century. The technocratic legitimation of politics carries, however, the danger of destroying true politics by reducing political problems to matters of the technical manipulation of resources.

Varcoe suggests that the technocratic/anti-technocratic controversies of modern times reflect the differing ways in which science and technology have developed institutionally and are perceived in different countries. He calls for a fuller investigation of the actual place of technique in human societies. People have desperately put their faith in science for the development of technology to deliver global solutions to social problems. But there is always a 'lag' between the increasing extent of complexity of modern societies and the degree to which technical mastery over those processes has been achieved. Indeed, technocracy is a product of such lags. The existence of these gaps induces ardent technocrats to overrate science as the medium which is going to save the situation. Science then develops a cultural authority which can be invoked in order to legitimate policies which new developments in technique, say computers or communications, are assumed to have made necessary. Techocratic thinking can in fact only offer a highly generalized range of solutions to what are complex social problems, which is ironically precisely the source of its perennial appeal as an ideology.

In the central sections of his chapter, Varcoe sets out the distinguishing structural features of technocrats as a group and discusses the historical origins of their often rationalistic and utopian ideologies. He also provides a useful discussion of their conservative, liberal and socialist critics, who, in their different ways, share a fear of the political and moral consequences of the technocratic tendency. He convincingly shows that technocratic scientism, which claims to be non-ideological, is in fact *continuous* with other contemporary ideologies, having provided many of them with their scientific rationale. Like other ideologies, it assumes that the world has a discernible direction of change, which is scientifically demonstrable, only in this case making it

13

explicit. One effect of the widespread use or advocacy of science for developing technocratic solutions to social problems is that science becomes politicized and the cultural ideal of science as pure inquiry is thrown into question.

Paradoxically, however, all forms of technocratic scientism are, Varcoe maintains, profoundly anti-politics. In trying to fuse scientific method and logic with the political organization of society, the tension between science and politics, which gives each its peculiar character, is abolished. He finds a view of power, compatible with this dissolution, in theories as diverse as those of Proudhon, Marx and Engels and the 'post-industrial society' thesis. Ruling politicians at the centre may be tempted to use techocratic solutions to try to solve problems in the periphery, masking their inability or unwillingness to manage the relationship by normal political means. Varcoe trenchantly maintains that technocratic political legitimation 'is destructive of the basis of democracy, understood as the openness of structures to the expression of political disagreement and dissent' (p. 93).

He concludes that the rise of technocracy and the decline of ideology are two sides of a coin. The more the empirical spirit of science has entered into the public's appreciation of social issues, the more ideologies – which were losing credibility, anyway, as complex modern social trends rendered them archaic – have declined. The more ideologies have declined, so the more politicians have looked to management solutions to economic and social problems at the expense of politics, understood as the socialized medium for the controlled expression of conflict. For that, ideologies are required. Thus, the erosion of ideological conflict has eliminated an important counterweight for holding in check the spread of technocracy, which carries the danger of rendering politics inoperable.

Agnes Heller's chapter is a philosophical meditation on the question: how can there be a universal foundation for morality in a pluralistic modern culture, in which all foundations and absolutes are apparently up for discussion and hence relativization? It is a compressed and closely argued piece in the philosophical style, which assumes a familiarity with the Kantian tradition. (See Burnheim 1994 for a useful introduction to Heller's work.) The implicit sociology in her analysis is a similar diagnosis of the later modern condition to that of Bauman in his *Legislators and Interpreters* (1987a) and other recent writings. They both

14

share the view that we now live in the age of competing interpretations, with no standpoint being accorded privilege. This decline in authoritative interpretations has occurred in a number of fields. The shift away from foundationalism partly reflects a shift in the function of intellectuals as a cultural élite. They are no longer legislators giving expert opinions and prescriptions, but now more appropriate for them is the role of interpreters, mediating between competing language games and forms of life, without presuming to speak from a position of cognitive privilege.

According to Heller, modern culture feeds on interpretations of interpretations, in a self-devouring process. The disappearance of authoritative communities of interpreters has created a situation whereby society consists entirely of 'contingent, fluid, ephemeral groups' (p. 108), interpreting anything and everything, picking and choosing cultural objects on a whim. Unlike people in pre- or early modern cultures, people today are able to step into and out of any tradition they please, because there is, she claims, no one, inherited, authoritative, dominant culture. The pre-modern cultural universe has thus been 'de-centred'. The current situation is highly individualistic: 'The interpretative subject is the monad of the omnivorous cultural universe' (p. 113).

For Heller, the crucial issue under these conditions is that of reliably grounding morality. In other words, as we understand her, she accepts that modern society is individualistic. On the level of culture and lived experience social life is contingent, fluid and individual – 'self-devouring' or 'omnivorous' in Heller's words. The issue is that this individualism cannot be a basis for grounding morality, which cannot purely be a matter of individual choice. However, it cannot any longer be grounded in metaphysics or based on the existence of God. So, morality is still a matter of choice, but there must be principles which cross contexts – that is to say, morality must be in some sense 'centred'. She draws on Kant and Emmanuel Lévinas in order to find a way of accepting the 'de-centring' of knowledge in modernity, whilst leaving morality 'centred'.

The backdrop to all the five chapters grouped together in Part II (those by Kumar, Bottomore, Coser, Mokrzycki and Wiatr) is the momentous fall of the communists in 1989. These chapters offer reflections on the significance of these events and their consequences, from both Eastern and Western viewpoints. The revolutions in the GDR and Eastern Europe, followed by

German re-unification and dramatic changes in the USSR, are, all these writers agree, events of world-historical significance. They signalled not only the ending of the Cold War but also a major upheaval in the sedimented lines of allegiance and difference within the socialist/communist camp and beyond. In the West the labour movement had for some time no longer appeared exclusively to embody radical hopes of emancipation. In its place, diverse new social and cultural movements have arisen. In the cultural field, much controversy has surrounded the debates associated with 'post-modernism'. All of these authors are concerned about the future of the young Eastern European democracies and the social and political consequences of the rapid implementation of free-market economic reforms in countries which still have large amounts of their economic infrastructures in public ownership and a significant socialistic (egalitarian) dimension to their national cultures.

Krishan Kumar surveys a wide selection of the outpouring of studies of the 1989 revolutions and maintains that these events raise classic questions in the study of revolutions. The kernel of this chapter is an assessment of the revolutions of 1989 in the light of theories of revolution and the European revolutionary tradition in general, epitomized by symbolic dates such as 1688, 1789, 1776, 1848 and 1917. He finds that the main weakness of most of the standard theories in trying to explain 1989 is their failure to take into account factors external to the nations concerned, residing in their international context as part of the Soviet empire. It was the withdrawal of the threat of the use of force by the Soviet government that was particularly important. All the internal ingredients for revolution – alienated intellectuals, delegitimation, etc. – had been present for decades prior. Modernization theory and industrial convergence theory are also of little use because they lack a theoretical device for understanding the dynamics of mobilization and political transformation.

The European revolutionary tradition provides Kumar with a rich source of parallels, continuities and discontinuities with 1989. The revolutions, he argues, were backward-looking and rectifying, containing no new principles or future orientation. They represented the peoples of the Eastern countries effectively 'rejoining' Europe, having been indirectly diverted by 1917 and its aftermath from the path to democracy. Novel in the 1989 revolutions was the global dimension of economic and political realities and the

16

role of television. He is sympathetic with the idea expressed by Bauman, Eisenstadt, Habermas and Rorty that the revolutions were not driven by a totalistic social vision, but partly by the comparison effect of 'post-modern', Western consumer culture. However, for Kumar, the content of the revolutions was more than a desire for consumerism, having also been conducted in the language of rights, democracy, freedom, private choice and private life. In that sense, they continue the promise of the unfinished democratic revolutionary tradition of Europe and the United States, going back to 1688 and 1776.

Tom Bottomore agrees that much of the vigour of the popular movements in 1989 in the East came from their opposition to the communist parties, with demands for citizenship rights being to the fore. These political demands also raised questions about the structure of the collective, planned economies, which had already been under extensive scrutiny in the years before 1989, with 'market socialism' already being taken seriously. But economic frustrations, the detestation of the communist dictatorships and nationalism all combined to give a conservative hue to many of the emerging coalition governments, giving fuel to calls for the restoration of *laissez-faire* capitalism in certain places. In this mood of overreaction against the communists, any conception of 'socialism with markets' was eclipsed, with, he believes, detrimental results.

For Bottomore, one effect of the changes in Eastern Europe has been to reinforce the widespread 'folklore' that publicly owned enterprises are necessarily inefficient and central planning a total failure. He shows in detail how these propositions are suspect. Failures of planning in the Eastern countries, he argues, had their source largely in the self-perpetuating dictatorship of the highly bureaucratized communist parties, not in any inherent flaws in planning as such. These dictatorships created attitudes inimical to the efficient functioning of the planned economies, resulting in corruption and the stifling of innovation. His message is that there is more than one kind of planning and many combinations of private and public ownership and organization are possible. The experience of Eastern Europe should merely re-open the question of democratic planning, not lead us to reject public ownership and planning in any shape or form. There is no reason why an optimal balance between varied forms of social and private ownership could not be found, consistent with the minimization of the detrimental social and cultural consequences such as unemployment and deepening social divisions, commonly associated with the lack of any regulation at all.

Lewis A. Coser looks specifically at the role of intellectuals in Central and Eastern Europe in the years preceding and following the political events of 1989. He argues that prior to then, outside observers failed to discern the repressed rebelliousness of Eastern European intellectuals, partly because it was hidden below the surface in the church institutions, where dissidence flourished. Unlike in the former Soviet Union, intellectuals in these countries always had higher status than their Western counterparts and occupied an important social position, providing spiritual leadership for the nation as a whole. They were aided in this role by their privileged access to Western ideas and experiences via travel and libraries. Now, after the euphoria of the revolutions has died down and economic deprivations are seen to be continuing to afflict these societies, they have largely not joined the new economic and political élites, but are once again taking on the role of social critics.

An audience for intellectuals is now beginning to emerge in East-Central Europe although, Coser argues, a certain disorientation has set in because of the sheer variety of intellectual opinions now being freely expressed, in a rigid culture ill prepared for them. It is a confused and potentially frustrating situation to which many intellectuals are ill adapted. Coser agrees with Bauman that communist parties in Eastern Europe have been severely weakened, but that intellectuals remain, vis-à-vis the state bureaucracy, a separate social category, possessing some class-like features, although not constituting a social class as such. In this structural relationship, Coser believes, lie the seeds of future conflict.

Edmund Mokrzycki, writing from Poland, reports that a paradoxical situation has developed there and in many countries in Central and Eastern Europe, following the fall of communism and the attempts by the state to implement economic reforms based on markets and competition. The pro-market reforms have stalled because of structural resistance being encountered from vested interests, including the working classes and peasantry, who have a lot to lose from the rapid introduction of economic competition. It is a strange situation in which the state, ideologically committed to such reforms, is enforcing them from the top on to

18

a society which broadly accepts the abstract goals, but in which significant sectors do not accept or resist the immediate measures to be taken to achieve them. There is no crystallized social force present whose interests are directly in line with the reforms, which could act as their bearers.

Mokrzycki reports that it is in this situation that the coming of the middle class is being seen in some neo-liberal circles as the hoped-for arrival of the saviours who can begin the process of renewal of the 'post-socialist' society. Some people even believe that this coming can be precipitated. He argues that on closer scrutiny the idea of the 'new middle class' in the Eastern European context reveals itself as an ideological artefact produced by an extreme form of neo-liberalism, promoted and stimulated in its development in order to support market reforms. It has no sociological characteristics of a class. This incipient class is said to consist of small private owners who, as entrepreneurs or capitalists, will be the builders of the new society. But it is a narrow definition which significantly excludes the peasantry, who constitute a quarter of the population of Poland, as well as the intelligentsia, both of which are in decline, pushed to the margins by the new commercial ethos and economic competition. He shows how, sociologically speaking, the so-called 'middle class' group is very diverse indeed, representing an amalgam of all the social classes and groups that existed under communism, shading over into a 'post-communist upper class'. This heterogeneous group – more a statistical category – does not resemble the Western middle class at all, its representatives merely posing under this label as they pursue their own ends in the struggle going on for the division of state property.

Jerzy J. Wiatr, also writing from Poland, tries to identify the key sources of the danger of political authoritarianism overtaking the young democracies which are emerging in Eastern Europe, if they are unable to contain conflicts of interest. In different degrees and in varying combinations in the various countries, he sees these as residing in the dissatisfactions arising from the new economic changes, in ethnic antagonisms and in religious fundamentalism. The economic changes have so far had the most visible impact on the stability of democracy. In countries which are still culturally committed to egalitarianism and justice and where people are accustomed to state welfare protection, Wiatr maintains that the impact of the free market, economic 'shock' strategy is likely to risk a popular political explosion strong enough to overthrow the reformist government before the positive effects of such reforms have had time to materialize; the Polish evidence suggests this. He sees the gravest danger in the possibility of authoritarian movements combining nationalism with populist socio-economic demands. Religious fundamentalism, particularly in Poland, is also dangerous in this connection, partly because it polarizes the society.

Wiatr sees as a likely scenario in many countries an anti-reform, populist and nationalistic form of authoritarianism, verbally committed to the continuing of the economic reforms, but carrying out repressive measures against 'enemies of the state', such as former communists. He concludes with four suggestions for policies which would aid stabilization of the democratic regimes and provide a countervailing weight against authoritarianism of the Right: reducing the social costs of the economic reforms and spreading their burden; negotiated compromises between government, new capitalists and trade unions, made legally binding; more actively involving the reformist post-communist parties in the reform process; and building political institutions conducive to the orderly representation of interests and their resolution.

We do not claim that this volume is a unified whole in any explicit sense. It was never intended to be a textbook of commissioned articles exploring a specific theme in a systematic way. That much it does share with the traditional *Festschrift* and its contributors understood it that way. However, we believe that together these papers do add up to something – intriguingly, they have emerged as possessing a significance which is more than the sum of their parts. Issues addressed independently in them often converge because they are some of the most fundamental and recurring questions in the sociological canon. These are particularly manifest in Part I and include the general problem of revolution. At the same time, many of the essays have in common their authors' concern to understand the current and emerging social and political condition of the new Europe, with particular emphasis on post-communist societies. These essays have all been brought together at a certain point in the development of modern European societies; this point is clearly closely bound up with the end of the Cold War, and has global implications. As such, these essays have a time-bound immediacy and significance.

In our view there is a very considerable research agenda

involved in understanding all this. We see these essays as a small part of a much larger enterprise. It will inevitably involve not only sociologists but also social scientists from other disciplines. It will be a long time before we can even begin to take the measure of the shape that these societies will have in the next century.

Part I
CULTURE

1

THE CULTURAL PROGRAMME OF MODERNITY AND DEMOCRACY

Some tensions and problems

S. N. Eisenstadt

Modern constitutional-democratic regimes have crystallized with the onset of modernity. As such they share some of the tensions and contradictions inherent in the cultural programme of modernity as it developed with the Great Revolutions and the Enlightenment (which in their turn had, of course, their roots in earlier periods of European history). It was above all the combination of the strong interweaving of this-worldly and other-worldly conceptions of salvation and the continuous struggle about access both to the sacred and to the political centre that created in Europe the potentialities for the crystallization of the new modern social order. These potentialities were greatly enhanced by the specific type of structural pluralism that developed in Europe – the multiplicity of social and political formations, of centres of power and continuous flexibility of political and communal boundaries.

But it was only with the Reformation, the consequent rise of Protestant sectarianism, the formation of modern states and the rise of capitalism that these potentialities gave rise to far-reaching transformations of the cultural and political order. This new cultural and social order crystallized in close relationship with the utopian conceptions that developed in the Great Revolutions of modernity (the English Great Rebellion, the American and French revolutions) together with the closely related philosophical trends of the post-Reformation era and the Enlightenment;

and with the concomitant transformation of the basic premises of Western civilizations, with the crystallization of the tradition of modernity.[1]

The various differences in the patterns of legitimation of the post-revolutionary regimes developed within the context of the basic transformations of the political arena and symbolism attendant on the institutionalization of the cultural programmes of modernity, as they crystallized in the Enlightenment and in the revolutions. Or, in more general terms, the most distinguishing characteristic of these revolutions has been the combination of far-reaching changes of regimes and the forcible overthrow of government. This was followed by consolidations of authority by new groups ruling through political (and sometimes social) institutions, instituting a new cultural vision – one could say a new civilization.

MODERNITY AS A CULTURAL VISION

The visions of the Great Revolutions and the Enlightenment entailed a far-reaching transformation of the conception of the relations between the transcendental and the mundane orders. They gave rise, perhaps for the first time in the history of humankind, to the belief in the possibility of bridging the tension between these two orders, to the possibility of realizing in the mundane orders, i.e. in social life, some of the eschatological, utopian visions. Such a belief could easily merge with the assumption of the overall relevance of the expansion of all aspects of knowledge for the formation of the social and cultural orders, giving rise to the tradition of modernity.

The radical innovation of this new tradition – even if this innovation could be seen as a transformation of the premises of the preceding traditions – lay in several major, often conflicting, tendencies and premises, all of them sharing a strong common denominator. This was the change of the place of God in the construction of the cosmos and of man and of belief in God (or in some metaphysical principles) as constituting the starting point for the understanding of both man and cosmos. Man and nature tended to be perceived more and more not as directly regulated (as in the monotheistic civilization, by the will of God, or, as in Hinduism and Confucianism, by some higher, transcendental metaphysical principles, or, as in the Greek tradition, by the universal *logos*) but as autonomous entities regulated by some internal laws which could be fully explained and grasped by human reason and inquiry.

These transformations in the basic conceptions about the relations between man, cosmos and God, as they developed in early modern Europe, were not initially necessarily anti-religious. Indeed, many of them had very strong religious roots, especially in the Reformation. At first they did not necessarily deny the place of God as the Creator of the Universe. Rather, they reformulated His place in relation to man, cosmos and nature. God, insofar as He remained in the picture, was more and more conceived of as Creator of that universe which has generated laws and which can be fully grasped by human reason and inquiry. Hence, the exploration of such laws became one of the major foci of this new intellectual tradition, providing, as it were, the key to the exploration of the perennial problems of the reflexive traditions of the Great Civilizations. At the same time, it was more and more assumed in this new tradition that exploration of these laws would lead to the unravelling of the mysteries of the universe and human destiny.

Such exploration was not purely passive or contemplative. Indeed, one component or assumption of this cultural programme was that through exploration not only the understanding, but also even the mastery of such destiny – a continuous expansion of the human environment – could be attained by the conscious effort of man. The exploration of nature and the potential mastery over it tended also, at least in some versions of this new tradition, especially the Enlightenment, to extend beyond the technical and scientific spheres into the social sphere in general and into the construction of the socio-political order in particular.

One of the central, though not universally accepted, premises of this new tradition was the belief in the possibility of the active formation, by conscious human activity and participation, of crucial aspects of social, cultural and natural orders. Society itself had become an object of human activities orientated to its reconstruction. This view of the possibility of the transformation of socio-cultural orders, of their continuous exploration as well as the potential mastery over them, implied – to return to that nomenclature – the blending of *Zweckrationalität* (instrumental rationality) and *Wertrationalität* (value-rationality), most fully epitomized in the arena of science itself. In this arena – but in

27

principle in all fields of this new tradition – the ethos of cognitive rationality combined in itself in a great variety of forms the elements of *'logos'* and *'mythos'* (see Blumenberg 1983; Habermas 1987b).

All, or at least most, of the components of the cultural vision of modernity have of course been challenged in the last decade or so. These challenges, which have claimed that the modern era has basically ended, giving rise to the post-modern one, were, in their turn, counter-challenged. Habermas, for example, has claimed that the various post-modern developments basically constitute either a repetition, in a new form, of criticisms of modernity which existed there from the very beginning, or yet another manifestation of the continual unfolding of modernity.

PROGRESS

The ontological conception entailed some very specific ideas of time, especially as related to the development of human history. Among the most important of these conceptions – many of which constituted far-reaching transformations of Christian eschatology – was, firstly, a vision of historical progress and of history as the process through which the cultural programme of modernity would be implemented. Secondly, it was assumed that through such historical progress the utopian orientations inherent in all the revolutions and in the basic premises of modernity (especially the concept of individual autonomy and emancipation) would be implemented. Such progress was, on the whole, defined in terms of such universalist values as reason, science and technology. There developed a very strong tendency to conflate science and technology with ultimate values, that is, to conflate *Wertrationalität* and *Zweckrationalität*. The major, opposite (romantic) tendency emphasized the autonomy of emotions and the distinctiveness of primordial collectivities. But within the new major programme it changed the strong utopias and semi-eschatological conceptions, even if certainly not the idea of progress. Present and future were thus brought closer together (Taylor 1979, 1989). Attempts were made to construct in the present, with a view to the future, a new social order and to justify it according to some transcendental and universalist criteria and the ideals inherent in it.

Thirdly, there was the strong tendency to emphasize the possibility of the active participation of social groups in the formation of a new social and cultural order, as well as a high level of commitment to such orders. Fourthly, there were very strong universalistic orientations – in principle negating the importance and significance of any specific political or national boundaries, but at the same time attempting to define a new, basic, socio-political order with broad, yet relatively definitive, boundaries. But, however future-orientated this programme was, it also developed references to an imaginary human communal past. It had as well a strong evangelistic and chiliastic trend which, together with its 'this-worldly' orientations, gave it the impetus to expansion.

This new cultural programme of modernity, especially as it crystallized through the Great Revolutions, constituted combined orientations of rebellion, protest and intellectual antinomianism, together with strong orientations to centre-formation and insti-tution-building. It was, as we have seen, these orientations, as well as the formation and institutionalization of centres, which distinguished the social revolution from other protest movements in history, and which gave them their specific modern revolution-ary connotation.

CITIZENSHIP

Such ontological conceptions necessarily transformed the basic parameters and premises of the political order, that is, its legitima-tion, the conceptions of the accountability of rulers and the structure of centres and centre–periphery relations. The advent of modernity was closely connected with the growing autonomy of various cultural and societal centres, and above all with changes in the relationship between the centres and peripheries; the per-meating of the periphery by the centres; and the growing impinge-ment of the periphery on the centre – often culminating in the obliteration of the differences between centre and periphery.[2]

Closely related was the transformation of the basic orientations to tradition and to authority. The authority of the past as the major symbolic regulator of social, political and cultural change and innovation began to give way to the acceptance of innovation as a cultural orientation and a possible component of the legitima-tion of authority.

This transformation of the basic premises of the social and

29

political order became closely combined with the full institutionalization of the ideology of citizenship in its modern version, i.e. as closely connected with the full development of representative institutions, and with the promulgation of modern constitutions. This ideology became connected with the expansion, through political struggle and protest, of the access to representation: to all citizens in all sectors of society, with the emphasis on the full accountability of rulers to the citizens.

The ideology of citizenship, with its roots in the political traditions of city-states, was also transformed by the new utopian visions, with the continuous quest for an ideal social order epitomized in the Great Revolutions. This was rooted in the transformation of Christian eschatology into the secular vision of the unfolding of human destiny. The search for the ways in which the concrete social order could become the embodiment of an ideal order became a central – even if certainly not the only – component in the modern political discourse and tradition (Montesquieu 1748; Strauss 1958, 1989; Bondanella and Musa 1979; Skinner 1978, 1981; Schmitt 1990).

PROTEST

In close relation to the utopian component in modern political life rooted in the imagery of the Great Revolutions, there took place far-reaching transformations in the symbolism and structure of the modern political centres, compared with their predecessors or with the centres of other civilizations. The crux of these transformations was the incorporation of themes and symbols of protest as a basic and legitimate component of the premises of these centres. Such incorporation constituted a major component of the project of the emancipation of man; a project which sought to combine equality and freedom, justice and autonomy, solidarity and identity.

In contrast with almost every previous civilization, themes and symbols of equality, participation and social justice became not only elements of protest orientated against the existing centre, but also an important component of the political legitimation of *orderly* demands by the periphery on the centre. Protest and the possibility of transforming some aspects of a society's institutional premises were no longer considered to be illegitimate, or at least marginal aspects of the political process. They became central concerns of modern political discourse (Mannheim 1940; Eisenstadt 1973).

The central focus of the political dynamics in modern societies was the continuous restructuring of centre–periphery relations, with the concomitant emphasis on, firstly, the incorporation of the symbols and demands of protest and, secondly, the restructuring of the relations between the changing civil society and the state. The various processes of structural change and dislocation which occurred as a result of economic changes, urbanization, changes in the process of communication and the like led in modern societies not only to the promulgation by different groups of various concrete problems and demands, but also to a growing quest for participation in the broader social and political order. (This quest, together with others for the incorporation of various themes of protest in the centre, and the concomitant possible transformation of the centre, were often guided by the various utopian visions and the programme of incorporation referred to above.)

Concomitantly, there developed political processes characterized by the gradual disappearance of ascriptive élites and a growing emphasis on criteria of achievement. Political discourse was transformed and revitalized by a number of related processes: the recruitment of élites; the diversification of the social bases from which they were recruited; the growing competition between different élites; the necessity to mobilize political support in open public arenas; and the close connection between the selection of rulers through such competitions and the promulgation of policies and the articulation and aggregation of political interests and demands.

TENSIONS WITHIN THE PROGRAMME

Among the most important tensions inherent in the cultural and political programmes or the cultural programme of modernity were those between liberty and equality; an emphasis on a vision of the good social order and the 'narrow' interests of different sectors of the society; the conception of the individual as autonomous and sovereign and the emphasis on the community; the autonomous civil society and the state; and between the utopian and the 'rational' or 'procedural' components of this programme.

In the political arena these conceptions were those between

31

the utopian and the civil components in the construction of modern politics; 'revolutionary' politics and 'normal' politics; the, above all, general will and the will of all; and in the concomitant oscillation between constitutional and totalitarian tendencies and regimes.

THE 'COMMON GOOD': A BASIC ISSUE

These tensions have become most fully articulated in a central aspect of the modern political process which is of importance from the point of view of the potential fragility of constitutional-democratic regimes. That is, the nature or contents of the basic issues around which this process is focused, especially the continuous connection between various issues around, and conceptions of, the common will.

Contrary to the assumptions of many rational choice analyses, the mobilization of support around leaders and programmes – effected mainly, but not only, through the medium of parties, interest groups and social movements – is based not only on aggregation of many discrete interests. It may also take place around the articulation and promulgation of different conceptions of the common good. Such mobilization also very often focuses, as Alessandro Pizzorno (1980) has shown, on symbols of identity – political, social or ethnic – as well as on the closely related conception of the common good of the good society. The latter is usually more closely related to the primordial and sacred components of legitimation. Such articulation and promulgation plays a very central role in the mobilization of political support.

It is indeed this combination of articulation and the aggregation of different interests and of different conceptions of common good that constitutes a continuous component of constitutional-democratic polities. And it generates continuous tensions within the political process that develops in these regimes. The most important among such tensions are those between two aspects of political struggle or process, the routine and the 'revolutionary', to use Bruce Ackerman's (1988) formulation. Between, on the one hand, that aspect of political struggle in which the aggregation of interests takes place and, on the other, the aspect in which different conceptions of the 'common will' and of the good social order, of symbols of collectivity and collective identity, are articulated.

These tensions are closely related to those between the majoritarian decision and the emphasis on basic rights; and between the autonomy of civil society and the incumbents of state power. They are also closely related to, but not identical with, the tension between the self-legitimacy of the rules of the game and legitimation in terms of some other – often 'ultimate' – visions present among the different definitions of democracy to which we have referred above.

CONSTITUTIONS

It is because the political process in the democratic regimes is so closely connected with some of the basic tensions inherent in such regimes (especially with the tension between an emphasis on rights as against that on majoritarian decisions) that also explains something else. That is, the special place of constitutions and of legal institutions, of the so-called 'rule of law' (a term which is often used in a rather general and loose way). Whatever the details of the different formulations in modern Western political discourse of the relations between the will of all and the common will, an explicit or implicit assumption of the constitutional-democratic regimes was that concretely these tensions are to be worked out in the constitutional arena, i.e. in constitutional arrangements in the representative institutions.

The promulgation of constitutions was not just a matter of the specification of the technical arrangements of government. It was above all the most important way to cope with the tension, or problem, of the relation between the will of all and the common will, as it became crystallized and continuously reformulated with the growing and continuous democratization attendant on the development of modern society.

THE BOUNDARIES OF THE POLITICAL

These tensions between 'routine' and 'revolutionary' politics are closely related to, and exacerbated by, two additional aspects of the political process in modern societies. Firstly, the tendency towards the politicization of many social problems and conflicts; and, secondly, the continuous redefinition of the scope of the 'political'. Modern constitutional regimes are characterized by the generally high level, unparalleled in any other regimes (again

33

with the possible partial exception of some of the city-states of antiquity), of potential politicization of many problems and demands of various sectors of the society and of conflicts between them. Such potential politicization generates also the possibility – strongly emphasized in the 1970s and 1980s – of the overburdening of the central political arenas, including all the three major branches, and the possible concomitant weakening of their capacity to function effectively and their ability to govern (Huntington et al. 1975).

These tendencies towards politicization are exacerbated by the fact that in all modern regimes the boundaries of what is considered as the appropriate scope of the open, legitimate, political arena and action have been continuously changing. The transition from the '*laissez-faire*' conception of the state – never, of course, fully implemented in reality – to the post-Second World War Keynesian regulatory policies and the institutionalization of the welfare state is perhaps the best illustration of such a change. But it constitutes only the tip of the iceberg. In fact, such changes have been continually going on in these regimes throughout their histories. As the illustration of the welfare state attests, they have been closely related to the specification of the different entitlements due to the different sectors of societies (Przeworski 1985; Maier 1987).

The specification of such changes, the drawing of the boundaries of the political, has in itself constituted – unlike in most other political regimes in the history of humankind – one of the major foci of open political contestation and struggle. Most of these changes in the boundaries of the political were results of political struggles rooted in the continuous social and economic changes which have been characteristic of development of these regimes.

The demands for the redefinition of the boundaries of the political have usually been promulgated by various movements of protest arising often in periods of change – but also in more 'stable' periods. It is in such periods of change that the articulation of protest usually comes forward as a major component of the political process. The most intensive themes and movements of protest are those in which the articulation and aggregation of concrete interests becomes closely related to the promulgation of different conceptions of the common good. It is because of this that such protests usually entail demands for a redefinition of the boundaries of the political, of the proper action of the state in relation to various sectors of the society and of the basic entitlement to which all the citizens and various such sectors can claim. And the demands are closely related to the processes of the selection of rulers.

The demands for such a redefinition of the scope of the political also usually entails the articulation of the basic tensions inherent in the democratic regimes to which we have referred above. That is, the tensions between the different conceptions of democracy and between equality and liberty; between conceptions of rights and majoritarian decisions; and the tensions between the Jacobin and liberal, or pluralistic, elements of this programme. Such Jacobin orientations, with their belief in the transformation of society through totalistic political action, are very modern, even if their historical roots go back to medieval eschatological sources (Cochin 1924, 1979; Talmon 1960; Baechler 1979; Furet 1982).

The Jacobin element exists – even if in many different guises, such as in populist movements, fundamentalist or fascist movements – in all modern, including the democratic, constitutional societies. It exists also in nationalist movements. As Norberto Bobbio (1984, 1986; Matteucci 1983) has very often emphasized in his works, the Jacobin element is very strong both in fascism and in communism. In a way they constitute mirror-images of one another. The communist regimes constituted, of course, the most extreme or pristine illustrations of the attempts to institutionalize a modern Jacobin regime.[3]

CIVIL SOCIETY AND THE STATE

The focal point of these tensions was the relationship between politically autonomous sectors of civil society in different modern societies (which developed, together with the concept of civil society, as a central component of the process of development of modern, especially post-revolutionary, regimes) and the state. One aspect of the revolutionary process was the transformation of a relatively passive, apolitical, sector of civil society into a politically active one, which promulgated not only the discrete interests of different groups but also different and competing conceptions of the common good.

In different modern regimes there developed distinct modes of civil society and of the confrontation between state and society.

Within the modern European (especially continental) societies, there developed the assumption that political forces, political élites and the more autonomous social groups (the state, on the one hand, and 'society' or 'civil society', on the other) waged a continuous struggle over their relative importance in the formation of the cultural and political centres of the nation-state and in the regulation of access to it. These tensions, i.e. the continuous confrontation between state and society, were above all promulgated by the numerous movements of protest which constituted a basic component of modern political regimes.

These numerous struggles between state and society developed in Western society in two opposite directions. One was that of the continuous expansion, growth and reconstruction of civil society in relation to the new expansion of democracy. This did not necessarily involve the diminution of the power or scope of activities of the state; rather it involved a continuously greater participation of sectors of society in the political arena. The other direction was that of the victory of state over society, most fully epitomized, even if in different ways, in the totalitarian regimes – the Fascist, Nazi and Soviet ones.

In these regimes – especially in the communist regimes which persisted for the longest period (seventy years in the Soviet Union and about forty-five in Eastern Europe) – there developed a rather paradoxical situation with respect to the relations between state and civil society. Given the intense processes of industrialization and education – in general of 'social mobilization' – in these countries, there developed within all of them the structural conditions for the development of civil society, i.e. multiple associations and the like. These structural kernels were, however, denied autonomy by the totalitarian party and state, which attempted to regulate them totally. But such regulation was often legitimized in terms seemingly similar to those of the constitutional regimes, in which the party was portrayed as the bearer of the real goals of civil society. Moreover, these various associations were formally regulated according to constitutional rules characteristic of the autonomous associations of the constitutional regimes. It was the combination of the repressed structural kernels of such a civil society and their seemingly (sham) constitutional arrangement which constituted a not insignificant factor in the delegitimation and breakdown of the communist regimes in 1989. It also constituted a potential – indeed only a potential –

springboard for future developments in post-communist regimes
(Eisenstadt 1992).

DIFFERENT REGIMES - SIMILAR PROBLEMS

These tensions are inherent in all modern regimes. In the democratic, constitutional ones, they give rise to some of the basic
paradoxes of democracy, for example those analysed by Larry
Diamond (1990) of élite choice versus popular participation; conflict versus consensus; representativeness versus governability;
and consent versus effectiveness. In the relatively stable constitutional-democratic regimes, these tensions may be attenuated,
but they are always simmering, ready, as it were, to erupt in
situations of intensive change.

In the pluralistic, constitutional societies – in the United States,
in Britain or France – this Jacobin element is hemmed in and it
constitutes only one component in the overall pluralistic constitutional arrangements, but the tensions are potentially there. In
the totalitarian regimes, the pluralistic ideologies and structures
were suppressed almost totally by the Jacobin ones, but they were
not entirely obliterated. Indeed, as we have indicated briefly
above and expanded in greater detail elsewhere (Eisenstadt
1992), it was the persistence in the communist regimes of some
of the plaudits of the institutional and ideological components of
modernity that constituted an important factor in their delegitimation and breakdown. In the post-communist regimes of Eastern Europe, the various 'pluralistic' elements, the more
autonomous forms of civil society, have reasserted themselves,
but the greatest challenge before them is whether they will be
able to institute a relatively stable, continual institutional
framework.

The fact that the breakdown of these regimes seems to lead to
the institutionalization of new and, on the face of it, constitutional-democratic regimes – more modern societies – does not
mean that such institutionalization will be easy. It is now fully
recognized that the transition is fragile. What are becoming
increasingly apparent are many economic pitfalls; great social
turbulence and dislocations attendant on the transition from the
communist command economy to some free market type; the
weakness in Eastern European countries of constitutional and
democratic traditions; and the continuous threat of the upsurge

of primordial, ethnic loyalties. There is always the possibility of economic collapse and general anarchy.

DIRECTIONS OF TRANSFORMATION

These problems, however, do not simply arise out of the breakdown of 'traditional' empires, the transition from some 'premodern' to a fully modern, democratic society; or from a distorted modernity to a relatively tranquil stage, which may well signal some kind of 'end of history'. The turbulence evident in Eastern Europe today bears witness to some of the problems and tensions inherent in modernity itself, attesting to the potential fragility of the whole project of modernity. These turbulences highlight tensions inherent in the modern political programme and process, which we have analysed above, and which are inherent in all modern regimes. In authoritarian and totalitarian regimes, as we have said, they are suppressed but never obliterated. The tensions and potential fragility of constitutional-democratic – basically of all modern – regimes are enhanced by the fact that modern regimes develop in highly volatile and continuously changing internal and international settings. The conditions conducive to their institutionalization and continuity are themselves inherently unstable.

In any situation of rapid change, modern societies may develop rather contradictory tendencies with respect to the development of conditions conducive to institutionalization, that is, to the perpetuation and continuity of constitutional-democratic regimes. Such situations generate changes in the following: the definition of the boundaries of the political, to which we have referred above; what is seen to be an appropriate range of activities for the state; the structures of centres of power; the extent of the access of different sectors of civil society to those centres; the nature of the linkages between the sectors, and between them and the state; and the types of entitlements extended to different sectors of society.

From the point of view of the construction of civil society and its relations to the state, in such transitional situations, developments could take several directions. One would include the development of new autonomous sectors of civil society; another the political activation of such sectors through the activities of multiple élites and counter-élites; and another the growth of various interlinking arenas between the state and society. The latter would include both the activation of 'older' types of association, such as consultative bodies, and the development of new ones, attuned in different degrees to constitutional-democratic arrangements.

Alternatively, the processes of 'transition' may develop in quite other directions. They may work to undermine the conditions favouring the development and continuity of constitutional-democratic regimes. The continuous social and economic transitions may easily change the distribution of power within the major sectors of society, eroding many autonomous centres of power, creating a power vacuum. Moreover, policies – such as, for example, those connected with the institutionalization of the welfare state – whose initial aim was to weaken existing semi-monopolistic centres of power may increase the political and administrative power of the state to such an extent as to obliterate independent bases of power.

Other possibilities exist. Many of the existing sectors of civil society, with their complex interlinking arenas, may become impediments to the restructuring of relations between civil society and the state. The very entrenchment of these sectors may lead them increasingly to represent narrow corporative or ascriptive sectors, and may weaken their initial acceptance of newly emergent common frameworks and centres. Finally, both the older associational structure and the new sectors of civil society may become undermined, giving rise to the development of highly volatile masses. In many such cases, these processes have been exacerbated by the emergence of new collective-national and ethnic communities, with ensuing internecine conflicts (Eisenstadt 1991).

The ubiquity of these tensions in the modern constitutional-democratic regimes points to one of the most important challenges before these regimes – namely how to create some common framework in which different views of the common good can compete without undermining the very possibility of the system working. It poses the question of the nature of the common basis or bases of acceptance of a constitutional-democratic regime – beyond adherence to the rules of the game – and the possibility that such common elements may exist in multiple bases of legitimation, so long as no one of them becomes predominant.

Since the Second World War, though not between the two

world wars, the constitutional regimes of the West, despite continual fears about the crisis of the state or capitalism, evinced to a
high degree the capacity for self-transformability. In the West, no
democratic regime has broken down since the end of the Second
World War. Indeed, the general trend has seemed to go the other
way, with the authoritarian regimes – in Spain, Portugal, Greece
and, most recently, in some Latin American countries – becoming
democratic. Similarly, several non-European countries – India,
Japan and Israel – have been able to maintain constitutional-
democratic regimes since the end of the Second World War, as
have also Germany and Italy, the two countries in which the
breakdown of democracy in the inter-war period was most
dramatic.

But even within these regimes, the possibility of crisis or breakdown cannot be entirely discounted. This is, of course, even more
true of the emerging constitutional regimes of Eastern Europe.
The initial stages of the breakdown of the communist regimes –
the relatively peaceful characteristics which distinguished them
from the Great Revolutions – suggested that they might also
evince some such capacity for self-transformability. At the same
time, however, the turbulences attendant on these transitions cast
new doubts on that capacity. Such doubts are due not only to the
specific conditions of these transitions, but also to the combination of conditions inherent in modern regimes, especially in
constitutional-democratic ones. Thus, the developments in Eastern Europe cast important light on the problematics of modernity,
on the inherent fragility of the great historical and cultural project
of modernity.

NOTES

1 On the premises of modernity, see Simmel (1900a, 1900b, 1926); Wolff
  (1950); Aron (1969); Eisenstadt (1973); Blumenberg (1983); Habermas
  (1987b); and Toulmin (1990). On the political process in modern
  societies, see Mannheim (1940) and Lasswell (1972). On the concept
  of centre see Shils (1975). On centre–periphery relations in modernity
  see Eisenstadt (1973: 203–58) and 'Post-Traditional Societies and the
  Continuity and Reconstruction of Tradition', in Eisenstadt (1972:
  1–29).
2 On the transformation of the political conceptions in modernity, see
  Dunn (1978: esp. part one; 1984) and Rousseau (1968). Among the
  classic accounts of the transformation of concepts of authority and
  legitimation in modernity, see Tocqueville (1835).

3 See also Frankel, 'Strukturdefekte der Demokratie und deren Über-
windung' and 'Ratenmythos und soziale Selbstbestimmung', in Frankel
(1990: 68–95 and 95–137, respectively). A very strong statement against
the emphasis on 'common will' in the name of 'emancipation' can be
found in Lubbe (1991).

2

THREE ASPECTS OF MODERNITY IN SIMMEL'S *PHILOSOPHIE DES GELDES*

Its epiphanic significance, the centrality of money and the prevalence of alienation

Gianfranco Poggi

Philosophie des Geldes (first published 1900; English translation, *The Philosophy of Money*, 1978) contains the most sustained treatment by Georg Simmel (1858–1918) of a theme that has always had critical significance for modern social theory, and to the analysis of which Zygmunt Bauman's work has signally contributed in our own time: the nature of modern society.

Towards the end of the nineteenth century, the problem of attaining an understanding of modernity was particularly acute within the German social and cultural sciences, since in Germany modernization had advanced both at a rather accelerated pace and in rather unbalanced fashion, leaving political institutions relatively unmodernized. Furthermore, many German academic intellectuals remained stubbornly attached to a proud sense that their national culture possessed utterly distinctive, uniquely valuable traits, which the advance of modernity placed under threat. Many of them were on that account resolutely (indeed, at times, pugnaciously) critical of other Western national cultures, which had earlier, and more spontaneously, accepted or indeed fostered, inspired and justified the transition to modernity.[1]

Georg Simmel, while appreciating and to an extent sharing some orientations and preferences associated with the prevalent

German view of *modernity as a threat*, basically stood aside from that view, or at the very least proposed a highly *nuancée*, discriminating version of it. Modern society, as Simmel conceived of it, evoked in him great perplexity, but no hostility or aversion.[2] In this essay I will argue this point with primary reference to *The Philosophy of Money* [*Philosophie des Geldes*],[3] whose 'true object', according to Cavalli and Perucchi (1986: 4), is 'the historical process of formation of modern society'.

Philosophie des Geldes, I suggest, conceptualizes and assesses modern society primarily in three ways. In the first place, it argues that through the process of modernization some valuable human potentialities, which pre-modern values and arrangements left unexpressed and uncultivated, or indeed positively concealed and repressed, come imperiously to the fore. In this sense, I would argue, Simmel views modernity as an 'epiphany', that is, as the express manifestation of powers intrinsic to the human species, but previously unrevealed. In the second place, Simmel emphasizes the extent to which modern society at large is shaped and biased by the specific features of an advanced money economy. Finally, Simmel sees modern society as particularly prone to a set of processes which together constitute the phenomenon of 'alienation'.

Before developing these arguments, let me note that however Simmel may have characterized the adjective 'modern' in the expression *modern society*, the noun 'society' itself is problematic in his thinking. In their book on the concept of *Society*, Frisby and Sayer discuss Simmel's understanding of it under the heading of 'Society as Absent Concept' (1986: 64; see also Frisby 1990: 39–55). They note that in his first book, *Sociale Differenzierung*, Simmel criticized two 'founding fathers' of sociology as different as Comte and Spencer for assigning 'society' a central position in their thinking. He felt that by the same token they unduly diminished the significance of individuality, reducing the individual to 'a point of intersection of social fibres'. Simmel chose to de-substantialize 'society', by placing at the centre of his own conception of sociology the 'sociation' process (*Vergesellschaftung*): 'Society ... compared with the *real interaction of the parts* ... is only secondary, only the result' of that process (quoted in Frisby and Sayer 1986: 55). *Philosophie des Geldes* restates this view in the context of a complex argument according to which the relationship of 'exchange' can be treated as paradigmatic of social relations in general.

> Exchange itself is one of the functions whereby society results from the mere proximity [*Nebeneinander*] of individuals to one another. For society is not an absolute entity which must antecede, and constitute the support and the framework of, its members' single relations.... Rather, it is nothing but the comprehensive concept or the general designation of the totality of those reciprocal relations.
>
> (208; *174*)

This does not mean that Simmel discards the concept 'society': in fact he uses it not infrequently (much more frequently, at any rate, than Max Weber), and does not always qualify it with an adjective. His *Soziologie*, for example, contains a very significant 'excursus' on the theme 'how is society possible?' But again what he means there is, primarily: how is it possible for individual human beings, constituted as they are, to enter into patterned relations with one another? More generally, Frisby and Sayer suggest, his interest is in those 'microscopic-molecular processes' which 'exhibit society in, as it were, *statu nascendi*' (1986: 61).

This interest led Simmel to investigate locales and instances of the sociation process which, on the face of it, are little affected by broader and historically more variable social contexts. He analysed, for instance, the 'sociability' characteristic of small gatherings convened merely *for fun* within circles of friends and associates. Yet such topics co-existed in his thinking with a keen sense of the significance of larger historical contexts. And, as I said, *Philosophie des Geldes* gives evidence of this specifically in its recurrent concern with the nature of modern society.

I have already indicated how I will organize my discussion of the resulting arguments in this text. Naturally, the three themes I distinguished above (briefly: modernity as epiphany; the broader impact of the advanced money economy; alienation as the human destiny under modernity) overlap, and some aspects of each recur in others. The succession in which I treat them, below, is meant not just to establish a scaffolding for the discussion, but also to emphasize the complexity of Simmel's views about modernity. For, it seems to me, the first argument conveys a largely positive view of modernity, whereas the other two are associated with a growing sense of perplexity. Yet, nowhere does *Philosophie des*

Geldes express that 'Catonian' rejection of the modern experience[4] so common among the academic intellectuals of his time,
especially (though by no means exclusively[5]) in Germany.

MODERNITY AS EPIPHANY

As I have already suggested, according to Simmel the process of
modernization has given fuller and more significant expression to
human capacities which previous conditions had left relatively
undiscovered and undeveloped.[6] Modernity speaks more profound truths about the human species than previous cultural
legacies and social arrangements had; and indeed makes possible
a better understanding of the making and the makings of earlier
conditions than could be attained while the validity of those
legacies and those arrangements was still undisputed (580; *421*).
(Incidentally, Marx expressed a similar insight in a famous aphorism: 'The anatomy of man is the key to the anatomy of the ape'.)

If we ask what achievements suggested to Simmel such a positive view of modernity, many of them appear to concern primarily
the way reality is typically conceptualized and interpreted in
modern society, rather than that society's distinctive institutional
developments. The advance of modernity, that is, brings what
could be called a 'cognitive gain'. Simmel suggests, for instance,
that 'the role of material components in the arts . . . has only very
recently been correctly understood' (436; *324*) – a statement
which unfortunately he leaves without further elaboration.[7] More
widely, Raymond Boudon's (1989: 477ff) thoughtful reconstruction of the contribution of *Philosophie des Geldes* to the sociology
of knowledge suggests that Simmel saw the typical modern understanding of the nature of knowledge and of the process of its
production as superior to earlier understandings.

Yet, according to Simmel, the boundary between the cognitive
and the institutional spheres is a flexible and permeable one; and
most modern achievements do establish the cognitive superiority
of modern thinking, but only to the extent that they accompany
ongoing changes in the structures of existence themselves. For
example, according to Simmel, modern conditions acknowledge
and affirm two aspects of reality which co exist with and indeed
presuppose one another, yet stand to one another in a tension-
laden relationship. To wit, the *modern mind* affirms and enhances

45

at the same time the subjectivity of subjects and the objectivity of objects:

> Essentially, what differentiates the intellectual world of classical antiquity from the modern one is that the latter, on the one hand, has deepened and sharpened the concept of the ego (conferring on the problem of freedom an extreme significance unknown in antiquity), and, on the other, has increased the autonomy and strength of the concept of the object, as it expresses itself in the notion that nature obeys unbreakable laws. Antiquity was much closer than later ages to that undifferentiated state in which contents [of knowledge] are represented as such, without apportioning them to subject and object.
>
> (30–1; *64*)

But what Simmel has in mind is not *just* an intellectual development; for in another passage he suggests that, over 'the last three hundred years', the modern juxta-position and contra-position between subjectivity and objectivity has found expression also in concrete structures of everyday existence:

> On the one hand, the legality of nature, the material order of things, the objective necessity of events become more and more clear and compelling; on the other, the emphasis upon the independent personality, upon personal freedom, upon autonomy [*Fürsichsein*] becomes sharper and stronger.
>
> (403; *302*)

Whatever the balance (or for that matter the causal relationship, if any) between the intellectual and the institutional side of it, I would emphasize that this 'parallel development' (ibid.) constitutes for Simmel the open realization, the *inveramento* as one says in Italian, of a basic anthropological datum. For, as Simmel sees the matter, the co-existence and the tension between subjectivity and objectivity are constituent aspects of human nature, evidenced in the ontogenesis of each individual. The early parts of *Philosophie des Geldes* contain several statements to this effect, which might remind readers of insights we have learned to associate chiefly with the thought of George Herbert Mead (1863–1931).

The points made in those statements could be summarized as follows: human subjectivity is the outcome of a process; it emerges only as a counterpart to the developing awareness of objects – the individual coming to perceive itself as an object by being addressed as such by others; finally, this feat rests on the human mind's (or soul's, or spirit's) mysterious ability to split itself up, or to stand outside of itself – not just to perceive, but to distinguish its perceiving activity from that which is being perceived, and above all (the biggest feat of all) to perceive itself as perceiving. To quote just one passage:

In fact, the fundamental capacity of our spirit [*Geist*] is that of judging itself, of imposing upon itself its own law. This does nothing but express or elaborate the primordial fact of self-consciousness. Our soul [*Seele*] possesses no substantial unity, but only that which results from the interaction between the subject and the object into which it partitions itself. For the spirit [*Geist*], this is not a contingent form, which could be otherwise without modifying what belongs to our essence, but rather the spirit's own essential form. To possess spirit means nothing else than to carry out this inner split, to make oneself into an object, to be able to know oneself. ... The subject endowed with soul knows itself as object and the object as subject.

(118–19; *117–18*)

Having insisted on the interaction between what I called the intellectual and the institutional aspects of distinctive modern achievements, I agree with Boudon that *Philosophie des Geldes* emphasizes achievements which, on the face of it, belong primarily to the intellectual sphere, and which concern particularly the possibility of attaining a correct knowledge of reality. The achievements I have in mind can be signalled by two characteristic expressions: on the one hand, the principle of the *relativity of knowledge*; on the other, the *de-substantialization of reality*. Once more, there is some overlap between the referents of these expressions, but not so much as to make it impossible to consider them separately. In the vocabulary of Simmel and his contemporaries, the notion that cognitive constructs, properly understood, had 'relative' validity did not have the sceptical implications it gained subsequently (Boudon 1989: 486). What it asserted was the following:

The contents of thought ... stand each as the background of the other, so that each receives its meaning and colour from the other, and, since they constitute pairs of mutually exclusive opposites, they both call forth one another to generate a possible image of the world, and each of them becomes the ground of proof for the other, via the whole chain of what is knowable.

(115; *115*)

Thus, whatever is true is so only with reference to some other truth, *and vice versa.* A telling simile for this relationship is provided by the notion of weight, which is intrinsically relative, in that the weight of any given thing is determined by reference to that of another; thus, of all things taken together it would not make sense to say that they possess any weight at all.

Ordinary cognitive praxis hides this relativity of all truth contents, by treating some of them as the undisputed ground of the validity of others but *not* vice versa – in the same way that, Simmel says, we are more aware of the attraction the moon exercises on the apple than of the attraction (not less real, though empirically much less significant) which the apple exercises on the moon.

As a body may appear to possess weight as a quality of its own, because only one side of the relation manifests itself, in the same manner truth may seem a determination inherent in a given representation in and of itself, because it appears insignificant vis-à-vis the totality of those currently assumed as unproblematical. Thus we do not notice the mutual dependency to which all elements owe their truth.

(116; *116*. NB: Free translation)

The superiority of modern over pre-modern thinking lies in the extent to which it takes on board 'the concept of truth as a relation of representations to one another, not as an absolute quality attaching to any one of them in particular' (103; *108*). For modern thinking the relativity of truth thus understood constitutes, according to Simmel,

not a qualification which attaches itself to, and weakens, an otherwise independent concept of truth, but the essence itself of truth, the manner in which representations become truths.... Truth is valid not in spite of being relative, but on account of being so.

(116; *116*)

There is little question that, so understood, the principle of relativity constitutes for Simmel a definite (though perhaps not *definitive*) advance associated with modernity. The same thing he says emphatically of a methodological strategy he connects with that principle – the preference for 'as if' statements. (In 1911 a contemporary of Simmel's, the philosopher Hans Vaihinger, was to expound at length his own understanding of that expression in a controversial book, *The Philosophy of 'As If'* [1924].) Simmel writes:

> The assertion that things behave in such and such a way must be replaced ... by the following: our understanding must proceed *as if* things behaved in such and such a way. This makes it possible to express adequately the way in which our understanding actually relates to the world.
>
> (106; *110*, italics added)

According to this same passage, the notion of relativity suggests that 'constitutive principles, which claim to express once and for all the nature itself of things, should instead be considered as regulative principles, that is, perspective points from which to advance knowledge' (ibid.). This suggests a relation between the first point, on whose account modernity for Simmel constitutes an *epiphany*, and the second – the modern de-substantialization of reality: it is relativism, Simmel says, that establishes 'the (mutual) conditioning of things' as 'their essence' (120; *118*). But de-substantialization has also aspects (determinants, concomitants, consequences) of a *non-cognitive* nature. It is not just mental contents that implicitly or explicitly refer to one another; rather, under modern conditions it becomes clear that reality itself comprises multiple aspects none of which stands by itself, but all of which presuppose, complement, converge with, contend with, accommodate to, subvert, posit one another. Modernity suggests powerfully (and revealingly) that inter-action, mutual effect (*Wechselwirkung*) is *all there is* to reality.

This, of course, is particularly clear in economic action, at the conceptual core of which, according to the first chapter of *Philosophie des Geldes*, lies the mutual exchangeability of objects. (In the above expression *Wechselwirkung*, mutual effect, widely acknowledged to designate the central concept in Simmel's social theory, the first part, *Wechsel*, means 'exchange'.) Money, in turn, embodies and makes visible that exchangeability. On that same account, it indicates 'that things attain their meaning from one another, and that the reciprocity of the relations in which they are suspended confers upon them their being and their determinate configuration [*Sein und Sosein*]' (136; *128–9*). Note that by the same token, according to Simmel, money does nothing less than disclose 'the formula of being in general'. For this further reason, the modern expansion and intensification of the money economy attributes to modernity, so to speak, *epiphanic* significance. It discloses that, on a correct view, reality is not an assemblage of self-standing substances, but results from the innumerable effects exercised upon one another by components, each of which derives its own identity from how it relates to all others.

This thoroughly processual view of reality, of course, constitutes the *ontological* counterpart to the *epistemological* conception referred to above as 'relativity'. As Donald Levine suggests, for Simmel 'the world can be best understood in terms of conflict and contrast between opposing categories' (1967: 25); but one might also say that the world *results from, consists in,* such contrast and conflict. This mutual implication between the appropriate conception of knowledge and the appropriate conception of reality, is particularly clear from the following passage:

> Thus, knowing is a free-floating process, whose elements reciprocally determine each other's position in the same way as masses of matter do so by means of weight; for, like weight, truth is a relative concept. If, on this account, our image of the world 'hangs in the air', this is all right, for so does the world itself.
>
> (100; *106*)

This last statement has, it seems to me, an ironic undertone. It conveys, on the one hand, Simmel's own resolute conviction of the intrinsic validity of the modern world-view and, on the other, his awareness that that view threatens the sense of assurance, or indeed complacency, many still derive from holding on to pre-modern views. If this is a correct rendering of the statement's intent, it confirms that, according to Simmel, humanity owed to modernity a keener consciousness of its own powers (and of the attendant burdens) than it had possessed under previous conditions of society and culture; and that in so (as it were) *endorsing modernity* Simmel self-consciously distanced himself from positions widely held in his own intellectual environment.

This is also evident if one recalls his statement to the effect that the modern consciousness surpasses that of classical antiquity in its twofold awareness of objectivity *and* of subjectivity. Throughout the nineteenth century, German intellectuals almost unanimously subscribed to the 'myth of Hellas'; for them, Homeric and Attic culture were the highest expressions of the human spirit, nowhere equalled in their originality, vigour and intrinsic validity. The many contemporaries of Simmel's who shared that myth (which, it has been recently pointed out, had some racist undertones – see Bernal 1987) must have found outrageous his suggestion that 'the moderns' were superior to 'the ancients' on a matter of such significance as the correct understanding of the relationship between objective and subjective aspects of reality.

Philosophie des Geldes contains other statements which probably had similar polemical value. It suggests, for instance, that 'what we call the objective significance of things lies from a practical standpoint in their possessing validity for a larger circle of subjects' (472; *348*), and that, at bottom, 'objectivity = validity for subjects in general' (59; *81*). Simmel also went near asserting a pragmatist conception of truth (99–100; *6–7*), and associated himself with epistemological positions which allow for 'the simultaneous validity of opposing principles' (107; *110*).

Finally, although he shared with the majority of turn-of-the-century German philosophers a strong appreciation of Kant's revolutionary emphasis on the significance of a priori components in the knowledge process, Simmel suggested that 'much that at one point had been considered a priori has subsequently been recognized as an empirical and historical construct' (112–23; *114*). Such views were entertained also by other German philosophers (such as Dilthey and, in a later generation, Cassirer), as well as by other sociologists (such as Durkheim); but, so far as Simmel was concerned, their burden was again that the advance of modernity had been associated with a definite cognitive gain. Of course, 'definite' does not mean 'definitive'; and Simmel never suggested that the modern advances had reached anything like absolute, final truth – a target the very possibility of which was contested by the modern epiphany.

GIANFRANCO POGGI

THE BROADER IMPACT OF AN ADVANCED
MONEY ECONOMY

The institutional environment generally associated with a money economy, which Simmel discusses at length in *Philosophie des Geldes*, develops more visibly and coherently to the extent that money widens its reach and attains sophisticated forms. I am thinking of money's association, for instance, with centralized political power, positive law or the liberal constitution, for these are all arrangements that in turn characterize modern society as Simmel construes it.

Here, however, I will emphasize more abstract phenomena, which to a greater or lesser extent cut across the modern institutional landscape and which *Philosophie des Geldes* connects directly with the growing empire of money. For modern society is characterized not only by the intensification and acceleration of the developmental tendencies of money itself, but also by the extent to which money becomes utterly central to it.

One of the several ways in which Simmel phrases this insight is a provoking comparison between money and God. In an important passage (305–6; *236–7*) he applies to money Nicolas de Cusa's characterization of God as *coincidentia oppositorum*, that in which all contrasts are conciled; suggests that biblical monotheism may have been among the factors predisposing Jews to deal with money in a particularly effective manner; likens the feeling of peacefulness which money may inspire, because of what might be called its *potentiality*, to a religious mood. He even argues that these similarities may help account for the recurrent hostility of religious people towards money concerns, since what makes God and money into rivalrous entities is not so much what differentiates money from God but what they have in common.

Other points mentioned before, but which deserve further mention, concern the peculiar mental and moral temper associated with modernity. The first aspect of this is the intellectualization of existence, and is connected with the instrumental nature of money (591–2; *429–30*). According to Simmel, within the context of action, evaluations and feelings tend to focus on *goals*, whereas a cool, cognitive orientation is primarily appropriate to means. The latter orientation, therefore, becomes prevalent in modern society, both directly, because of the central significance acquired by that 'tool *par excellence*', money itself; and indirectly, because under modern conditions money allows the construction of lengthier and lengthier means/goals chains, where more and more of the apparent goals have no *ultimate* significance, but matter purely as means, as way-stations to further goals (592; *430*). Furthermore, 'the intensification of intellectual, abstracting capacities characterizes our time, in which money more and more becomes a pure symbol, indifferent to its own intrinsic value' (171–2; *152*).

A second, related feature of modernity, clearly associated with the increasing dominance of money, is the premium placed on a quantitative orientation to reality. 'Money appears as the exemplar, the expression or the symbol of the modern emphasis on quantitative aspects.' Simmel characterizes this emphasis as the prevalence of 'the interest in how much' over the interest in 'what and how', and states that it 'belongs to the very basis of our intellectual constitution' (368–9; *278–9*). That quantitative orientation engenders a disposition to calculate, and an emphasis on precision; once more, these are associated with money, as well as with another phenomenon in turn related to money: the modern conception of time as a continuous and uniform flow which lends itself to objective, precise reckoning.

> The penchant for measuring, weighing, exactly calculating characteristic of modern times ... seem to me causally connected with the money economy, which makes continuous mathematical operations necessary in the course of everyday existence. ... The mathematical character of money introduces into the relationship between aspects of existence the same precision, reliability in the determination of parity and disparity, lack of ambiguity in understandings and arrangements, that the general diffusion of pocket watches imposes upon other external aspects of our existence.
>
> (613, 615; *444, 445*)

Note that, according to Simmel, the quantitative orientation to reality finds expression in very diverse aspects of the modern institutional environment: for instance, in the recourse to majorities for settling political conflicts, or in the view of 'the greatest happiness for the greatest number' as an ethical rule (612–13; *443–4*).

A third feature of modernity is the acceleration of the tempo of existence (706–7; *505–6*). This is clearly connected with money's distinctive ability to mobilize and transfer values, enhanced in an advanced monetary economy by the increasingly symbolic character of money, thanks to which a great number of transactions can take place very rapidly, for instance on the stock market (438–9; *325–6*). The growing significance of money imparts a quality of restlessness to modern existence:

> The speedy circulation makes it a habit to give and to receive money, each specific quantity of which becomes psychologically less significant and valuable, while money itself acquires greater and greater importance, for monetary transactions affect the individual more widely and intensely than under less agitated conditions.
>
> (247; *199*)

And the tension this imparts to modern existence is less likely to be broken by periodic lapses into relative inertia than is the case in societies resting on a natural economy, with their more direct dependence on the rhythms of organic growth (677; *486–7*).

The association of money with individual freedom is also enhanced under modern conditions. A developed money economy allows (or perhaps compels?) individuals to enter into more numerous, wider, more diverse networks of relations with one another. But the relations in question are more and more anonymous, and thus only to a lesser extent commit, nurture and display the individual's personal qualities (397–8; *299*). Their scope is generally narrow (392–3; *295–6*); their terms are dictated by objective considerations (404; *303*); the associations resulting from them are 'soulless' (468; *346*). Paradoxically these very features of most of the relations the individual entertains allows him/her to withhold from them, and to cultivate and express out of their reach, preferences and inclinations peculiar to him/herself, to maintain a reserve vis-à-vis his/her counterparts in those several, unco-ordinated, discontinuous, discrete relations (397, 451; *298, 335*).

But there is a dark side to this phenomenon, which Simmel connects expressly, in a passage worth quoting at length, to the increased recourse to money, related in turn to ongoing modernization:

> The relationships of modern man to his milieu generally develop in such a way as to distance him from those closest

to him in order to bring him close to those more distant. . . .
In this general picture we find that distance increases within
properly intimate relations, while it diminishes within more
external ones. . . . The extent and intensity of the role money
plays in this twofold process manifests itself at first as the
overcoming of distance. . . . But money seems to me more
significant as the medium of the opposite tendency. . . .
Money transactions create barriers between those involved,
since only one of them receives what he *actually* wants,
what activates his specific sensations, while the other at first
only receives money, and must seek what he wants from a
third party. The fact that each enters the transaction with
a wholly different *kind* of interest imparts a new element
of estrangement to the antagonism already resulting from
their contrasting interests. . . . In this manner, as I said, there
emerges an inner barrier between people, one however that
is indispensable for the modern form of existence.

(664–5; *477*)

Those discussed so far are aspects of modernity connected with
the formal properties of money, and thus intensified by the growing scope and sophistication of an advanced monetary system.
We may now return to a point made at the beginning of this
section, concerning the central position money occupies in
modern society. If we consider in this light the nature of money
itself, rather than its formal properties, we realize that such position expresses and enforces in turn the centrality of economic
values, the dominance within modern society of the processes
pertaining to the production and distribution of wealth.

As we shall see in a moment, Simmel is emphatically aware
of this aspect of modernity; but *Philosophie des Geldes* chiefly
investigates its significance for the culture, the mentality, the life-
style of modern society, rather than showing how it shapes (and
results from) the distinctive structural arrangements of modern
society, its stratification system, the nature of its major component
groups, and the pattern of the relations obtaining between them.
(Characteristically, the final chapter of the book bears the title
'The Style of Existence', not 'The Styles'; and throughout *Philosophie des Geldes* Simmel reveals both his awareness of the class
phenomenon and his relative lack of interest in it.)

Within these limitations, *Philosophie des Geldes* argues most

eloquently and in a very sophisticated fashion for the pervasive-
ness and depth of the effects the money phenomenon has upon
modern society. Here, I will only consider some of the general
statements directly addressing the relationship between money
and modern society.

> At present ... the whole shape of existence, the relations
> of men to one another, the objective culture receive their
> colour from the interest in money.
>
> (304–5; *236*)

> Money becomes the central and absolute value.
>
> (369; *279*)

> The utter heartlessness of money mirrors itself in the culture
> of society, which it determines.
>
> (468; *344*)

A correlate of this overpowering presence of money is 'the
materialism of modern times, which even in its theoretical significance must share a common root with their money economy'
(360; *273*). Under modern law, for instance, it is difficult to seek
remedy and compensation for individual interests, no matter how
unjustly damaged, unless those interests are of a patrimonial
nature, and a money equivalent can be given for them; most of
the values that cannot be evaluated in those terms are practically
disregarded by the apparatus of justice. This is, as it were, the
downside of the 'extraordinary simplification and uniformity'
achieved by the modern legal system (503; *369*).

A concomitant of such materialism is, of course, an accentuated
secular orientation, individuals' growing inability or unwillingness
to keep themselves attuned to transcendental beliefs and values.
This phenomenon, Simmel notes, had already occurred during
the decadence of the society of classical antiquity (305; *236*); but
it has particularly damaging effects in (post-?)Christian societies.
For, with Christianity,

> [f]or the first time in the history of the West, a real ultimate
> purpose of life was offered to the masses, an absolute value
> of existence, beyond all that was petty, fragmentary, contra-
> dictory in the empirical world: the salvation of the soul and
> the kingdom of God.... [In this way] Christianity allowed

the need for an absolute, ultimate purpose to sink such deep roots, that even those souls that now reject it inherit from it the sheer longing for a definitive purpose of existence as a whole.

(491; *361*)

Therefore, modern secularization – in which, I repeat, the advance of the money economy plays a critical role – leaves man particularly deprived: he has lost any sense of ultimate purpose, but still longs for one (491; *361*).

A final aspect of modern society which one may relate to the central positions money holds within it is what Simmel labels the objectivity of the modern life-style. Money, operating as the universal link between all aspects of reality, brings everywhere its distinctive features of impersonality, abstractness, calculability, etc. Individuals are thus made to feel that they inhabit an immense and diverse but unified, self-enclosed realm of objects, all parts of which relate to one another and to the whole as if mechanically, leaving no place for emotion and for a sense of purpose or hierarchy.

Insofar as money itself is the omnipresent means to all goals, all elements of existence are geared together into a colossal teleological complex in which none of them is first and none is last. And since money measures all things with pitiless objectivity, and their resulting value determines their connections, there emerges a web of material and personal aspects of life which approximates the unbroken cohesion and the strict causality imparted to the cosmos by the laws of nature. Everything here is held together by money value in the same way that nature is held together by all-activating energy. Both energy and money value vest themselves in thousand different forms, yet the uniformity of their nature and the reversibility of all their transformations connect anything with anything and make of anything the condition of anything (593–4; *431*).

A world centred on money is thus a unified world, but one which gains its coherence only from objective relations, not from giving expression to a meaningful design on which individuals may fasten their commitments and their hopes. In Wittgenstein's inimitable statement, instead, the world is all that is the case.

In so analysing the hold upon modern society of an advanced money economy, Simmel began to introduce markedly negative

GIANFRANCO POGGI

motifs into his appraisal of modernity. It is difficult not to detect
a strong critical charge in a phrase like the following: 'If modern
man is free – free because he can sell everything and free because
he can buy everything . . .' (555; *404*). Those motifs are even more
clearly in evidence in *Philosophie des Geldes*'s arguments about
alienation.

THE PREVALENCE OF ALIENATION

To Simmel (it is doubtful whether the same thing can be said of
Marx) alienation is an anthropological phenomenon, not one
connected exclusively to the circumstances of modernity. He connects it, particularly in *Philosophie des Geldes*, with the notion of
objective spirit he derives from the idealist tradition. Alienation
represents a fateful vicissitude in the relationship between subjects and objects; it expresses, on the one hand, their mutual
dependency and their similarity of nature (indicated, in the
expression 'objective spirit', by the noun 'spirit' as against the
adjectives 'subjective/objective'), and, on the other hand, their
tendency to diverge (their *Diskrepanz*, Simmel calls it), their
repeated, frustrating failure to acknowledge, to correspond to,
one another.

The whole process follows from the very nature of objects.
These, besides being publicly accessible, external realities which
'bind time', are of necessity externally bounded, internally
bonded, structured entities. That is, they only exist in certain
configurations, have a given form, distinctive qualities. Although
they are the product of past action, such qualities are of consequence for future action: they open up certain possibilities and
foreclose others. The root of the difficulty is suggested by the
etymology of the term 'object' itself, and of its German equivalent, *Gegenstand*. Both the Latin *ob* (as in 'obstacle') and the
German *gegen* (=against) suggest something which resists, and
which must be mastered or overcome if the subject is to have its
way with it; for, alternatively, the object itself will have its own
way with the subject. An important late essay of Simmel's, 'Der
Begriff und die Tragödie der Kultur' ('On the Concept and the
Tragedy of Culture'), characterizes this second outcome as
follows:

The spirit brings about self-standing objects, over whose

58

path must take place the development of the subject from itself to itself. But by the same token is initiated the autonomous development of those very objects. This development continuously consumes the energies of subjects, drags them along *without* leading them to fulfil themselves. Thus the subject's development can no longer follow the same road as that of the objects, and if it follows that road it runs itself into a cul-de-sac or a vacuum.

(1911: 142–3)

Although anthropologically grounded, the alienation phenomenon, according to *Philosophie des Geldes*, attains such unprecedented intensity in modern society that it becomes a critical aspect of it. In modernity, the machinery of civilization yields as if automatically an overwhelming number and variety of objects. While most individuals have some access to a varying but relatively high proportion of those objects, none has a chance of *mastering* more than a ridiculously insignificant proportion of them. Rather, they mostly 'traffick' with objects – material and immaterial – and become dependent on them, without understanding them and often without truly appreciating them. A subheading from chapter 7 in *Philosophie des Geldes* characterizes in lapidary fashion the resulting, fatal *Diskrepanz*: 'Increase in the Culture of Things, Lag in the Culture of Individuals.'

Under modern conditions, the alienation phenomenon flows, in the first place, from the processes whereby material and immaterial objects are *produced*. Two overlapping aspects of those processes make it very difficult for their protagonists to recognize themselves in their products, to sense that they embody and represent their own powers.

The first aspect is the advanced *division of labour* characteristic of modern production (628–31; *453–6*). This makes the production process very complex, and locks its individual participants into narrowly circumscribed, highly specialized working roles. Mostly, their operations are imperiously prescribed, directly by the machines to which they attend, and indirectly by the managerial requirements of a complex productive unit which they cannot survey and understand.

The second aspect is the *capitalistic structure* of modern industry. Simmel argues its effects in ways that may remind readers of Marx's discussion of 'alienated labour' in *The Paris Manuscripts*, although these were unknown to Simmel himself and his contemporaries. Workers, he says, are typically 'separated' from the means of production; from the work experience itself, which is carried out under the control of employers and their agents; and from the products of labour, for these are commodities, and as such possess 'laws of motion of their own, a character foreign to that of the producing subject himself' (631–3; *455–7*).

Furthermore, the 'growing estrangement between the subject and its products' (637; *459*), induced by the division of labour and by capitalism in what Marx would call the *sphere of production*, finds a parallel in that of *consumption*. Normally, under modern conditions, individuals consume and otherwise make use of objects which are produced not for them but for the market, and reach them through complex distribution arrangements: '[S]o many intermediate passages stand between the producer and the consumer that they wholly lose sight of one another' (633; *457*). Besides, the offerings of the market are so numerous, diverse and changeable that the consumer has no chance of acquiring a thorough, self-confident familiarity with most of what he/she owns and uses. As is particularly clear in the case of fashion, products incessantly and invitingly present themselves to the individual as if they were part of 'a self-activating movement, an objective force which evolves through powers of its own' (640; *461*). As a result, even in their capacity as consumers individuals feel overwhelmed by the objects which surround them, and which they cannot easily assimilate; and this feeling is enhanced under modern conditions.

Furthermore, as I have already stated, most objects only play an intermediate, instrumental role within very lengthy means/goal chains, and have no intrinsic, consummatory significance of their own. This has two 'alienative' consequences. In the first place, trafficking with such objects (as producers, consumers, whatever) only activates and fosters – at best – the intellective faculties of the people involved. Such faculties fasten on those objects' instrumental import and disregard their insignificance from the standpoint of values and emotions.

This preponderance of means over goals finds its culmination and its most comprehensive expression in the fact that the periphery of life, matters outside of life's spiritual significance, have come to dominate over its centre and over ourselves.

(672; *482*)

What this engenders, or reinforces, is again the view of the world as 'all that is the case', as a complex of units and events held together only by causal processes, in which it is difficult to find purpose and meaning. In order to exist in a world so conceived, individuals must, as it were, bracket their own subjectivity, and concentrate on tinkering with objects, operating them as effectively as possible. This engages them in an effort at mastery over means: but the set of means they can realistically seek to master is generally very small. Besides, as Simmel notes in a different context, often a serious effort to master something takes the form of subordinating oneself to what one wants to master (318; *245*). This is reflected in the central position technology occupies in modern society: '[T]he control over nature which technology offers us is paid for by our enslavement to it' (672; *482*).

Insofar as this occurs, there opens up another 'road to alienation': the tendency for means to become goals in themselves. And here, again, money comes in, and nowhere as triumphantly as in its modern, highly developed forms. Again, money is intrinsically and exclusively instrumental; it owes all of its significance to its ability to give access to things other than itself, which alone can directly satisfy human needs. But this ability money possesses to such an extent, it can open so many doors so easily and effectively, that, paradoxically, it becomes the pinnacle and the centre of most people's aspirations, ambitions, wants, and tends to acquire a powerful hold over their passions. 'Money is the absolute means which on that very account acquires the psychological significance of an absolute goal' (307; *238*).

In modern society more than anywhere else, the multiplicity and complexity of means/goals chains, Simmel writes,

> is brought about by money, for money constitutes an interest which connects otherwise unrelated chains, to such effect that any one of these can serve as the premise of another wholly unrelated to it in substantial terms. . . . What counts is the fact . . . that everywhere money is conceived as a goal, and thus degrades to means an extraordinary number of things which properly constitute goals.

(593; *431*)

The sovereignty and centrality of money interests in modern society, then, amounts to a massive phenomenon of alienation, connected with other modern manifestations. Advanced forms of the division of labour, for instance, are only possible in a money economy: '[O]nly the exclusively monetary relation [between the employer and the worker] has the utterly matter-of-fact and automatic character which is indispensable to the construction of very differentiated and complex organizations' (65; *468*). 'Only money allows cultural objects to develop the degree of autonomy, the compelling form, which makes them resemble the way nature holds together' (651–2; *469*).

To bring to a close this argument, I will mention a few criticisms of the modern 'quality of life' voiced by Simmel in *Philosophie des Geldes*. First, the universal hold of the money economy has a strong *devaluing* effect on the things that money commands; to quote Oscar Wilde's famous aphorism, people know 'the price of everything and the value of nothing'. Simmel phrases this criticism as follows:

> The fact that ever more things can be had for money, and the related one, that money becomes the central and absolute value, has the consequence that things eventually are only valued to the extent that they cost money, and that the quality of value we see in them is merely a function of their higher or lower money price.... The significance of money replaces the significance of things.
>
> (369–70; *279*)

A psychological correlate of this development is the growing prevalence, particularly within the upper strata of modern, urban society, of what Simmel calls *Blasiertheit* – the blasé attitude. This consists in the loss of a capacity for discriminating appreciation of values. The blasé person 'experiences all things as being equally dull and grey, as nothing worth getting excited about' (334–5; *256*).

In the second place, the properties of money act back upon the individuals who are, as it were, the titular protagonists of the economy and the society which find in money their centre. Consider, for instance, the 'characterlessness' of money. As David Frisby points out, there are frequent intimations in *Philosophie des Geldes* of the emergence of a human type both celebrated and criticized in a famous Austrian novel, Robert Musil's *Man Without Qualities*. Frisby writes:

> Money's indifference to human goals and its facilitation of the reduction of individuals to fragmented functions ... suggest that the individual has not merely lost control over one of the purest of social forms but is actually faced with his or her disintegration as a total personality.... Individuals ... are unable to act except in order to perform ... fragmented functions.
>
> (1981: 146)

Furthermore, the centrality of the money economy and, in association with this, the existence of multiple, lengthy means/goals chains impart to modern society a quality of growing abstractness and artificiality. Individuals deal with less and less concrete, down-to-earth experiences, as a result of the following progression. As Simmel construes in the first chapter of *Philosophie des Geldes*, economic value is based on a comparison established (with a view to exchange) between pre-existent, primary values. But then money comes to stand for economic value itself, and in this capacity becomes the medium of increasingly extensive and complex sets of transactions. Furthermore, over time, money undergoes a process of increasing de-substantialization and symbolization: that is, what people under modern conditions tend to treat as 'absolute value' – money itself – bears a more and more arbitrary and abstract relation to economic, let alone primary, values: 'The economic relations, priorities and fluctuations of concrete things appear as derivatives from their own derivative, that is, as representatives and shadows of the significance which their money equivalent possesses' (181; *157*).

A significant implication of this is the growing economic significance of purely speculative activities in the financial market; these deprive of all stability the relation between the ultimate value of objects and its representation by, say, a bond or debenture bought or sold on the market for negotiable instruments. According to Simmel, such circumstances allow unrestricted play to 'the psychological impulses of caprice, of greed, of ungrounded opinion' (438; *326*) – a view which cannot fail to strike a chord in those aware of the increasing significance of purely financial manoeuvrings in today's economy.

In sum, it is not just that, in modern society, 'Things are in the saddle / And ride mankind.' The point is also that more and more of the 'things' in question bear only an exceedingly remote and fanciful relation to human feelings and wants. What seemed to Thoreau his contemporaries' foolish concern with dispensable possessions (see the opening section of *Walden*) is many times surpassed, on the evidence of *Philosophie des Geldes*, by Simmel's contemporaries (and many more times by ours). According to him, this imparts to the modern experience an increasing sense of unreality, of illusoriness, which he attributes also to the growing significance of technology (670; *481*). In a later essay, he quoted St Francis's definition of the ideal attitude towards material things, *nihil habentes, omnia possidentes*, and suggested that the opposite applies to modern individuals: *omnia habentes, nihil possidentes.*

Because modern technology *is* superior to pre-modern, we are led to think of it as intrinsically significant, that is, we fail to ask ourselves what valuable ends it might assist us in achieving. Once more, this impoverishes the quality of our lived experience, by centring it on matters and processes which should by rights lie at the periphery of it (672; *482*).

Sketchy as it is, this treatment of 'alienation in *Philosophie des Geldes*' may inspire in readers some doubts towards my earlier contention that Simmel does not espouse the bleak vision of modernity characteristic of German 'cultural pessimism'. Let me remind them, however, that the theme of alienation complements two other ways of characterizing modernity (its epiphanic nature, and the centrality of money to it), at least the first of which is prevalently affirmative; and that, as I have indicated, Simmel does not construe alienation as a phenomenon *exclusive* to modernity.

Furthermore, although he, unlike Marx, does not think that alienation can be abolished, erased from the trajectory of the human species, Simmel thinks that single, gifted and heroically committed individuals can overcome it. They can do so by steadily reaching beyond what they know and possess, treating it as a horizon to be transcended, an attainment to be challenged (in the words of Rilke) *immer wieder*, ever anew. There is definitely an élitist streak in Simmel; if the masses are, sadly, condemned to acquiescence and complacency, and thus to a surrender to alienation, to a few individuals it is given to surmount the masses' fate, to express the human spirit's capacity for self-transcendence in their capacity for critical appreciation of material and immaterial objects, and for exacting, abiding commitment to cultural values.

NOTES

This essay draws on chapters 6 and 7 of Poggi (1993). The first draft of this book was completed in 1989–90 while I was a Fellow at the Center for Advanced Study in the Behavioral Sciences (Stanford, California), whose support is gratefully acknowledged.

1 For a sophisticated review of the theoretical *querelle* about modernity, see Blumenberg (1983).
2 The same thing could perhaps be said of Max Weber. But Weber 'thematizes' modernity only infrequently; his analytical focus is primarily on the notion of rationalization, and in the light of it he sometimes disemphasizes the break between modern and pre-modern Western society-and-culture. (See, for instance, the '*Vorbemerkung*' to the 1920 edition of *The Protestant Ethic*.) Furthermore, his concept of modern capitalism antedates that break with respect to the era of the Enlightenment, where German social and political thought tended to place it.
3 I will cite this text by giving page numbers first in the recent edition from the *Gesamtausgabe* (Simmel 1900a) then, in italics, in the English translation (Simmel 1900b). Wherever a translation is given, however, it is my own.
4 I borrow this imaginative expression from Moore (1966: 352).
5 The extent to which some critical concerns about modernity were shared across national boundaries by European intellectuals of the Simmel generation is apparent for instance in Hughes (1959).
6 For a similar formulation, see Levine (1991: esp. 105).
7 We may, however, connect with it a footnote in a text by Simmel recently translated as 'The Problem of Style':

> Material has ... a great importance for style. The human form, for instance, demands quite a different type of expression if it is presented in porcelain or in bronze, in wood or in marble. For the material is in fact the general substance, which offers itself equally to an arbitrary number of different forms, and thus determines these as their general prerequisite.
>
> (1908: 71)

3

TECHNOCRACY AND DEMOCRATIC POLITICS

Ian Varcoe

Technocratic theories are symptomatic of a profound cultural crisis, as are anti-technocratic views which accept the idea of a growing dominance of technique and its social bearers or representatives. They have sprung up in the absence of a social theory that would explore systematically and illuminate the relations between industrial processes of production and human social, motivational and political organization. At the same time, they exploit the methodological uncertainties of social science. In particular, there is lacking a sociology of technology which would seek to understand the place of technique, linguistic and social as well as material-instrumental, in human life and history, although of course some progress has been made. Fears of technocracy as well as its advocacy are symptomatic, too, of the defensiveness into which humanistic and literary culture has been thrown by science, and of the mingled sense of promise and disappointment, resentment and enthusiasm which has surrounded the question of the broader cultural meaning of developments in the social sciences.

'Technocracy' grows from the fact that science and technology appear to be ever-present, expanding realities, but their expected benefits are not. The utopia of the dissolution of power has not come about, either from within, or through the importation into social life and the implantation there of the ethics and method of science. And in the hands of those who desperately require total solutions and seek them restlessly, technocracy has come to seem perilous as well as a source of hope. Technocratic thinking (and action) of a positive, affirmative kind is characteristic of the early stages of industrialization when cultural strains are greatest and the impact of modern industry is most in evidence. At these times, the question of the future of power in the society is a critical one. Or technocratic thought is characteristic of societies – like the United States – which have achieved a position of cultural and economic dominance such that observers are not compelled to face up to the facts, and strains, of comparative powerlessness and cultural subordination. In addition, technocracy can be sustained as a credible political reality, where, as in France, there is a combination of comparative cultural isolation with considerable centralism. Here technocracy is associated with *dirigisme* and planning.

TECHNOCRACY AND CULTURAL POLITICS

The central disjunction to which technocracy draws attention is one which involves a combination of social complexity and advanced technology, but which is marked by a persisting gap between technical and social sophistication; between the level of technical control and that of understanding of, and ability to manipulate, the socio-technical environment. Technocracy is, at the same time, a phenomenon of lags; of the gaps of which it is painfully aware and from which its proponents seek to escape through the salvatory medium of science. Science is, in this sense, raised far beyond its own inherent authority within its defined province. It becomes a cultural authority and source of legitimation of political power.

The gaps of which technocracy produces such a sensitive awareness are those between, on the one hand, a dominant, culturally superior and universally attractive source of growth in activities worthy of the highest aspirations of humankind as well as in material power (e.g. research and development in developed, scientifically productive countries and regions); and, on the other, a materially and culturally deprived and ineffective set of cultural regions (e.g. poorer countries and regions without a strong science base). This, in a world made conscious of a certain basic cultural cohesion and identity (cf. Gellner 1968). It is of importance, but still secondary, that these gaps are also an element of stratification, and that power and powerlessness to effect outcomes in the world of affairs is involved. Much concern has, for example, been expressed about the technology gap between Europe and the United States.

European countries, being smaller, are spending more than

67

they can afford on scientific research.[1] The results of this research are still most effectively exploited by the United States. Because of its size and its scale of investment, the United States can get more from a proportionally smaller, although absolutely much larger, investment than the Europeans. It can keep in the forefront of a wider range of fields of science than them.[2] Also, there is a drain of highly qualified manpower trained in Europe, attracted to the United States by the prospect of working in the forefront of research.[3]

This gap has, however, been mistakenly understood as implying an underlying 'logic' of technological development in all these societies (Floud 1971). All seem to be pressed into spending a great deal on research and training larger numbers of qualified research workers. The United States, on this reading, only appears to be the leading country, the one most affected in this way.

What is not seen is that United States' dominance is interpreted politically by the smaller countries in terms that induce them to spend more themselves. However, it is not so much their common technology or industrial processes that impel them, but rather their political perception of the gap and their response to it, in the face of an electorate inclined to measure other things in terms of scientific and research strengths. (Whether or not they are right to do so is another question.)

Technocratic assumptions are thus more easily and appropriately held in the dominant country which perceives others tending to follow a path it appears to tread rather effortlessly. These assumptions are: universality of direction of change; immanence of change; a single source of change; and a fundamental subsystem responsible for change.[4]

A necessary distinction is that between the technocracy of the centre and that of the periphery (Shils 1975). Technocratic solutions are canvassed when the dilemma of isolation as against expansion must be confronted by either a society or a smaller social group such as a profession (King 1968). The choice is one between, on the one hand, seeking a more inclusive role which the importance of a social function (of, for example, a profession) or a country's 'world role' (in the case of a national society) is said to warrant; and, on the other, a renewal of defensive husbanding of elements of culture and social organization which are thought to be of supreme value and for which the 'outside world' (the wider society, or other societies) is judged not yet ready.

Technocracy provides an answer to this question. It can be of either an *expansionist*[5] or a *minimalist*[6] kind. The latter ensures purity of principle and concentration on purely technical tasks. In each case, cultural clash, the possibility of assimilation of alien elements, is avoided.

Peripheries are either *defensive*[7] or *proprietary*[8] in relation to the sources of technological change and scientific discovery. These sources are the previously described regions of social space which are the more highly charged and which exercise a leading role. They would do so through the impact created by the diffusion of innovations which they bring, more rapidly and potently than others, into being. They do not necessarily actively seek a corresponding political dominance through cadres and planning agencies devoted to the management of the diffusion. Those to whom innovations are diffused must necessarily adopt an attitude of heightened, often fevered, expectancy. They may indeed have cause to be fearful. If so, they will probably not care about science itself or its relation with the political authorities, the would-be technocratic leaders of the expansive centre.

A minimalist centre which seeks to hide its influence and which feels that something of its effectiveness would be lost by association with the worldly authorities may still be drawn out, and some of its leading members forced to assume the role of 'statesmen' and mediators (King 1968), by quiescent (defensive) peripheries turned resentful (proprietary). Intellectuals play a leading role in the awakening of peripheries, just as they do in the minimalist or expansionist centres.

Peripheries may consistently express a sense of deprivation in relation to science, considered as a cultural good to which all have an equal right. Or they may, only slowly and with great difficulty, turn their attention from the discomforts of their immediate situation to its remote sources in a cultural location (a centre) that emits more influences than it receives; these become intermittent and disjointed in their differential impact on peripheries. Innovation is not disruptive for the source of origin which is prepared for it in having brought it to life; it has the attendant technologies and is more able to cope with the side-effects.

In the case of a peripheral region's attempt at appropriation of science (or its results) as a cultural good to which it feels it has a right of access, it is the corruption of those goods, i.e. of science, which is charged. Science, the common property of all humankind, is said to have been appropriated by the political authorities for political ends which are masked by science. The charge is one of technocracy. Although science is absolved from having been an active partner in its own corruption, the charge of technocracy politicizes science. It assumes that science can be used, however neutral it may really remain, in the pursuit of worldly influence. In the face of such charges it is futile for those who believe otherwise to defend the purity of science. For one thing, the fact that critics believe science now to be implicated is enough to move its affairs into the public domain. For another, the case for the purity of science is often acceptable enough in principle to critics who none the less deny that scientists *themselves* can guarantee it. Those who reject science itself – its values and ethos are held by critics to be inhuman, impersonal, general and therefore empty, etc. – remain beyond the reach of argument. (But then, they do not believe sufficiently in the worthwhileness of science to be concerned about its corruption by those who rise to political influence in the world by riding on its back.)

However, to most critics it is power, capitalism, the unholy alliance between the military and industry which is responsible for the true science having been diverted from its proper course, i.e. the disinterested service of humankind, into channels alien to its proper aims and import. Closely related to this attitude is the one which asserts that the weak and disinherited are, wittingly or otherwise, already possessors of the true science. The concept of a science alternative to the existing one – not merely one with different objects of research[9] – is, however, much more difficult to sustain than the corruption charge, both logically and in the world as presently arranged. Anything remotely resembling scientific activity has for too long been removed from the province of even the educated non-scientist in the rich countries of the West to make its practice independently of existing powers a possibility. It is today a professionalized science.

In the case of applied scientific research – most indeed of the broad spectrum of activities known as research and development – the technocratic intent is already plain: the use of science for the development of new techniques for the solution of problems. Still, the charge of the corruption of science, of its technocratic distortion in the service of political ends, is likely to be levelled where there is a substantial gap between the centres of the directed diffusion of its results and the peripheral regions of society or social space where its effects actually come to reside.

At the periphery, circumstances may be very different from those envisaged at the centre. What appears to the centre as a neutral application of science within a framework of common, unexceptionable values is, in reality, a failure to realize that the gap can be mediated only by one of a variety of political processes, from bargaining to the exercise of authority unilaterally. It is a failure of acumen. In such situations, science is abused, even by its friends.

TECHNOCRATS: ARE THEY A CLASS?

Technocratic theories involve the idea that power in society is passing to the category of persons who have technical or scientific qualifications. By 'technical' one is thinking of the applied social as well as the natural sciences, including the qualifications possessed by those who have been to a business school or have otherwise been formally trained in the methods of modern management. Often, however, the term 'technocrat' is not applied very strictly at all, and is meant simply to suggest the new people, who hold public and private positions of some responsibility, but who do not do so on the basis of property ownership or the possession of a political following. The 'technocrat' represents a different basis and type of power. Their prototype is perhaps the modern official, who owes his or her position to the fact of being qualified for the office. The office, not the person or their private fortune, is the source of authority.

It seems central to the idea of a ruling group or class that its members should be conscious of the fact, and that they should consciously defend the principle they claim to represent. This is not just for the purpose of legitimating, or providing for acceptance among the ruled of, the power that is wielded; it is, in a more narrow sense, ultimately bound up with ruling itself. This is, above all, a purposeful activity involving the conscious pursuit of ends and the active defence of a set of means against rival ones, and against the possessors of those means.

The claim that the *techniciens* are, or are on their way to becoming, a new ruling élite or class is unconvincing.[10] However, rising classes are not given to announcing their arrival in advance, so to speak.[11] By the same token, the very ubiquity of *techniciens*, the fact of their having entered the service of many groups, including organized labour, in contemporary society, and their growing indispensability may have put them in a position in which their own assertion of their capacity to rule could command a widespread acceptance in the event of a crisis.

An empirical approach to these matters prompts an awareness that a long period of time may elapse between the first appearance of representatives of the new people of influence and their actual assumption of a dominant role in society. During this time, their ultimate intentions need not be clear to themselves, or to others, and they are capable of working alongside other, more obviously powerful groups. However, although a group's interests are subordinated to another's for a period, these interests do not cease to exist. There would be nothing to stop the technically qualified from ceasing to serve others if it were in their interests to do so and if the right circumstances presented themselves.

In addition, the comparatively small numbers of the technically qualified is offset by the fact of their being strategically placed in effective control of vastly expanded and technically more effective processes and machines (Bourricaud 1949: 203). If nothing else, there has been in the last one hundred years or so a relative shift away from mechanical processes in which manual labour plays a significant role, to systems dependent for their operation upon the application of organized intelligence. These range from administration to the production of nuclear energy.

People intimately associated with the new technologies may come to play a variety of political roles. Given their relative indispensability, the question of which one is important. There is even the possibility that they will defy attempts to assess their likely behaviour based on every interpretation of the previous conduct of ascendant and descending classes. The newer educated cadres, or some section of them, could come to prominence through a conjunction of as yet unexplored social forces – *entre l'avant dernier et le dernier acte.*

TECHNOCRATS' IDEOLOGY

Since the eighteenth century, the creation of new knowledge and the implementation of new techniques have had an increasingly explosive impact upon the rest of society.[12] This has been accompanied by a persisting perception[13] of the disproportion between progressively more sophisticated technique and the relatively slow rate of change of other aspects of belief and action (Ogburn 1932). Institutions such as those of religion, the system of property, relations of authority, the family, work and patterns of consumption have been seen to adapt slowly and incompletely to developments in material culture. The contrast[14] between the potential afforded by vastly augmented material and intellectual means[15] for achieving given ends and the existing institutional arrangements[16] has excited the curiosity of, and provoked the sense of moral outrage among, successive generations of thinkers. Intervening between the possible and the actual realization of a given potential, these institutions serve to hold up, smother and distort the society's performance in the achievement of the goals of individual well-being and social harmony.

Where thinkers have differed is in the location of the source of the obstruction within the social framework (e.g. traditions, social classes), and in the course of action necessary to overcome them. They have differed both in the conception of the passage to a properly ordered future (e.g. peaceful, revolutionary) and in their vision of the utopia of which the future would consist (e.g. division of labour or its absence). (Surprisingly few have been untouched by these conceptions, or have actually questioned the validity of the distinction between technology and the non-material, non-rational elements of culture upon which they rest.)

Technocratic conceptions are well known for predicting the end of power and coercion in human affairs. Theirs has been a preoccupation with the functional achievement of tasks, taking priority over, and removing the heat from, disagreements arising from the organization of production and administration. Differences between people arising from the facts of ownership or reward would become inessential[17] in a society in which the power of decision rested with those who were qualified for, and actually carried out, the essential tasks, upon the fulfilment of which all depended.[18] Any remaining differences in a society ordered in this way would be seen to flow from the fact that not all are necessarily qualified for, or expected to make, social contributions of the same worth. These necessarily remain different, although the differences will be accepted as legitimate by virtue of the requirement of effective task performance which remains the basis for the well-being of all.[19]

The technocratic utopia is one in which the tension between

73

advanced technological processes and outmoded and retarded social and political arrangements has been removed. It is one in which those who are best able to see and respond to the newer technical imperatives are in a position to make their influence felt. With this influence comes the dissolution of coercion.[20] Organization and technique now being adjusted, there will be no need for the exercise of force, which is a sign of inefficiency. The appeal of the technocrats is thus explicitly to a future in which there will be no more ideological ferment, because no more politics. The administration of things will replace the old government of people.[21]

What is paradoxical in this conception is that its employment of rationality, which is the source of its powerful appeal, is, at the same time, the source of its negation as a political weapon. Technocrats are necessarily highly pragmatic creatures. It is for this reason that their thinking has been regarded in two ways: (1) as peculiarly insidious, constituting a new kind of penetration of hitherto-known political behaviour and argument (e.g. Habermas 1971); and (2) as a comparatively harmless pragmatism that is destined to be overcome and forced to face up to its own limitations in the face of genuine and permanent conflicts of interests, in which technocrats necessarily participate as subsidiary, and only intermittently influential, elements (e.g. Bettelheim 1949; Lefebvre 1967); that is, technocratic thinking will be repeatedly swept away in the ideological conflict of classes. Neither interpretation is true. Technocratic thinking is linked to existing traditions; but at the same time, it has real force.

THE FAITH IN SCIENCE

The members of the newer educated élite groups may be said to possess a military, juristic or capitalistic complexion. However, they do so as competences or abilities possessed, rather than as the right of issuing commands requiring obedience, ultimately by virtue of the superior sanctions at the disposal of authority.

Among them, there has been uncertainty as to what they might stand for.[22] A persisting feature is the denial that theirs is a demand for effective political power commensurate with that wielded by previous groups in history. The principle of office is undoubtedly of importance in setting off the newer right to rule against previous forms, but what unites it with the technocratic form is that modern officials are almost universally recruited on the basis of the possession of specialized competences as attested to by the possession of paper qualifications. The increasing weight attached to these, and the fact that actions in pursuit of a plan or some other pre-determined administrative programme are considered to flow directly from them, distracts the attention of the possessors of qualifications, and of critics and commentators, from the claim to the right to rule implicit in actions having some discretionary component.

The emphasis on trained, specialized competence as a basic principle of social organization rests upon an appreciation of the difference which modern science has made to the ancient idea that knowledge is power. Applied science has been seen to transform human life through the medium of medical advances, changes in the methods of transportation and communication, etc. To many thinkers, the question has also arisen of applied science transforming human institutions.[23]

Since the Enlightenment, reason is held to be the common possession of all people. Authority, apart from that of reason itself, is understood to require a submission unbefitting the dignity of the individual. The prospect of the ending, if not of all authority, at least of that which cannot be justified by reason is also the promise of an end to the use of force and constraint in human affairs, just as, in the economic sphere, the application of rational methods to production can be seen as heralding the end of necessity.[24]

It is held that scientific truths alone are susceptible to rational, unconstrained acceptance. Up until the dawn of the scientific age, the ultimate realities were held to be mysterious. Access was permitted only to a priestly minority. The proper discharge of their responsibility towards the laity consisted in a form of pastoral care. A partial ignorance on the part of the latter was considered to be part of the divine scheme of things. The steps towards the attainment of grace, if this were possible, were marked not by a progressive rational penetration, but by a deeper spiritual appreciation of ultimate reality as revealed by God. The discoveries of science, in contrast, are available to all who are qualified by virtue of sustained interest to assess them.

The charge is made by religious or anti-rational critics that scientific rationalism is corrosive of human solidarity, that it has no higher purpose; and that it offers no prospect of contact with a transcendental level of reality. Against this, the defenders of scientific rationalism argue that scientific inquiry is guided by an ethic. The investigator is required to submit before empirical truth. This supplies a bond among all who accept the discipline of science and acts as a check upon personal self-interest. A conception is provided of the scientific community as a model of a free society; and of the moral qualities of the scientist as the standard of conduct for all who would be active participants in it (Polanyi 1951, 1962).

THE FEAR OF SCIENCE AND THE STRAINS OF TECHNOCRATIC CULTURE

This has not satisfied the critics. They point out that the compulsion to bend before the facts as interpreted by science can be used to justify the exercise of force in human affairs, and that technology can supply new means for the exercise of tyranny. The critics warn of the threat which the incorporation of the findings of science poses to human values, and see faith in the eradicability of 'politics' from human life as confirmation that they never can be.

To the critics, the rationalistic utopia[25] is corrosive of the 'moral' and 'political' categories which define conduct and are constitutive of human life. Coercion and the exercise of power, as much as the blind adherence to established institutions and behaviour patterns, are thought to be endemic in society which must remain inherently recalcitrant to being placed on a new, unproblematic footing. The great majority of human beings are, on this view, simply incapable of submitting to the stern, and perhaps ultimately self-destroying, disciplines of reason and experience.

This broad tradition of thought encompasses, in different ways, philosophical conservatives as well as the more liberally inclined. Included in it are positivists like Durkheim, who, while methodologically in the camp of positive science, considered society to be a fundamentally moral phenomenon. The Philosophical Radicals were very close to the scientistic tradition. They did not share the fear that Reason threatened human values or the belief that human action itself was intractable to re-organization on scientific lines. It is not the methods of science but the faith in its authority that is decisive. This issue divides those for whom science stands in tension with values from those who hold that it alone extends the promise of an advance to a better and more harmonious world.

Several forms of twentieth-century thought manifest sensitivity to the strains induced by an increasingly technocratic culture. These are partly an autonomous development within the conservative, socialist and neo-Marxist (as practised by the Frankfurt School)[26] traditions. They are also a reaction to the technocratic elements in Marxism–Leninism, corporativism (Fascism, National Socialism) and the social democratic labour movement on the continent of Europe, particularly in Germany. The common element in these otherwise diverse movements was the unqualified acceptance of certain technological 'givens', from which flowed the 'need' to re-organize society[27] in such a way as to liberate more fully the potentials for national growth, power and economic well-being of the people. On the political plane, this means the freeing of the specialized expertise of groups of qualified practitioners from various interferences.[28] Waste and inefficiency are said to be caused by profiteering or by 'irrelevant' groups which interpose themselves between the leaders and the rank and file. A more direct, rationalized command structure is called for, in which the managers, in James Burnham's (1962) sense, will play a larger role.[29] In Nazi Germany and Soviet Russia this reform programme was total in that it applied to the entire political organization of society.

The opposition to technocracy remained diffuse because of the initial diversity of the sources of the negative appraisal of technology; and because technocracy nowhere became an effective political force in its own right, despite the predictions of publicists like Burnham. It was overlaid with the repudiation, far more explicit than that of technocracy, within the Western democracies, of other things that the Soviet and Nazi regimes had inaugurated. Of particular concern was the suppression of a system of democratic political representation and civil liberties, brought about in the countries affected by a totalitarianism determined to suppress all forms of 'interference' in the 'direct' relation between the leaders and the led.

In the twentieth century, the preoccupation with the political implications of modern industrial technology – the effect of which has been to spread the engineering mentality both within the social organization of the factory and in social life generally –

has been a decidedly intellectualist one, associated with revolutionism and reaction:[30] strikingly absent in the 'ideologial breakdown between the enthusiasts and the indifferent' has been any 'simple left and right alignment' (Maier 1970: 28). The artistic, intellectual and social movements which have sprung up in response to an increasingly urban-industrial civilization have shown different degrees of both these political attitudes in their praise for, and condemnation of, what the modern technologies and their associated social arrangements have been said to bring. Often the response has been a fervid sense of mingled hope and despair in which reactionary and progressive elements have been indistinguishably mixed.[31]

Artistic and general intellectual culture offers many examples of this mingled sense of liberation and oppressiveness. The former was in the forefront of the brief flowering of Soviet art, immediately following the 1917 revolution, in which technology was married to social purpose. The latter feeling is carried particularly by those for whom modern life has come to mean only a growing fear of rationalism, bureaucratic centralism and latterly totalitarianism; and, in the case of fascist aesthetics, revolt against this took the form of a reconciliation with a technology seen now as celebrating the irrational: will and violence (and in the case of the Italian Futurists, eroticism and death). This profound sense of ambiguity is associated with the change of pace of European industrialization; the growth of the newer, science-based industries; and the consolidation of the city. It has inhibited the development of a specific, technocratic political doctrine or world-view. Instead, technocracy has remained a way of thinking. It is a strand or element in political philosophies which claim in some way to be progressive.[32]

A central figure in creating and disseminating these aspirations is the modern secular intellectual, as someone either with a scientific training or conscious of the lack of it. The intellectuals are also the bearers of the anti-scientistic tradition. They are the source of romantic attacks on science and technology, although they have also inspired on occasion what Thomas Mann termed 'a highly technological romanticism' (1947: 24). Current conditions exacerbate the old ambivalence.

This is now becoming increasingly intensified. It is true that the effect of the revolution in modern methods of communication and warfare has tended to be to make the world more of a unity.

However, it is equally true that technology creates gaps within and between countries which may be perceived to be more impossible to bridge than previously existing ones of physical distance and inaccessibility. The habit of thinking in 'global' terms has always been the prerogative of intellectuals. They have always had a more intermittent attachment to the symbols of class and nation.[33]

The effects of the discoveries of modern science have been to reinforce this habit of thinking in 'totalistic' terms. At the same time, the reaction against these tendencies has been more sharply experienced and voiced more articulately by intellectuals who find themselves caught between an increasingly dominant world culture (of science) and the disjunctions it induces everywhere. Part of the traditional restlessness of intellectuals lies in their occupying this position.[34]

There has always been an ambivalence towards science. The point of origin of the modern attitude is the nineteenth-century German academic tradition. Scholars attempted both to consolidate historical studies scientifically and, at the same time, to perpetuate a philosophical tradition in which there was a radical disjunction between the necessity of nature and the free actions of free human beings as expressed in history and culture. The ambivalence towards science is continued down to the present day in the ever-present conflict between 'specialism' and general culture. The 'specialist area' seems to be the condition of effectiveness within modern science and scholarship and the basis of its organization as a community. A broad knowledge appears to be both the residuum of an older idea of cultural organicism and the ideal of the person as a rounded source of humane expression. The conflicting pressures are: (1) of general cultivation, which seems to be the condition of intellectual performance – range and breadth being necessary to the selection of problems of sufficient profundity; and (2) of specialization. The attendant feelings are, on the side of specialization, of intellectual isolation and ineffectiveness, and, on that of general cultivation, of being an anachronism and of ineffectualness.

There is on the part of modern intellectuals both admiration of, and disdain for, science in a world which appears increasingly to be made after science's image. On the one hand, science has done so much to improve the lot of humankind. On the other, it seems to be the source of new divisions and injustices. As a 'neutral' tool, it is implicated in the aims of its various users. Even in its neutrality it is somehow condemned for its heartlessness. It is resented because of its very indispensability and neutrality even while its critics borrow its forms of expression.

The modern scientific intellectual regards him- or herself as part of the wider intellectual community, and belonging to the Western tradition. Even so, he or she cannot but be aware of being different from the occupants of traditional intellectual roles – both in their very specialization and in the fact that they are separated by a wide gulf from even the most intelligent and actively curious of the educated public. Above all, the modern scientist is implicated in the bringing about of changes through the medium of new techniques. This has never been true of the literati, who may have held administrative power or been close to rulers but were never placed, as scientists have been, in a position of continuous proximity to matters affecting the military and economic interests of nation-states.

Coupled with this is the continuing uncertainty as to whether science itself is a world-view or merely a technique devoid of any higher purpose and incompatible with, or at least distinct from, the traditional religious faiths. Moreover, since at least the early nineteenth century, there has been a tendency for the enthusiasm for science and the reaction against it to go in waves.[35] This has given to modern culture a marked cyclical tendency. In the twentieth century, the 'swing effect'[36] seems to have occurred more quickly. There has been a rapid oscillation[37] between a belief in the redemptive power of science and a disgust and disenchantment with what it is said to have produced.[38] This has created a deeply characteristic modern tension.

TECHNOCRATIC THINKING AND IDEOLOGIES

Technocratic thinking does not constitute an absolute break with previous forms of ideological thinking. Indeed it has given the latter some of its principal characteristics. These it still shares.[39] Nor is it to be regarded as inconsequential because premature.[40] On the contrary, it expresses a permanent feature of modern societies, that is, how might developments in technology and industry affect the structure of power within those societies? And which groups are best qualified, and on the basis of qualification most likely, to assume power?[41]

Technocratic scientism professes itself anti-ideological; yet it bears the marks of ideology. Arising out of modern scientific culture, its adherents claim that it constitutes a solution to all traditional political dilemmas, and that it provides an infallible, because 'scientific', guide to the future of humankind.

However, it differs from the ideologies of other non-scientific movements in that its appeal is to reason. This creates certain difficulties for the doctrine, considered either as a set of formulations about modern science and its role, or as one about the nature of political power in the technologically advanced societies.

The claim that those technically qualified to do so should be allowed to run society does not differ from other similar claims, either in the apparent variety and incompatibility of the groups to which it is directed (e.g. Marxism), or in the fact that it is often presented in the guise of objective social-scientific analysis of the way developments are actually tending (e.g. liberal economics). Neither are the circumstances, the cultural and political context in which ideas of this kind are formulated, so inchoate as to render the ideas themselves incoherent. 'Technocracy', and the broader tradition of scientism in which it is embedded, remains a body of ideas, like other such ideas, shaped by a setting and a set of experiences which provides the frame in which the thinker is placed, even while remaining unaware of the larger meaning and tendency of development of the forces which are located, or of which he or she forms a part.

The profoundly paradoxical aspect of the attempt to secure the logic and methods of modern science as an aspect of the political organization of societies is that both science and politics appear to lose their character: they tend to lose their tension with each other which gives them their identity. This is, at the same time, the source of the perennial appeal of the idea. The 'superior' rationality would unite the rational scientific universe with the world beyond it in an overarching synthesis.

The claim is frequently made on behalf of political doctrines that they are comprehensive and part of a cumulative development. Like scientific theories, they are thought to have emerged not as simple successors to, but as replacements for, their predecessors – and to be distinctly more 'adequate' than them. Highly 'ideological' politicians uncompromisingly and explicitly demand the immediate and consistent extension of political ideas to social reality. In their style, there is more than an echo of the rigour and exactitude demanded by scientists of their experimental techniques.

In those doctrines which envisage a planned or strategic approach to social organization, the conduct of political life is linked explicitly to the methods of science. As the agents of the execution of this new approach, they see various kinds of expert, e.g. economists, administrators and trained revolutionists. Such doctrines are generally impatient of all forms of customary and evaluative approaches to existence. Moral sentiments, and the appeal to the righting of long-standing injustices, play only a secondary part in them.

Waste, inefficiency and the deformation of the life of the emotions are things that flow from a system of authority based on principles other than those of the technical 'one best way'. They are certainly seen as undesirable. But the benefits likely to flow from their removal are not considered the primary goal of action. Nor is the removal of authority itself, as in anarchism. Of principal and overriding importance is the pressure, born of human cognitive faculties, to secure an order in which reason is the sole determinant of action and the exclusive content of belief. What ultimately matters in this conception is the rational perception of the underlying principles of nature and society, and not the imperatives of securing an augmentation of state power on behalf of the masses, or of abolishing authority itself in the name of the unique and irreducible powers of self-expression of the individual personality.

Technocratic thinking takes from science the scheme of means–ends rationality: the idea of determined and determinable techniques involving the manipulation of certain variables, based on a theoretical, and not merely rule-of-thumb, appreciation of the technical field of operations. The picture is one which stresses the origins of the purely intellectual side of science in practical, technological advances.[42] Although it has only been advanced in these terms in recent times, the description goes back to Saint-Simon, and beyond him, to Bacon. The sciences, like the arts, were pre-eminently useful activities. Their productiveness was contrasted with the idleness of courtly life and the destructiveness of the military aristocracy.

For technocratic thinking, politics is understood as concerned with matters of human association, not necessarily with power, authority or rule. Politics is, in principle, separable from power, and a politics without power is conceivable.[43] This idea was familiar to both Proudhon and Marx and Engels. It was also present in the classical liberal notion of the self-regulating market mechanism which rendered state functions secondary, if not unnecessary or positively harmful. It also lies behind theories of post-industrial society.

These envisage a peaceful, universal transfer of authority. This will lead to the dissolution of hierarchical power as it has been known up to the present; to the replacement of commands by competences, applied to objective needs; and to the dispersion of authority to functional groups. The number of these, their diverse relations to each other and their indispensability, it is expected, will turn them into independent, necessarily interdependent, centres of decision (Bell 1967).[44] Central to the perceptions of those who see such a new social order in the making is, on the one side, the apparent abatement of the social struggle between classes, and, on the other, the establishment since 1945 of some of the leading universities and scientific research institutions, particularly in the United States, as the recipients of an augmented, and not entirely disinterested, patronage. The group of qualified scientists and engineers employed full-time in research and related activities is, accordingly, larger in the United States than in any single European country.

It is larger even than the whole of the European scientific community combined. But it is not much larger, considered as a proportion of the total labour force, than the leading European complements. In terms of the variety of disciplines and specialisms represented, and the degree of excellence with which they are cultivated, the American research and development system is unrivalled in the world. By contrast, in Europe 'it is a question' not merely of resources, but 'of the "inefficiency" of science and technology systems supported by traditionalist attitudes and mentalities' (OECD 1981: 54).

In the United States there has developed a highly flexible and varied institutional framework surrounding scientific research and training. There exists a variety of institutions between the traditional university department,[45] that more recent phenomenon the industrial research laboratory, and its counterpart in government. Also there are special forms of contractual relationship and specialized institutes as well as a more complex and variegated system for advice-giving in executive government. They have no equivalents in Europe. In Europe there has not been the same freedom or willingness to innovate. Relations between government departments and universities, and the latter and industry, do exist in Europe. But they are not part of a constant effort at co-operation, of which a system of 'improvised federalism' is the natural result in the United States. In Europe, in the case of the university, as well as that of government, there has been no fundamental change of structures which have a very long history and traditions of autonomy. Modifications have been made in the way of additions to structures[46] which remain otherwise adapted more to a stable situation rather than one of change.[47] In the United States it is necessary for the knowledge-producers, in particular, to seek out their clients and persuade them of the potential economic returns from the adoption of innovations.[48]

Correspondingly, European scientists have found themselves generally less involved than American ones outside the sphere of their technical work. And the number of their professional attachments to groups or institutions in the society has generally been less than that of scientists and engineers in the United States. Apart from the very few called upon to give advice at the highest levels in both continents, the sense of exclusion from the sources of power has perhaps been greater for the European scientists, the majority of whom have enjoyed a more settled status – but less of the acclaim, sense of social worth and the patronage of the political authorities – than have scientists in the United States. The exclusion from authority has been particularly painful for those who have come to be impressed by the extent to which science is put to social use and have been displeased with the manner of its utilization. One of the most potent sources of left-wing scientism among scientists[49] is this sense of exclusion from authoritative positions. Scientists feel that they are not consulted about matters in which they are knowledgeable and which vitally affect them and their fellow citizens. However, this sentiment has a long history.

SCIENTISM

Technocratic thinking is continuous with other major contemporary ideologies. In common with them, it asserts that the world is tending to, and must, change in a given direction under the influence of determinate forces. In this sense, it contains, as a principal substantive element, that which other systems only assume methodologically, namely a belief in the authority, cognitively and morally, of science. In the history of modern ideological developments, the sense of the immanence of change and the assurance of its inevitability, because it is actually discernible in the nature of things, have tended to run side by side and borrow support from one another. There has, at the same time, been a continuing tension.

Thinkers imbued with scientism have consistently sought to break the epistemologically 'corrupt' association with philosophies of history of the traditional sort. They have, at the same time, been under continuous threat of being repudiated by adherents of these philosophies, insofar as the latter wish to remain true to the spirit and principles of 'humanism' (e.g. the Frankfurt School). The relation of dependence between social theories which aspire to the status of philosophies of history and scientism is not likely to be severed. The scientistic spirit has given these systems some of their principal characteristics. From scientism is derived the following: (1) The importance of generally applicable solutions to problems, developments, etc. (2) Determinism: this involves the idea that the universe as a whole is a system.[50] Standard conditions regularly affect outcomes in determinable ways. Within the system, changes (development) derive from a single source or set of sources which are common to the line of general development which is in progress. (3) The belief that some 'level', aspect or sub-system of the system under examination is more fundamental than any of the others; that it provides the key to unlock the mysteries of the system as a whole; and that this stems from its greater potency. It is the model upon which the other parts are based. It is the pattern after which they are moulded.

Scientism induces the following: (4) A propensity to look for causes outside the social or the psychological realm. Explanations are preferred ultimately deriving from biology, but, better still, physics, as being more determinable in a scientific sense. At least, non-human ecological factors, including technology, are preferable to subjective ones. (5) A tendency to locate the sources of political and cultural changes in the collective interchanges with nature, by means of technology. The economy, in the widest sense, is thought to be fundamental. In addition to being determinable in the scientific sense, it is the point of contact between the objective realm and the uncertain sphere of values, actions, etc. And, through its relationship to the basic question of survival, it has acquired primacy. (This last is probably reinforced by a theory of the instincts[51] in which self-preservation is the most basic, the least malleable, of human motives, reminding us of the common nature which humankind shares with the animals.) These features scientism still shares with certain social theories.

Scientism, on the other hand, if it is not to remain a purely philosophical-epistemological movement, requires historical carriers. Only a social theory can identify these and educate them in their historical role. Between them, these two tendencies of modern thought have done much to keep alive the Manichean vision of a human nature divided between, on the one hand, the pressure, inherent in a technological civilization, to submit to the imperatives of increased technical effectiveness; and, on the other, the apparently ineradicable need to live on a higher plane than that of the merely expedient. These attitudes are projections respectively of the faith in, and the fear of, science.

FROM PHILOSOPHER-KINGS TO RULE BY MANAGERS

Technocratic outlooks are to be distinguished from ones possessing a greater moral-political content by their exclusive employment of means–ends rationality. They are thus impelled by their own internal logic to give up the qualities that would permit them to be effective as *idées-forces*: rhetorical force and compulsive holding power over their adherents. Their careers are thus different in certain respects from those of the generality of doctrinal viewpoints.

Technocratic viewpoints have undergone attenuation in situations characterized by an intensity of commitment on the part of participants to one or other of the great philosophies that have dominated political life in the last two hundred years or more. As a focus of emotional attachment and a morally compelling guide to action, technocracy is, in its own terms, superfluous. It is unnecessary, not simply in the context of the utopian reality which it defines as about to be brought to realization, but in its very form and structure, i.e. as a doctrine.

Technocratic programmes have, quite rapidly after their initial formulation, hardened into familiar outlines, by being largely assimilated by those who interpret and receive them into contemporary social analyses. The process starts initially as a sense of frustration with an economic, political and social situation which seems to the proponent of the technocratic viewpoint to thwart technical potentialities that require only minor social adjustments to achieve fulfilment. The diagnosis and remedial action proposed, then tends to come under attack from more value-laden viewpoints of the Left and the Right. This vulnerability of technocracy to dilution and distortion is an expression of the difficulties confronting liberal solutions in the altered ideological circumstances of the twentieth century. For example, from the German revolution of November 1918 to the summer of 1919, when the chief protagonists, Rudolf Wissell and Wichard von Moellendorff, resigned from office, such a process was in evidence as leftist *Räte* (councils) ideas, corporative-socialist schemes (of Max Cohen) and *Gemeinwirtschaft* conceptions (Moellendorff 1932) came into competition during the months-long debate on the constitution of post-Treaty of Versailles Germany.[52]

A similar though more extended cycle is visible in France, in the gathering of strength and its subsequent sudden loss, by the Redressement Français – a big business pressure group with a pronounced technocratic character[53] – from the franc crisis of 1925 to the end of the decade. Like Rathenau's schemes in Germany (1916, 1917), Ernest Mercier's movement in France was feared by the Right, but courted for a time by the Left, in the latter case by syndicalists. In the end it was denounced by the Left, much as the *Gemeinwirtschaft* (collective economy) idea proved too uncertain a concept for the orthodox SPD left to swallow in Germany.[54]

Technocratic remedies arise in moments of acute social tension. They tend to be developed by thinkers with an intense commitment to rationalism, and perceived by them as neutral solutions to social and economic crisis. They tend to be taken up and intensified in such a way as to become transformed into conservative[55] or left-wing dogmas. (Here one might cite the syndicalist schemes of Georges Valois[56] or the tensions within the British social relations of science movement between moderates and a figure on the Left like J. D. Bernal.) Ideologically, the reconciliation of technics with nation and class was achieved. For example, on the Right: 'If up to 1936 the focus of Nazi economic policy had been recovery from the depression, the four-year plan con-

tained the additional goal of reducing German dependence on
the world economy through technical innovation. Fundamentalist
slogans of national economic autarky went hand in hand with
technical advances' (Herf 1984: 201). Similarly, on the Left: 'the
Soviet public was reminded that the proper role of the technical
intelligentsia was not a concern with major policy questions but
with "following orders" ' (Bailes 1978: 117). Defined as a small
stratum, not as a class, the intelligentsia were *specialists* and
therefore suspect to Marxism. And yet they were indispensable
(therefore dangerous) in a socialist society that was becoming
industrialized.[57] Technocratic proposals tend to lose their distinctive and original form. In both cases, it is the initial deterministic
element, that is, the initial taint of scientism inherent in technocratic viewpoints, that permits the radical development to occur
by extension, extrapolation and admixture of substantive social
aims. Only when these ends have been rendered problematic by
changed factual circumstances – as, for example, in the case of
the United States after the Second World War – can a new
softening of the lines of social opposition prepare the way for
the sense of *rapprochement*. This is the basis for the original
sense, empirical in spirit, that 'times have changed'. And it is the
ground from which technocratic viewpoints tend to spring in
the first place.[58] This at least has tended to be the pattern
in Europe.[59]

For this reason, the ideological context in which technocratic
viewpoints make their appearance is of the utmost significance in
settling the question of their impact on the rest of society. In
post-war Europe, the issues that have come to be associated with
the theme of technocracy remained within the field of *social*
theory. Harold Wilson's speeches to the Labour Party in 1964,
emphasizing the unity between the scientific and technological
revolutions and modern socialism, are a striking case in point.[60]

In recent years, the technocracy/anti-technocracy debate has
shifted somewhat from being a primarily European one, conducted on a mainly philosophical level, to being a sociological
one, conducted on a comparative, transatlantic basis. The issue
has come to be seen as one of the validity of a general theory
of advanced (or post-)industrial development, originating in the
United States, but with some European adherents. Criticism has
taken the characteristic form of a charge of unwarranted techno-

cratic patterns of thought – as well as of conclusions in which *techniciens* figure too prominently.

CONCLUSION

What, if anything, remains of the faith in science as a principle of politics today? The technocratic mentality in politics has helped to keep the impassioned search for a set of principles alive. It has done so at the same time that such a search is being continuously weakened at the hands of politicians. They, conscious that their grip on the destinies of their societies has become more uncertain than ever before, eschew 'ideology'. They turn to economic management as the principal means and the goal of economic life.

The empirical spirit of modern science, insofar as it has penetrated the study of society as a scholarly undertaking, and entered into the public's appreciation of social issues, has contributed to the decline of ideological thinking. At the same time, however, a strongly ideological context, in which values are actively canvassed and fought over, seems to be a necessary condition for holding in check the spread of technocracy, understood as the illegitimate extension of scientific ways of thinking to questions that do not admit of scientific answers, and the elevation of scientists and technicians to a position of responsibility for which their knowledge and skills alone do not qualify them.

The enthusiasm for science (as opposed to its practice) is not alien to the ideological spirit. On the contrary, it reinforces it. It also borrows from the ideological tradition, to which it is closely akin, and which it continues under a new guise. The technocratic ideology is a continuation of the philosophies of history. All of these have proposed a new beginning and a final end. This is the case with the idea that scientists will solve all questions, and that they will rule society in science's name and under its benevolent auspices. Under what conditions will the enthusiasm for science and the ideological tradition reinforce and interpenetrate one another? Under what conditions can they be induced to dissolve those elements in the other that are harmful and misleading?

It is possible that the two will diverge more and more. Possibly, in the future they will flow more in separate channels. It is possible, however, that the ideology of science will take over the position formerly held by political and religious faiths. This would be the worst outcome. Scientism, understood as the application of science to politics, would render inoperable politics, understood as the technique and the medium for the socialized expression of conflicts. These necessarily require and are fed by an input of ideology, which must continue if politics is to continue. Since politics in this sense is not eliminable by reference to the facts of the case, the only effect which science can have is to give persons who exercise authority in its name a role which is apolitical in name yet political in substance.

The conditions under which knowledge is created and applied in modern societies gives scope to the technocrat because it weakens the position of the generalist politician who is not equipped to question his or her advisers. A necessary distinction is that between the 'technocrat' and the *technicien*; the latter is, in an equal degree to the generalist, forced into a position of relative powerlessness by the pressures towards increasing specialization. Being increasingly specialized, the *technicien* is forced by his or her indispensability in the running of technical processes and his or her limited role in the overall co-ordination of tasks to accept the guidance of middle-ranking persons. These are the true technocrats. Their room for manoeuvre is greater than that of the *technicien*; and their knowledge is often greater than that of the heads of political bureaux who require the service of technocrats to mediate between themselves and those who actually maintain and operate modern technology (Bon and Burnier 1971: 107; Suleiman 1977: 141).[61] Intellectuals function, as they always have done, as publicists and ideologists. In the past they have often been the source of romantic attacks on science; as intellectuals attached to the managers and even scientific intellectuals (who often have little interest in social matters), they tend to support rather than hinder the spread of technocratic patterns of rule. In practice, however, there is often a considerable cultural gap between the intellectuals and the ordinary scientist or manager.

The exercise of authority is weakened to the degree that specialized knowledge becomes the basis of administrative action. Political decisions tend to lose their character as actions where they are seen to flow from the facts of a given situation. The task of assessing the facts in the light of values ceases to occupy the attention of political leaders when they become heavily reliant on the force of expert opinion. Political authority tends to lose its character and its vulnerability to criticism in the light of alter-native values on the part of the persons subject to it.

Similarly, democratic rights of participation are undermined by the substitution of administration on the basis of expertise for rule by elected representatives. This is part of the familiar critique of bureaucracy. It is, however, given an added impetus by the technocratic emphasis on the prerogatives which are due to the qualified. Under these conditions, a meritocratic principle tends to be substituted for a democratic one. Participation is replaced by consultation. Democracy itself comes to be inter-preted as a technique of management. For the ethical claim to self-rule through the choice of representative is substituted a procedure: the seeking of the opinion of subordinates on matters considered likely, on technical grounds, to affect them.

Scientism in its technocratic form acts against politics as an ideological process in which different and irreconcilable ideals are pitted against one another. Scientism does this by weakening and systematically undermining the faith in the traditions which are the bearers of historically created ideals. These ideals, in turn, require the persistence and re-creation of tradition in order to survive in an increasingly rationalized world. The traditions and structures which have been created by the force of ideologically inspired actions in the past are required by ideology if it is to continue to function effectively as the ground and the substance of politics. They are required also if the tempering of ideology in politics is to be properly effected by a respect for the practicable – the balancing of alternative courses of action. This balancing is an empirical activity. But it is one which is none the less distinct from the scientistic conception of the 'one best way' or the technic-ally most expedient, or the most aesthetically satisfying.

The principle of realism is the proper influence of the scientific temper in politics. Its illegitimate application is the attempt to extirpate all that the past has bequeathed, including the values which are derived from the past. The values continue to motivate people. In conducting his war on the great formative ideologies, the technocratic politician does not act outside politics. Ideologies are inherent in the nature of human society itself. The techno-cratic politician borrows the language and the style of ideology – and appeals to the ideological disposition in his hearers – in an ultimately fruitless, but none the less extremely damaging, onslaught on an inheritance which is formative of all politics and of democratic politics.

The technocracy of the Right and the Left is anti-political. It is based on the desire to eliminate politics from human life. Politics are believed to be corrupt, to involve compromise, to be compounded by half-measures and mistaken, because not scientifically determined, perceptions of goals. Goals are thought to be only half-perceived. And often they are sacrificed to the more immediate ends of simply maintaining or enhancing a short-term tactical position within the ever-fluctuating and unsatisfactory, eternally incomplete and half-realized condition that is politics. Ultimately, the goals which the practical politician seeks to attain are unrealizable and the judgements he or she makes, measured by the stern criteria of meaning operative in the purer realms of abstract philosophy or pure science, considered to be without enduring meaning – sometimes even without content.

Technocratic viewpoints express frustration with representative institutions and even human life itself, as it is lived. They are characteristically the possession of the non-propertied and the politically ineffective or dispossessed. They are used by excluded or dissatisfied groups – and by those who are rendered hopelessly complacent by the totality of their power – to by-pass or discount traditional political institutions and to justify their own discretion. The technocratic philosophy reflects a consciousness of having expertise but not being in a position to use it for discriminating and active purposes. For example, Italian Fascists in the 1920s sought to use technology to stress the role of a new ruling group originating outside the traditional classes which by mastering machines would sweep away petit bourgeois democracy and nineteenth-century sentimentality.

It is no accident that technocracy has always tended to attract the non-propertied. The Saint-Simonian doctrine applies as much to the managers in the 1920s and 1930s as to the scientists. It says 'knowledge is power'. And the doctrine (which is a form of knowledge) is used to gain and hold on to power. Power is then to be 'dissolved' in the final realization of an encompassing rationality from which none may demur.

Just as technocrats are covertly political, so technocracy is covertly ideological. It offers a technique of action to those who desire above all an active philosophy. Uniquely, this is offered by science in modern times. Science promises a progressive, ethically relativistic, evolutionary philosophy from which any political content and any realistic appraisal of other groups and values, including what its proponents regard as the retrogressive, has been drained. The belief that knowledge is power is supposed to galvanize the technocrats to action.

Even their own doctrine is reduced by the technocrats to a technique (of politics). Yet this doctrine is destructive of the basis of democracy, understood as the openness of structures to the expression of political disagreement and dissent. As social theory, technocratic thought suffers from the incapacity to offer other than general solutions which must remain inadequate in a world marked increasingly by complexity and divisions. Technocracy offers the opportunity of a systematic critique directed against an overly systematic or premature synthesis. But, in the process, critics as well as adherents do not so much learn from science, understood as the disciplined study of nature, as misappropriate and misapply what are seen as its fundamental tenets – but which are in reality a doctrinal distortion of its meaning for a limited section of humanity.

Science seeks novelty in neglected, particular aspects of phenomena. It stresses the revisability and fallibility of human cognitions and creations vis-à-vis the reality it tries to understand. The scientistic spirit attempts blindly to apply a technique of discovery to all things. In doing so, it damages scientific endeavours and confuses their wider cultural meaning. And it degrades and seeks to pull down an already too frail political life.

NOTES

1 For example, in 1990 the US gross domestic expenditure on R and D (GERD) was 152,925.0 (in current Purchasing Power Parities dollars) representing 2.7 per cent of GDP. Switzerland, Sweden, Japan and Germany, all 'technological leaders', had a higher percentage. Total GERD was a fraction of the US figure in every case (OECD 1991: 50).
2 OECD (1988: 44) reports 'a higher publication rate for the U.S. across a range of sub-fields'. See ibid.: 79–90, for statistics of national publication counts. Also Martin and Irvine (1986).
3 For example, in 1986 some 11,000 scientists and engineers arrived in the United States from other countries, representing some 7 per cent of the annual increase in this professional category (OECD 1992: 143).
4 Technocracy, in the shape of the 'post-industrial' society, contains

assumptions reminiscent of Marx's dictum that one country will show to the others the image of their future. In Europe, the confident belief in the discovery of the 'economic system', its prime mover, and the necessary path that all must follow, was a response to certain powerfully impressive facts of the early stages of industrialization, even though the form of this response was not warranted by the facts alone. In the same way, in the United States in the late twentieth century, the assumption of a world role, which has distorted American life and society in several ways, has been misinterpreted by theorists, still in the grip of essentially nineteenth-century assumptions about society and social life, as a portent, heralding the dawn of a new post-industrial age. Various observations are called on in support of these claims (Bell 1967: 645, 683, 699, 931).

5 E.g. A profession: computer science. A country: the United States after 1945.
6 E.g. A profession: pure science or mathematics. A country: nineteenth-century Japan's autarkic modernization policy.
7 E.g. Intra-society: Michael Polanyi and the Society for Freedom in Science before 1945. Society: nineteenth-century China.
8 E.g. Intra-society: J.D. Bernal and the idea of planning science before 1945. Society: Italy's view of itself as the 'proletarian nation' in the 1920s or the Soviet Union in its response to Taylorism in the early 1920s.
9 See in this connection Hessen (1931). This paper inspired radical scientists in Britain. In the newly formed Soviet Union itself the official view was that science and technology now served the masses. By contrast, a bourgeois science and technology, because it is rooted in class-divided social relations, serves the ruling class by assisting in the domination of both nature and humanity. Bourgeois science is kept separate from technology and is regarded as 'pure'. But this merely masks the domination which is inherent in it. Max Scheler reached a similar conclusion, although his starting point – the neo-Hegelian rightist tradition in German conservative thought – was very different. For him science and technology were both *Herrschaftswissen* (knowledge for domination). That is, the very conceptual forms of science were shaped by the aim intrinsic to it of asserting control over nature. More recently, Herbert Marcuse (1941, 1966) has argued in the same terms that, in the eye of science, nature is *a priori* viewed as something to be used. Calculation, prediction and control are what matter. Technology follows from this, and nature (and human beings) is mastered. If exploitation and domination were ended, science, too, would have to change, and in its very concepts. Jürgen Habermas (1971) has dissented from this. For his somewhat more subtle view, see Habermas (1971, 1976). For a polemical rebuttal of these views, see Grove (1980).
10 Nor has any systematic evidence ever been produced in support of such claims. That they are not a class has been most trenchantly argued by those who ask: 'In what sense are the techno-bureaucratic groups conscious of their existence as a cohesive social force?' The

negative answer which this question almost always evokes has, however, not succeeded entirely in allaying the fear that power is shifting in the *techniciens*' direction, or in preventing the re-emergence of claims, offered either in the spirit of neutral prediction, or of warning, that it will do so. Behind these latter claims is the suspicion that it is somehow not in the nature of technocratic influence to manifest itself in the political form that experience has led us to expect of newly arrived and rising groups. The rejection of an *a priori* approach to the question of the meaning of technocratic influence has usually been accompanied by certain general observations on the subject of power shifts in society.

11 In Europe, a long period of time elapsed between the first appearance of representatives of the business community and their eventual severance of their alliances with the formerly dominant landowning classes. A great deal of effort had to go into the business of attempting to convince other groups of their right to rule. Such efforts, and the generation of the capacity to make good the claims made on the group's behalf, virtually required, as Marx himself acknowledged, a period of incubation in which the nascent contenders for power could establish their position (Gurvitch 1949: 96).

12 As time has gone on, this has happened more dramatically. There has been an impact, if only in the visible rate of growth of knowledge and techniques.

13 This perception has been more or less sharply focused.

14 Ever-present and occasionally stark.

15 The *locus classicus* for Marx's presumed anticipation of a post-industrial (or knowledge) society in which scientific knowledge becomes effectively indistinguishable from technology is the statement: 'modern industry makes science a productive force ... [and] presses it into the service of capital' (Marx 1867: 335).

16 This contrast was most forcefully expressed by Marx and Engels (1848).

17 This was, for example, Durkheim's view. See his discussion of Saint-Simon (Durkheim 1928). Also Bouglé and Halévy (1924) and Bouglé (1931).

18 Classically expressed by Saint-Simon as the opposition between power and ability. 'I do not say: a new power is growing alongside each of the two old powers but an *ability* is growing alongside a *power*.' Only by replacing powers with abilities can 'society, taken as a whole ... really exert sovereignty which consists now of a principle deriving from the very nature of things' (1819–20: 86–7).

19 Nowhere has this been more sharply expressed than by F. W. Taylor in his testimony before the United States House of Representatives:

The great revolution that takes place in the mental attitude of the two parties under scientific management is that both sides take their eyes off the division of the surplus as the all-important matter, and turn their attention toward increasing the size of the surplus until this surplus becomes so large that it is unnecessary to quarrel over how it shall be divided. . . . Both sides must recognize as essential the substitution of exact scientific investigation and knowledge for the old individual judgement.

(1920: 102; see also Lewin 1921)

20 'In the old system the people was regimented [*enregimenté*] in relation to its leaders; in the new it is combined with them. They received commands from the military leaders whereas they receive only guidance from the industrial leaders. In the first case the people was *subject*, in the second it is *participant* [*sociétaire*]. For such is in reality the admirable character of industrial combinations that all those who join in them are in reality all collaborators, associates, from the simplest worker to the most opulent manufacturer and to the most enlightened engineer. . . . Each receives a degree of importance and benefits proportionate to his ability and his stake – which constitutes the highest degree of equality both possible and desirable. . . . Industrial ability finds it as repugnant to exercise arbitrariness as to impose it' (Saint-Simon 1819–20: 150).

21 As Saint-Simon put it originally:

[The Jacobins] have committed an enormous political error; they have . . . tried to perfect government action whereas they should have subordinated it and should have acknowledged administrative action as supreme. . . . They should have drawn the conclusion that the scientists, artists and the leaders of industrial production were those to whom administrative power should have been entrusted, i.e. the task of directing the national interests.

(1825: 129–30)

22 It is one of the ironies of contemporary interpretation of those élites that their beliefs about themselves have either gone unnoticed by commentators, or they have been treated as curiously all-embracing and unspecific, synonymous with the underlying assumptions of the sciences whose applications they are employed in working out.

23 Social arrangements could possibly be re-ordered according to the dictates of the rational spirit. This is the wider meaning of the technocratic ethos in which reason is set against authority.

24 Namely the pressure of unsatisfied needs for food, shelter, care, etc. For an interpretation of American history and in particular the form of its political institutions in these terms, see Beard (1947).

25 The scientistic dream is of a commonwealth freed from the encrustations of tradition and irrational attachment to the symbols of authority. Every individual directly and independently employs his or her cognitive faculties in the perception of the facts of any given situation. Cf. Shils (1972: 18, 56).

26 The classic texts are Benjamin (1930) and Horkheimer and Adorno (1944).

27 For Lenin, communism was: 'Soviet power plus the electrification of the whole country.'

The Soviet Republic must at all costs adopt all that is valuable in the achievements of science and technology [regarding work organization]. The possibility of building Socialism will be determined precisely by our success in combining the Soviet government and the Soviet organization of administration with the modern achievements of capitalism. We must organize in Russia the study and teaching of the Taylor system and . . . adapt it to our purposes.

(Lenin 1918; Carr 1952: 105–15; Bailes 1977: 376n; 1978; Maier 1970: 50–1; and Devinat 1927, for details of the sixty or so work study institutes established in the Soviet Union)

Other examples include the attempt in Germany in the 1930s to build national recovery and social integration on an economy permanently geared to an immediate preparedness for war, utilizing for the purpose Goebbels' 'steely romanticism' (*stählernde Romantik*). ('National Socialism was dedicated to emancipating technology from capitalist exchange' [Herf 1984: 193, 201].) And from the turn of the century throughout Western Europe, the definition of socialism by the trade-union-dominated labour movements in terms of an ever-increasing share of economic rewards for the workers in societies organized around large-scale production – a programme which sharply accentuated the tensions between these revisionists and revolutionary Marxists.

28 Expressed most notably in proposals for economic parliaments. Of the many that have been mooted, only the German one reached the point of being embodied in the (Weimar) constitution. (See Bernhard 1923; Finer 1923; Bowen 1947; and for a measured analysis, Maier 1975: 142–5.) A nation-wide scheme of industrial self-regulation was prepared at about the same time in France (ibid.: 73–6; and Kuisel 1981: 46–8).

29 One particularly striking example is Eugène Letailleur's call for a 'national technique' (*l'idée d'une technique nationale*) in the November 1919 Bloc National elections in which a genuinely right radical tone was discernible. Science, technology and cartels would be promoted; factories would become hierarchies of disciplined experts; and parliament would simply represent economic interests. Lysis [Letailleur] (1919). Discussed in Maier (1970: 39; 1975: 101); Kuisel (1981: 291–2n).

30 For a discussion of this theme in the context of Weimar politics, see Grebing (1969).

31 As, for example, in Nietzsche and those who absorbed his ideas at the turn of the century (Herf 1984: 29–30); in the thought of Sorel; and in the fascist aestheticization of technology as the expression of the irrational, of will and violence (ibid.). Generally, as Charles Maier has written, technocratic or engineering models of social management in the inter-war years 'appealed to the newer, more syncretic, and sometimes more extreme currents . . . Italian national syndicalists and fascists, German "revolutionary conservatives" and "conservative socialists", as well as the so-called left liberals . . . and finally the Soviet leaders proved most receptive' (1970: 28). Similarly, in the

97

extraordinary variety and febrility of pre- and post-First World War (particularly Weimar) art (Gay 1969) there is a sense both of the appalling weight of the past, and of the possibility of the achievement of a new dominance over an increasingly man-made, urban environment. In architecture – for example, the Bauhaus, and in France, Le Corbusier – this found expression in the use of materials such as concrete and steel and a functional concept of design.

32 There has been nothing comparable in range, or the breadth of the community of its active adherents, to the great social and political philosophies. There has been no distinctive development in the direction of a fully articulated doctrine having mechanism and technique at its centre.

33 However, on occasion that attachment has not been less intense for being more principled.

34 And in being the leaders of nativistic reactions against increasing globalization.

35 Cohen (1980) sees trust in science and its benefits at its zenith in the eighteenth century. Then, a natural order was seen in the universe at large which could perhaps be applied to man. The cumulation of scientific knowledge suggested the possibility of a parallel progress in society. For Condorcet, humankind's development was a series of stages (like the stages in the earth's history seen by Buffon), each of which was related to science. A more perfect state and a more equitable society were in prospect. Cohen quotes Descartes, to the effect that by use of method one does not have to be especially clever or good to receive divine revelation: 'what one person did, everyone could repeat ... people could find truth and test it for themselves. Science was essentially democratic; it had reached every social level.' Fear and distrust of science reached peaks around the time of the Copernican revolution; Darwin's and Freud's work; and the rise of statistics. Over the past one and a half centuries, it has tended to increase (ibid.: 57).

36 Toulmin writes of 'the continuing pendulum-swing of general public sympathies and attitudes first towards, then away from ... science' (1972: 24). Public attitudes to science are 'a generational or secular phenomenon, as predicable as the tides', when one considers 'the whole history' of such attitudes. '[A]nti-scientific attitudes seem to have peaked at intervals of 130 years or so, if not every 65 or 30–35 years' (ibid.).

37 One could almost write the history of creative achievements in social theory and of modern revolutionary movements in culture and politics in terms of the tensions created by this.

38 This tendency has not been experienced everywhere to the same degree; nor has it always manifested itself in the form of a creative, intellectual response. In the United States up until the ending of the Second World War, tendencies favouring a technical definition of human problems and development did not provoke the kind of intense intellectual debate or the wide public reaction familiar in Europe. The ideas of F. W. Taylor and the school of management

science which took his name never provoked the critical reaction that it did among European, especially French, industrial psychologists and sociologists. Even the friends of American management thought in Great Britain drew upon it selectively, adapting it to native traditions going back to Benthamite radicalism and non-conformism. The 'Taylor movement' formed part of a fairly continuous tradition, given substantial intellectual expression by Thorstein Veblen (e.g. 1921) at the turn of the century, and expressed particularly through the organizational efforts of Henry Ford and the Bedaux engineers; it was turned into a general system aimed at utilizing the physical sciences for tasks of social engineering by the self-styled technocrats who gathered under Howard Scott's leadership at Columbia University in the 1920s. (On technocracy see Chase 1933; Frederick 1933; Raymond 1933; Scott et al. 1933; Kraemer 1933; Resar 1935; and more recently Wutke 1964; Elsner 1967; Layton 1971; and Akin 1977.) This tradition was almost entirely lacking in critical self-awareness of the kind which had become familiar in Europe with the spread of the influence of the irrationalist philosophies of history. It lacked the political sensitivity which, in Europe, was intensified by the social tensions of the pre- and inter-war years. By the end of this period, the pragmatic spirit was still deeply entrenched in American culture, despite the world recession of the 1930s; it had been, and continued to be, more or less continuously expansive. The United States had, moreover, been physically isolated from totalitarianism and war in Europe.

39 As Habermas suggests (1971, 1974).

40 As Bettelheim argues (1949).

41 This question is continuous not at variance with the long-established preoccupation with the likely course of change in the advanced industrialized countries. The differences which it does create, however, are the ones alluded to: (1) that the overtly political appeal is played down in favour of a neutral transfer of authority – this is not supposed to be the scene of the sort of struggle for power associated with previous conflicts; and (2) that the groups involved are likely to remain somewhat separate in their activities, loosely linked together by the structure and ethos of modern knowledge and sharing no uniform sense of historical destiny.

42 See Hessen (1931) and note 9 above.

43 This idea was familiar to Aristotle and to the Middle Ages. Not until Machiavelli were the two concepts fused.

44 Cf. Saint-Simon (1821: 185). In the industrial society 'individuals in their overwhelming majority will be grouped in industrial associations, more or less numerous, but interconnected . . . so as to form a general system of organization directed . . . towards a great common industrial goal'.

45 Itself usually a larger and less hierarchical structure than its European counterpart,

46 Such as funding procedures for projects of 'timeliness and promise',

99

supplementary to annual budgeting, together with governmental and industrial contracting for research.

47 As indicated, for example, by the inclusion of research funding in institutions' annual budgeting based on student numbers.

48 'More than 70 per cent of U.S. research funding for higher education is allocated as separately budgeted research in the form of competitively awarded grants to individual researchers and teams' (OECD 1987: 44). The institutional setting of science and technology is discussed in Price (1958, 1965) and Ben-David (1968).

49 See in this connection the studies by Wood (1959: 121–57) and Werskey (1971, 1978). An important document is Bernal (1939).

50 This idea is forcefully conveyed in Needham (1937). His Herbert Spencer lecture exemplifies most of these points: (1) the entire universe from the start of time is a 'cosmic process'; (2) increasingly higher levels are generated – physical, biological and social; (3) these three orders are continuous. Evolution is an orderly process of growing complexity. Relations among an increasing number of parts become more complex. This is balanced by greater efficiency and centralization. The whole becomes more and more independent of its environment. Collectivism – classlessness, common ownership – is the highest form. The transformation to it is comparable to that 'of lifeless protein to the living cell'. It is higher in the same way that the human brain is superior to the twenty or thirty ganglia of the annelid. The reasoning is similar to Spencer's, the conclusions are different.

51 However, it need not be. Augustin Cournot (1875), an important technocratic thinker, held that instincts were being transcended: the vital (instincts) was being replaced by the rational.

52 The issue was political representation of experts.

53 Saint-Simonian themes were prominent (for the link, see Mason 1931). At the start of the decade a neo-Saint-Simonian group was active in France (Bourbonnais 1923).

54 See Kuisel (1967: 65–87; also 1981: 88–90; and, for the longer-term technocratic trend in France, 1973). For the German debates, see Maier (1970: 45–8, 50–1; 1975: 144–5, 159–60); and Bowen (1947: 195–205).

55 Charles Maier provides the following examples: Italian Fascist technocracy waned 'alongside [the] emasculation of any independent economic or administrative expertise' (1970: 43). In the Weimar Republic '[t]he enthusiasm for rationalization ... accompanied the four-year political domination [from 1924] of the conservative and bourgeois parties, not the governments with SPD participation' (ibid.: 56). The same thing occurred in France in the late 1920s. Of the Redressement Français: 'the ideological implications ... were actually far less radical than those of the movements earlier in the decade'. Indeed, 'Mercier's [its leader's] own social analysis reflected a bourgeois conservative traditionalism, far from any right-radical *ressentiment*' (ibid.: 58). In fact, technocracy came into conflict with both fascism and Stalinism between the wars, as engineers urged pragmatism and reality-orien-

100

tation. In both cases the conflict was resolved in favour of the ideologues. Broadly, scientists and engineers were co-opted by Hitler (Herf 1984: 201) and persecuted by Stalin (Bailes 1978: 114, 120).

56 Valois, a disciple of Georges Sorel, started as a spokesman for the Action Française; later formed the Faisceau, a semi-fascist organization of mainly war veterans; and ended up advocating a syndicalism of the producers: a pure technocracy (Kuisel 1981: 81–2; Béracha 1930, for a collection of syndicalist writings).

57 Stalin's attitude to the technical intelligentsia grew directly from Marxist–Leninist ideology; 'it cannot be dismissed simply as a form of paranoia' (Bailes 1978: 120).

58 The tendency of which this cycle is a part is the enthusiasm for science and the reaction against it. The superseding of the initial technocratic viewpoint is part of the enthusiasm. The sense of disillusion with radical-conservative and Marxist answers (i.e. with the enthusiasm for science) is part of the reaction against scientism – paradoxically, however, it is the seed-bed of a new technocratic way of thought. (Even the reaction to scientism breeds 'scientific' solutions. There is no escaping it.)

59 However, the New Deal fits the pattern.

60 Just as in the post-war United States, so in Europe, there was a large measure of dogma and counter-dogma in the debate over the role of qualified manpower. But in Europe it was less than in the United States a matter of a compelling world role and the accompanying institutional changes that it appeared to force upon society, or of putting an already pre-eminent economy on a footing of permanent preparedness for war. (The United States was a *Wehrwirtschaft*: 66 per cent of total government-funded research in 1984 was for defence [OECD 1984].) It was one of how older social and political assumptions needed revising in the light of aspirations towards a society that was felt to be in principle capable of using technology more effectively (Nichols 1969). Marxists and technocrats all shared this assumption.

61 These pressures are heightened where areas of quasi-administrative jurisdiction grow up. Such is the case with international organizations to which member countries send delegations, which may even be led by ministerial representatives – but who are not independently elected or subject to close parliamentary scrutiny; and with negotiations between national governments and organized corporate forces such as trade unions, regional authorities and local administrations within these governments' own societies.

4

OMNIVOROUS MODERNITY

Agnes Heller

Among the various things it does, culture processes and distributes spiritual food and drink. This task is normally accomplished in institutions (e.g. philosophical schools, workshops, churches, regular festivities) where the healthy spiritual food is properly distinguished from the unhealthy and the unsavoury kind. Very different criteria may be applied by the cultural epicureans, but some standards are always applied. Pre-modern cultures were far from being omnivorous; they grew on a very restricted cultural diet. Some of the staple foods were of just average quality; others were considered better. Food and drink of the best quality was usually favoured by the upper strata of the social world in which they had been processed (though not necessarily also created). Cultural food is roughly custom-made. It befits the rank and aspirations of the members of a cultural community, it defines their taste and, in reverse, it is defined by their taste.

The early moderns developed a highly ambiguous relation to culture-processing. They resented the distinction between a healthy and an unhealthy diet, yet not that between refined and less refined food or drink. The distinction between a healthy and an unhealthy cultural diet was perceived as a limitation on freedom, whereas that between a less and a more refined taste was seen as proper to the service of freedom. After all, members of lower classes could acquire the most subtle of tastes if they tried hard enough. Moreover, while ethical/hygienic limitations on culture-processing are normally prospective in character (only certain kinds of food and drink are admitted into the circulation of culture), culture-processing along the lines of 'low' and 'high' can also be performed retrospectively. If no spiritual food is in principle excluded from the diet, mistakes in judgement of taste can always be corrected and rectified. The representative cultural drama is acted out against the backdrop of a collective epic.

The collective epic is about the total abandonment of the staple diet. It tells the story of how the modern cultural animal has become omnivorous. The representative cultural drama is about the unrecognized genius. Many tears are shed for the young artists who starved to death, yet whose canvases now sell for millions of dollars, or for the crazy composers whose beloved ones preferred to marry undistinguished officials, while a few decades later these are the 'geniuses' with whom all music-loving girls become infatuated.

Yet the collective epic has finally devoured the cultural drama. Genius-hunters have turned out to be just little fools; and painters do not starve today just to enter the Grand Gallery of Immortals tomorrow. If they can paint pretty well, their paintings will be bought by art galleries, taken care of and evaluated, and the same galleries will also take care of the artists' future. The early modern project to open the gate to all kinds of spiritual foods, yet to keep it well guarded with a view to distinction, did not work out as planned. Once the processors of spiritual goods ceased to distinguish between healthy and unhealthy (unsavoury) cultural diets, the separation of 'low' from 'high', and 'refined' from 'unrefined', had soon to follow suit. When no distinction is made prospectively, retrospective judgement will become ephemeral and fluid. As Bauman (1987a: ch. 9) suggested: following the era of the legislators and the critics, the interpreters will carry the day.

THE ECLIPSE OF TIME

If the spirit of technology were indeed the sole imaginary institution of the modern age, we could hardly understand how our culture became omnivorous. The technological imagination is strictly future-orientated: in technology, the latest, the most recent, is always the best. The product of yesterday quickly becomes outdated – it is destined to end up in the rubbish bin. Such a constant movement towards the new and the newest is one of two major motives of contemporary culture. There is another one as well, which moves in the opposite direction, in terms of which the older that something is, the more precious it becomes. This is true even if it concerns certain products of modern technology. A car of the latest model is of great value, but a car of the oldest model is of greater value. Both novelty and patina are precious and imagination plays its role in both cases. The newest is regarded as the best, not only because of its greater usefulness, but also because it carries the aura of a form of life which is associated with 'elegance', 'luxury', and the like. And the oldest is regarded as the most valuable for a very similar reason. It carries the aura of a bygone form of life which was elegant or simple, peaceful or dramatic, but by all means different from ours – a form of life that is no more. Project and nostalgia are extremely different, but they belong together, for the present feeds on the future and the past.

There was a moment when the technological and the historical imagination seemed to merge: this happened in the post-Hegelian grand narratives, in both their liberal-progressivist and Marxian-eschatological versions. But since the great utopia has faded, the technological and the historical imaginations have completely parted ways. History has become politics, whereas the historical imagination has turned wholly past-orientated, as though Hegel's frequently abused prediction had come true: modern men and women turn their backs to the future, at least as far as cultural practice is concerned, and they face the past.

The past has been opened up and it now stands wide open. Moreover, there are no longer privileged pasts (as there were still for Hegel). Be they the past of ancient Mexico, New Guinea or Egypt, it makes no difference. All spaces and all times are at the disposal of the interpreter. In political terms, people continue to plan, sometimes even ingeniously, and they can still think big. But culturally, nothing is expected from the future. Since the generation of Lukács and Heidegger, no one has dreamed about the renewal of great cultural creativity, because it has been assumed (so far, without much ado or regret) that grand cultural creativity is (to the extent we can see it) a matter of the past. At any rate, the future cannot be interpreted. One may still dream about the coming rejuvenation of original creativity, but one can barely discuss it publicly.

As our omnivorous culture continues to feed on unlimited interpretation, historical consciousness becomes vague, or, rather, self-reflective. The oldness of the old – the 'patina' – still remains decisive, but the intimate relation between time and work is less emphatically sought. Precise philological 'dating' has lost its original importance for taste, though not for the wallet. Thus not only the two-thousand-year-old original work, but also its imitation made two hundred years ago, is precious; both are old and beautiful and both have 'patina'. The old is by definition old if it elicits nostalgia. Whether a building is Gothic, Neo-Gothic or Neo-neo-Gothic still makes a difference, yet not in the same way or to the same extent that it did just thirty years ago. What matters more and more is whether and to what extent one can squeeze some meaning out of an edifice of the past for oneself and for others. The archaeology of the interpreters becomes more and more timeless.

INTERPRETATION

The interpretation of works is an activity of devotion. The object of devotion is the form, the ipseity or personal identity (*quidditas*) of the old text or the old thing (the *interpretandum*), and not its matter, content or message alone. When a tale is recounted in several ways, as often happens with myths and histories, devotion (if there is any) is vested in the story itself. The original version is not the text, but the archetype of all texts; thus no text can become the target of devotional cultivation. For the authors of the Gospels there was no devotional text; the Redeemer's life and death alone was the sacred object of their devotional practice. They were not supposed to interpret at all, but to act as truthful chroniclers. But for the orthodox Christians a few centuries later, the texts of the Apostles became sacred objects of interpretation.

All kinds of interpretations of all kinds of works are activities of devotion, regardless of whether the stories they tell are themselves sacred or secular. Or rather, lay stories become quasi-sacred in and through the practice of interpretation. This happened with the philosophical works of Plato and Aristotle and with the Pythagorean fragments. The more devotional the interpretative work on the text, the greater importance the author of the text will assume. This also happens the other way around. If a text is attributed to someone of high reputation, it becomes an object of devotional practice; the works of the pseudo-Hermes Trismegistus, Dionysius the Areopagite or Ossian are well-known cases in point. The cultivation of the genius is the modern version of this story. After all, 'genius' stands for divine inspiration.

Interpretation ties us to the other, to the author of the text or the thing. Normally this author is a person, although early modernity invented and cultivated 'the people' or 'the folk' as a so-called 'collective author'. The other, however, cannot be entirely other, but it also has to be us. What is completely other is not sacred to us; it does not carry authority; it is not worthy of our interpretation. If, on the other hand, something is entirely us, it is neither authoritative nor sacred, thus it is equally unfit for (devotional) interpretation.

Defining the texts (things) worthy of devotional interpretation and determining the ways of proper, or licit, interpretation belong to the activities of the cultural processing of spiritual food. They are the forms of this kind of food-processing. What needs to be determined are the following: first, who is 'us' and who is the other who belongs to us, or to whom we in the last instance belong? Further, which texts carry authority for us and which are simultaneously also sacred? Finally, which texts carry authority for us without being sacred, because they are sources of wisdom and keepers of secrets worthy of being deciphered?

The spirit of interpretation was not essentially modified up until the last decades of the twentieth century and it remains to be seen whether the recent change was as radical as it seems to have been. Interpretation remained devotional. Throughout early modernity, the work (the object of interpretation) was regarded as authoritative and a keeper of secrets – a kind of hieroglyph that offered itself for decipherment. Authorship remained crucial for authority. To be sure, there is no reason to turn to an old work and interrogate it unless one is convinced that deep and surprising discoveries can still ensue from those sources that have been questioned a thousand times over. A work of art or philosophy, or a text of religious worship, is always a star witness. It can constantly be brought back to the stand, for one can expect that if only we could ask a new question from a new angle, it could still come up with a fresh and original disclosure.

One can wonder whether deconstruction, which is a kind of radical hermeneutics, is so far off the traditional mark. Deconstruction violates the texts, reads text against the text; but apart from cases in which deconstructionists treat contemporary authors, they conspicuously restrict themselves to the most frequently interpreted texts. This is particularly true of Derrida.[1]

Sometimes one has the impression that one is seeing an interpreter in despair. The star witness (e.g. Plato, the Zohar or Immanuel Kant) stubbornly refuses to offer new answers, to disclose unrevealed secrets (and revealed secrets are no secrets) if interrogated in the old fashion – that is, with eyes downcast, in a low and trembling voice, overwhelmed by awe. One has to bully the witnesses, to shake him/her up, so that s/he may finally offer new testimonies. An answer that has been repeated many times over becomes boring – the text that does not disclose new secrets is a corpse. Deconstruction, as with radical hermeneutics in general, is also a kind of devotional interpretation, for it keeps the texts alive through ridicule, irony, 'unmasking', negation – that is, through provocation.[2] There is still something new (in the old) under the sun.

THE RETREAT OF AUTHORITY

The spirit of interpretation did not change from the time of the Roman Empire until the last decades of our century and it is questionable whether the present change goes beyond the surface, although everything else did. The broader the 'us' (the community of the interpreters) became, the less selectively chosen became the objects of interpretation. During the Renaissance, the distinction between the holy and the worthy text had already been substantially blurred. Afterwards, the cluster of the worthy started to widen and to grow. If 'us' means 'us Germans', then the saga of the Niebelungen and the fairy tales collected by the Grimm brothers will be included among the worthy *interpretanda*. If 'us' means 'us moderns', then everything that can only be fathomed as being 'already modern' will become a worthy object of devotional interpretation. And if 'us' means 'humankind', then actually everything that was ever created by the human mind and hand may eventually become such a worthy object – the carrier of authority and of secrets.

But who decides whether a text is the carrier of authority and the keeper of secrets? Who selects the texts that are worthy of devotional treatment? There is no longer such an authority. In this respect it has become true that 'anything goes'. Take any statue, religious text, ceremony, verse, song or the like, and question them in a devotional spirit – they all are supposed to answer you and to disclose their secrets.

Modernity has become omnivorous because the institutions of text-selection, text-processing and text-preparation have lost ground and finally disappeared. This has reinforced the tendency towards the slow disappearance of all cultural élites. At the beginning, the 'authority deficit' of the old culture-processing institutions favoured, rather than hindered, the establishment of élitist cultures. Actually, early European modernity was quite successful in its attempt to produce a cultural élite based on merit rather than on birth. But this is a matter of the past. In a topsy-turvy way, deconstruction still preserves the vestiges of the habits of cultural élitism. Even the slogan that there is no difference between low and high culture is 'avant-gardist', for it still breaks a taboo (perhaps the last one). And for two centuries, it was taboo-breaking that both constituted and maintained the cultural élites.

Where there is a fairly circumscribed 'us', such as 'us Jews' or 'us humanists' (Talmudic Jews and Renaissance humanists), there is still a community of interpreters. This community encompasses the living and the dead and also the not-yet-born, for the latter are supposed to join the community. Though just recently the expression 'community of interpreters' has assumed a solid philosophical position, there is no such community now, nor is there one in sight. There are texts which are interpreted only by one single person. It is actually a feat if someone finds an obscure piece of work which has not yet been treated, nor even seen by anyone. Other texts are squeezed dry by members of groups which consist of the followers of famous (contemporary or recent) interpreters. It rarely happens that two people invited to the same dinner have ever read the same books or seen the same paintings or that they maintain ideas about the same philosophical text. Instead of a community of interpreters, we have fragmented mini-communities, contingent, fluid, ephemeral groups that are kept alive by academic, professional or political lobbies. They interpret in the same way as Adam had once worked: in the sweat of their brows, and for their living.

'A WORLD ACCORDING TO ONE PERSON'

Everything can be interpreted, worked upon in a devotional practice, but now it is – finally – the single person who chooses the proper *interpretandum*. The single person is contingent, so is the *interpretandum*. This is how the great promises of the Enlightenment have come true. The merely particular no longer mediates; the individual directly relates to the species. The species does not stand here for the empty category of 'humankind'; rather, it encompasses whatever the human mind and/or hand has ever created. The individual has a choice, irrespective of the contingent space and time of his or her birth.

Gadamer (1975, 1976, 1988) maintains that the choice of the *interpretandum* is not entirely accidental, for it remains interlocked with tradition. Furthermore, he says that the interpreter mediates between the present (life-experience) and the *interpretandum*, and, finally, that the relationship is mutual. Gadamer has become old-fashioned at a time when his work has become widespread. Nowadays, it is not the 'present' that the interpreter mediates with the past and vice versa. There is no 'present' in the traditional sense as Gadamer still understood it, for there is neither a representative 'us', nor are there, for that matter, representative 'others'. The mediator is the person, as an individual subject, who ice-skates freely, and quickly, among all traditions, and who whimsically picks his or her *interpretandum* once from here and once from there. The naked 'I' is the Eye.

Although there is hardly a 'present' in the traditional sense, there are presents (in the plural), because every eye of any naked 'I' looks upon all its *interpretanda* from a spatial/temporal point (from the mini-point of view) where this 'I' stands. But this 'I' is naked insofar as it has got rid of all traditions (if it had any); it can represent the always present 'present' exactly in its nakedness. Nowadays, no real emperor has clothes on, or rather, no real emperor wears the same clothes throughout his whole life. The cloth obliges; it ranks the person who wears it among one or another tradition. The real emperors or empresses of the omnivorous culture change their clothes all the time; their 'reality' is their nakedness; this is their 'I', the viewpoint of their eye. Like actors, they change costumes, they slip from one period costume to another. These period costumes (the *interpretanda*) are not mediated by one another, because their choice has been contingent. Yet the choice of the nakedness of the 'I' is not contingent, because this is contingency itself, not an attribute but an ontological constant. The same person can interpret a Mayan vase, a biblical verse, an inkstand from the early 1920s, a movie of yesterday (or the interpretations of any of the former) – it will not make any difference. But it makes a difference that all this does not make a difference. What I will eventually pick as my next *interpretandum* does not make a difference, yet it does make a difference that I can freely pick this (or any other) *interpretandum*. Ontological contingency and omnivorous culture are two sides of the same coin.

The paradigm of language is inadequate to the proper description of the contemporary cultural universe. In the cultural tower of Babel, one changes languages all the time. Language itself loses its power; the power remains with the speaker. The question will be: who is the one who speaks? This is a well-known question. The speaker is the carrier of authority; the carrier of authority reveals the authentic message. But in the case of the (post-)modern speaker, the message is not carried by the speaker, because it is not mediated. (Post-)modern speakers broadcast messages which originate in themselves (as far as they know and as they exercise will). The speakers' authority rests solely on the fact that they are the ones who speak. Every speaker is an authority on his or her own. Which *interpretandum* he or she chooses and in which sequence is decided on the spur of the moment by him or her alone. This authority is empty insofar as the person is naked, unclothed by tradition; she is simply identical with the 'I' who speaks.

The meaning of the *interpretandum* that comes to light through interpretation is warranted only by the single (naked) person who speaks. The meaning extricated from the things (texts) by the single person, for the single person, can be now identified as the subject. It is not the epistemological subject in the traditional manner, for the ever-changing novel meaning does not necessarily convey new knowledge, and it certainly does not warrant the veracity of its exploits. The subject (of world-interpretation) stamps the *interpretandum* with her own face. Every interpreter pays in her own coins. She is the one who has stamped them through her interpretation. The meaning squeezed out of the *interpretandum* is her meaning, or rather it is the meaning for her; yet it is not 'private'. It is still the other(s) from whom meaning is squeezed out, and the interpretations remain devotional.

That which becomes manifest in the series of interpretations is a world according to one single person, a world stamped by the face of that person: the subject. All significant naked subjects have their own worlds in this way: insofar as they choose their *interpretanda* themselves, insofar as they suck meaning out of them. As all the monads of Leibniz's[1] (1840) metaphysical universe mirror the whole world, though each of them does it in its own unique way, so all modern significant persons – as subjects – produce the whole (modern) world, in relation to their (self-chosen) *interpretanda*, in their own unique way. All subjects (unique worlds) together warrant the life (survival) of the (post-) modern, omnivorous culture.

Rather than being a member of a community of interpreters, the cultural emperors and empresses of the omnivorous universe – the naked selves that change from one period costume into another – are all centres of their single and unique interpretative universes. They 'have' worlds of their own, and they are the centrepoints of their worlds. They choose, again and again, among the inexhaustible and limitless wealth of *interpretanda*. The whole world, all the things and texts of the world, surround them as if they were whores; they pick one after the other and then they pick a third. Whichever text the naked self chooses, this will become a bearer – though not *the* bearer – of meaning. The emperors and the empresses of the omnivorous culture offer their coins for more general use. Others – who are not emperors or empresses (sovereign subjects), but non-sovereign subjects, the courtiers of the royal subjects (the representative interpreters) – will accept those coins as token meanings for cultural commerce.

To avoid misunderstandings: the naked emperors and empresses of the omnivorous universe – the sovereign subjects, the omphaloses of a cultural world who take their pick from everything that surrounds them (all the things that have ever been produced by human mind and hand) – do not take over the function of the old culture-processing institutions. They do not present the 'proper' texts, the authoritative texts for others; they do not create a (new) tradition, for they do not stand in any tradition, not even negatively. Rather they provide an ephemeral point of attraction. The subjects of the empires of the sovereign emperors and empresses are subjects of lesser power and authority. They do not stamp their faces on coins, though the shadow of their faces can still be recognized on all the coins they handle. They are in line waiting for the well-processed spiritual food – the new, the unexpected, Their world will also always change, but not through their own sovereign gestures.

111

It makes a difference that one is contingent, that one is free in one's nakedness – free to step into, and out of, any tradition. It makes a difference when compared with the pre-modern and early modern individuals who inherited a culture (a language), who knew their limits, who ran against those limits, who had a style, or at least preferred a style. It makes an even greater difference if a modern person becomes aware of his/her contingency, for this is the first step on the road that leads to self-authorization; that is, to becoming a speaker who speaks but only in *his* or *her* own name, and resigns the pretension to speak for – or instead of – others. Here stands an interpreter who resigns the divine mission of the prophet and does not pretend to continue the divine vocation of Hermes. But without Hermes there is no hermeneutics. If personal meaning is squeezed out of all of the open, and no longer resistant, pasts (not traditions!), by and through interpretation, interpretation ceases to be a proper hermeneutical exercise.

Both the promise of infinite possibilities and the warning against infinite impoverishment are written on the cradles of the modern (contingent) persons, precisely because nothing has been written on their cradles. While Nietzsche (1895) said that it is easy to dance in chains, it is certainly difficult to dance where there is no choreography at all. Without choreography only a series of free improvisations remain, for the dancer has to improvise all the time. The dancer chooses all the steps. She does not know whether her dance is pleasing or displeasing, whether it conveys a meaning to the onlookers. Free interpretability, free authorship, being a subject, is also a curse; nothing helps, limits, prescribes; there is no crutch to lean on. Moreover, one cannot be sure of whether there is, or ever will be, an audience at all; one improvises, yet the theatre may remain empty. Nothing is known in advance.

To act as an interpreter in an omnivorous culture is pretentious, yet it is not a sheer blessing. The naked emperors and empresses of the omnivorous universe are also frightened – as if they had to learn to orientate themselves in a dark room. Men and women interpret one thing (text) after the other in order to squeeze some meaning out of them, whereas the meaning of this exercise itself becomes problematic. Who cares about it? Who is interested in it? Who curses one because of it? Who loves one for that which one does? Some reject these questions with impatience or indignation. After all, they say, why should these questions be raised at all? Interpretation is just a kind of play. One plays without reason; one plays for a while with this toy and then with others; when one gets tired or bored with one toy, one grabs another.

But culturally omnivorous creatures are driven by the same kind of spiritual hunger and thirst that drives the creatures of a mono-cultural universe. It is the hunger and thirst for meaning they seek to satisfy. And if the spiritual food is not pre-cooked and presented on a platter, the single person needs to look for it and choose it. While pillorying the field of the 'Absolute Spirit', one still asks the questions 'Why?', 'For what reason?', 'To what end?' – all the questions children ask and adults fail to answer.

CHOOSING THE MORAL SELF

So far, two different statements have been made on the (post-) modern mode of interpretation. First, all things (texts) in the universe have become worthy of interpretation; second, the single person is the centrepoint of the universe which presents to her the sum total of *interpretanda*. Every interpretation is 'a world according to' a person. The interpretative subject is the monad of the omnivorous cultural universe.

These two aspects of (post-)modern interpretative culture are connected. The single person selects whatever suits her from the practically infinite interpretative possibilities. In the language of Walter Benjamin (1940): all things of the universe wait to be redeemed – they are redeemed, for they are resurrected in inter-pretation. It is just that the omnivorous universe does not present some items for salvation and others for damnation at the (always repeatable and repeated) outset. Everything can be saved. It depends on (single) persons and their quest for meaning whether, how and when they will be so redeemed.

The two aspects of the (post-)modern universe of interpretation can be rendered in two entirely different spatial metaphors. The process of interpretation resembles a circle. The person sits in the centre of the circle; he or she is the omphalos of the world. In contrast, the cultural world itself is infinite, both extensively and intensively. There is no – there cannot be any – centre. The interpretative universe both centres and de-centres. It becomes de-centred, and this is precisely why it can be approached solely from the vantage point of a centre.

The pre-modern universe (the Cosmos) has been centred. It was limited (*peras*), in contrast to that which had been thought of as the unlimited (the *apeiron*, the chaos). There was no Chaos in the Judeo-Christian Cosmos where God (Truth, Power and Goodness) sat in judgement. A universe is centred if we know where (who) the centre is (e.g. God), and if the humanly possible true and good are achieved through the approximation of the centre. In a centred universe, both (true) knowledge and (good) action aim at reaching the same centre. Of course, no one can really hit the centre, for humans are imperfect and their knowledge, power and goodness are limited. But when we approximate, if only from afar, we still know that we approximate and what we approximate.

The same is the case in interpretation proper. The meaning, or, rather, the divine message, of a text is approximated. Even if we cannot decipher the message in full, we speculate about the message. Esotericism offers an interpretative cue that helps one to hit closer to the centre. As long as there is one single centre, the pursuit of true knowledge, moral goodness and interpretative meaning are not yet disentangled. All of them are a kind of knowledge, all of them share an ethical (moral) quality, and all of them render meaning to texts that had been opened up for interpretation.

Knowledge has become de-centred in the Cartesian universe. Science deals with the infinite dead matter and its laws. The discovery of the 'secrets' of nature go on *ad infinitum* and where there is an infinite progression (or regression) that lacks life, goodness or power – for it cannot be personified – there is no centre. Yet if knowledge is de-centred, it cannot present any other meaning than the pursuit of knowledge itself. Consequently, modern sciences do not unearth meaning, not even for scientists; although 'being a scientist' can provide meaning for the life of persons who chose to become scientists.

The ancient distinction between *ratio* and *intellectus* is not just reconfirmed, but developed to the extreme. What the ancients called intellect (and what Kant termed *Vernunft*) has to resign many of its pretensions, first among which is its confidence in approximating (or intuitively hitting) the centre. Knowing and thinking are different, so Kant (1787) argues; many things that we can think we cannot know. *Vernunft* can transcend the limits of theoretical knowledge. We can think big, but we cannot know big. The epistemological (transcendental) subject[2] constitutes things, the very world that we (the human race) can get to know or comprehend (*erkennen*) in and through the process of infinite regression. There is no approximation here, for there is no centre; or, if there is one, we cannot come to know it, for there is no intellectual intuition (ibid.).

Yet Kant never accepted the de-centring of morals. While presenting the strongest case for the de-centring of (scientific) knowledge, he confronted the moderns with a Moral Absolute, the Moral Law qua Centre. God disappears but the Law remains and the Law is simple and understandable for all; it can be, because it should be, approximated. We know when we approximate it, or at least we know whether we have truly done our best to approximate it, even when we do not know the source of the Law (for knowledge must remain de-centred).3 Furthermore, there is as little interpretation in morals as there is meaning in knowledge. If one undertakes to interpret the categorical imperative,[3] one cannot approximate it any longer; and if one tries to squeeze meaning out of world-constitution, one mixes up categories and ideas, ends up in confusion and commits 'transcensus'.

Kant's Third Critique[4] has to bridge the gap between centring and de-centring, between morality and knowledge; and the gap can be filled only with that which is missing from the two major realms (the noumenon and the phenomenon[5]), namely with interpretation and meaning. Interpretation and meaning are also connected to the third question: what can I hope for?

The Third Critique (particularly the first part, 'Critique of Aesthetic Judgement', although to a lesser extent the second part also) deals with culture (Kant 1790). Within the Third Critique, the chapters on the sublime and on the arts address the question of meaning and the problem of interpretation.

Something else is also going on in this text that may be of great interest with regard to our reflections on the omnivorous cultural universe. In the case of the judgement of taste, Kant insists that all cultural elements are ephemeral and contingent; in fact, *sensus communis* is something that one might rather term 'anthropological', for it issues from a kind of pre-established harmony between our faculty of understanding and our imagination. Moreover, it is (later) assumed that our reason (*Vernunft*) is somehow also party to this kind of pre-established harmony.[6] The shy and tentative Leibnizian move does not necessarily hint at the divine telos (as it did in Leibniz), for there is nothing that we can know in this case, but it pinpoints the paradoxical character of an *a priori* judgement rooted in a kind of feeling. Kant confronts us with the question of whether there are limits to our choice of *interpretanda* to the same extent as there are to the choice of the object of taste. True, cultural or social limits no longer exist; but does the same apply to anthropological ones? To enumerate examples here (e.g. peacocks are considered to be beautiful in every culture) is to no avail. Here Kant was right: no merely empirical evidence (if there is any) could prove this point. We still assume that there might be anthropological limits to what we can see (hear) as beautiful. Can we also assume that there are anthropological limits on the exercise of gathering meaning? Can a culture factually be entirely omnivorous? This question remains a question, or, rather, a question mark.

In one sense I fully subscribe to Kant's intuition: if knowledge is constantly de-centred and morals remain centred, then culture is 'the middle term' (the mediator) between knowledge and morals. At a second glance, the conditional tense ('if' ...) seems to me superfluous. As long as the discourse of the natural sciences remains what it now is, the approximation of a centre in science is out of the question. And one cannot think further – if there is a 'further'. And as long as morals remain, there will also be a centre. And I do not desire to think further – if there is a 'further'.

In scientific discourse and inquiry, that is, in the realm of cumulative knowledge, an infinite regression (or progression) of knowledge is to be expected. What was once called the subject became useless here. Metaphors such as language game, paradigm, discourse, system, structure and so on describe the processes of the accumulation of knowledge more adequately than does the Transcendental Subject. Here language speaks, the language of ghosts, of abstractions. At the same time, all attempts to model (or to remodel) morals in the fashion of knowledge prove to be disastrous, both in theory and in practice. Constant regression in morals results soon in nihilism and it cannot be continued *ad infinitum*. If one rejects nihilism and one also maintains – with philosophers from Kant to Lévinas (1989) – that morality has a transcendent or transcendental foundation beyond the pale of reason, then one will not even try to recommend a new theory that still encompasses knowledge and morality alike, as happens in 'discourse ethics'[7] (Habermas 1984, 1987a).

Therefore, if morality is to remain, it also remains centred, but in a way quite different from cultural interpretation. In the omnivorous cultural universe each subject is the omphalos of the universe, that is, the centrepoint of all interpretations. Persons increasingly become subjects the more they themselves choose the *interpretandum* that suits them from all the practically unlimited candidates, squeezing meaning out of it from their own point of view as single monads. But in morality, this will not do. With morality the centre is never the individual subject, the actor herself, but rather something that is termed 'the good', decency, the honest way of life and so on. Briefly, it is always the Other(s) that occupies the centre. Moral persons do their best to approximate this centre, though they never hit it. As a moral person one is not a subject in the same sense as one in the capacity of interpreter. The moral person is subjecting himself/herself to a kind of moral law at the very outset.

The fundamental model of moral striving has not changed much as it has been carried through the modern era, in spite of the successful deconstruction of the pre-modern social and political universe. What has changed is not the attitude of centring morals or the resolve to approximate the centre. The change occurs and new difficulties arise at two other points.

First, tradition does not tell us exactly how to become a good person. These days, it tells us very little. Yet since the moral person is not the omphalos of her own world, but always turns her face towards the Other(s), the gap between the resolve to be decent and the actual approximation of the centre is not closed by the single subject, but found out together, intersubjectively. There is a devotional element here, but it does not relate to the process of squeezing out meaning; at least not directly. Second (and from the standpoint of the single person this 'second' is the 'first'), the subject appears here in an 'instant' and this instant is also the manifestation of the Universal. This 'instant' is the transcendent/transcendental moment (we can use one or another category according to our philosophy). I speak here, in the wake of Kierkegaard, about the existential choice.

The transcendental moment is the choosing of myself as a good person. This gesture is the most personal, yet also the most universal. It is eminently personal, for I choose myself and no one else; moreover, I choose nothing but myself; I do not even choose goodness (as a value or a goal) but just myself as a good person. At the same time, it is eminently universal, for whenever I choose myself as a good person, I choose under the category of universality, because everyone can choose to be good and everyone could make this choice good. (Whereas all other kinds of existential choices are made under the category of particularity – for example, the choosing of oneself as a philosopher.) But in choosing myself as good, I choose myself as a person who is *not* the omphalos of the universe. Moreover, at the instant of the choice (the instant is also a metaphor, because the choice is atemporal) I 'have' no world, for I isolate myself completely from the world: being born again – becoming – happens in isolation. The existential chooser has no world, so she certainly does not interpret one either.

Interpretation reappears in the life of a good person *after* the existential choice has been made. Moral interpretation is hermeneutics proper and this time in a traditional sense: it is mutual; it aims at mutual understanding; it is constant; and perhaps it may arrive at the fusion of horizons. This kind of interpretation is also of a cultural character. One can speak about moral culture and moral aesthetics without putting these expressions in inverted commas. But this kind of interpretation, the mutual one, the one that can achieve the fusion of the horizons of the community of interpreters, is far from being omnivorous. Furthermore, the aim of interpretation is not to satisfy our thirst and hunger for meaning in general, but to bring about sufficient mutual understanding between single persons allowing for the establishment of meaningful emotional relations and attachments.

MORALITY, CULTURE AND SCIENCE

We came to the conclusion that the culture of interpretation – our omnivorous culture – can be placed in our philosophical topology somewhere between science, on the one hand, and morals, on the other. In one sense, culture centres, in another sense it de-centres. Insofar as it de-centres, it shares a decisive quality with scientific knowledge. Insofar as it centres, it shares a decisive quality with morals. However, interpretation in our omnivorous culture de-centres in a different way than scientific discourse does and it centres in a different way than morals do.

Let me repeat that the centrepoint of (post-)modern interpretation is the subject itself. This is the only place that the subject now can occupy. One can add: at last, the subject has found its only legitimate place. It is the meaning-squeezing subject, the world-constituting monad, that we encounter here. This centre has nothing to do with a moral centre. Interpretation is not a moral exercise. To mistake correct moral interpretation (if there is something like that) with morals is as great a blunder as to mistake correct knowledge of something with good morals. Morality is always about action. A person who can offer a splendid interpretation of moral paradoxes may act as a scoundrel when the chips are down. Certainly, there is space for interpretation in morals, to the same extent that there is for knowledge; sometimes it even assumes great importance. But it is, and remains, always subjected to the ultimate moral gesture which is as much above and beyond interpretation and interpretability as it is beyond knowledge and knowability.

De-centring in meaning-providing interpretation and de-centring in knowledge also work in two entirely different ways. Knowledge is de-centred because of the unlimited, infinite regression-process (the 'bad' infinity) in knowing. One cannot approximate here, for all centres are merely temporal, they are further and further removed. A temporal centre is not a centre in a metaphysical sense. Horizons cannot be fused here either, because as our knowledge charges ahead, our horizon moves also. Finally, de-centred knowledge is cumulative, in and by discourse. One discourse may replace the previous one, but a community of scientists always remains the collective author of inquiry. Certainly, interpretation also plays a role in the knowledge-gathering and -accumulating process (for example, every experience or fact is, and must be, interpreted), but these interpretations, too, are absorbed by the discourse. A merely personal interpretation is not yet scientific; it becomes scientific when it ceases to be personal. In science it is untrue that each and every person has his or her own world. There are shared worlds here; abstract and not concrete worlds, worlds to be known, worlds where no one – not even a scientist as a person – could possibly dwell.

De-centring shows an entirely different face in (post-)modern interpretation. There is no cumulative interpretation. There is no progression (or for that matter no regression) in the realm of interpretation. In this regard, interpretation resembles morality more than it does sciences; after all, there is no such thing as the accumulation of morality (though legal-political institutions can go through learning processes). There is no need here for a tightly knit community of interpreters; if there is something similar, it fulfils institutional requirements (requirements of the academy or of the media of communication), not those of the cultural practice of interpretation itself. Each interpreter is supposed to interpret something different from every other interpreter, or at least to interpret it differently; this is not a shortcoming, but a merit. In reverse, if a chemical experiment cannot be repeated twice, one sees a shortcoming rather than a merit.

As far as cumulative knowledge is concerned, the infinite is as much ahead as behind – there is also an infinite regression in the (scientific) knowledge of the past (e.g. the genesis of our planet) just as there is of the future. Strictly speaking, there is no difference between past and future in scientific inquiry (except in the merely social sciences – if there are such things at all).[4] The infinity of the omnivorous culture lies, however, solely in the past and in the past of the present. Scientific inquiry cannot become omnivorous. The kind of spiritual processing that used to be widespread in cultural interpretation has moved its habitat into scientific institutions. Here there are rules – there are things unfit for inquiry. Not because they are unholy or beyond dignity, but because they do not promise results. There are routes that are totally barred for the members of the scientific community, for example the routes of magic and sorcery – and also the routes of strict and direct metaphysics. A host of practices are now considered 'unscientific', but no single interpretation (if it is new and surprising) is unfit.

CONCLUSION

What Heidegger (1927) termed 'Being-towards-Death' is the authentic manifestation of the omnivorous culture. It is not only that individuals reckon with their own finitude and conduct their lives in view of this finitude, but also that this old and well-known attitude also assumes a new character. Given that every subject has a world of his/her own, acceptance of Being-towards-Death on the individual plane also means acceptance of the end of the world. Our individual life is accepted, and not merely perceived, as finite; because our whole culture, our whole world, the sum total of all the worlds of monads, all worlds seen from all the subjective perspectives, that is, modernity as such, is accepted as something mortal. Moderns are the first specimens of the human species that live consciously in a mortal culture. We now know (or believe we know) that all cultures were mortal, but the denizens of ancient worlds did not know it, so their cultures were neither perceived, and even less accepted, as mortal, but were rather seen as immortal or eternal. There was never in this sense a Being-towards-Death. There is now.

If we begin sincerely (authentically) to reflect on our culture, we confront historicity as our foundation (*Grund*). The foundation of the modern world and the modern individual is transient; it is not supposed to hold; it is contingent, conditional. So are we. Historicity is historical time; we, too, are historically grounded. This is why we exist, and can choose to exist, towards death. The omnivorous culture is the culture founded on historicity; it is Being-towards-Death. Infinite possibilities of interpretation emerge within finitude; all interpretations echo the experience of finitude. In contrast, a culture that knows itself as One and Eternal is always self-sufficient.

The practice of accumulating knowledge (modern science) does not manifest the consciousness of Being-towards-Death – not because it is ahistorical, but because historicity does not make any difference here; it is meaningless. True knowledge is temporal – so what? New and perhaps better or simpler knowledge will replace it. Where there is no centre, where no meaning is provided, the problem of authenticity/inauthenticity is not to be raised.

Morality remains centred (for if it ceased to be centred, it would cease to exist altogether); the Other sits in the centre of this circle. Here the first gesture is and remains also the ultimate one. The source of this gesture cannot be known and the gesture itself cannot be interpreted. The decent person suffers injustice rather than commits it; she does the right thing irrespective of the consequences she might suffer or enjoy; she does not use other persons as mere means; she loves her neighbour as much as herself. One can express the same thing in many different ways. Yet as far as morality is concerned, culture and the discourse are just costumes; they do not change the *what*, only the *how*. There is the Circle – the Good is at the Centre; one tries to approximate it. The Centre is Eternal. So is the approximation.

As moral beings, men and women do not exist towards Death, for they do not exist in Time. Morality is not historically grounded; by definition, nothing transcendent is historically grounded. When Epicurus said that as long as we live there is no death – he consoled us mortals with a kind of moral therapy. Authentic moderns (contingent individuals) could dismiss this therapy – we are, after all, historically grounded. And yet, historicity cannot take root in the essence of the good person, for this essence is ahistorical; it is eternal.

My conclusion is that our modern, omnivorous culture holds fast to infinity within finitude. In a similar way, morality holds fast to eternity within finitude. Or can we reverse the connection? Could we say that the omnivorous culture holds fast to finitude in infinity and morality holds fast to finitude in eternity?

NOTES

1 Cf. Derrida (1974), where his interpretation is devoted to Rousseau's works. Other works where this is the case include Derrida (1982 and 1987).
2 See Derrida (1974), as well as Caputo (1987), for an extensive discussion of deconstruction.
3 For a discussion of the moral law, see Kant (1788).
4 For further discussion of this point, see Heller (1990).

EDITORS' NOTES

[1] The reference here (and later in this chapter) is to the doctrine of monadology in the philosophy of G. W. von Leibniz (1646–1716). He argued that individuals (monads) are unique and exist separately from each other, each viewing the world from a different point of view. Since God is the creator of each monad, a 'pre-established harmony' exists between them, inclining them towards each other. This commonality makes possible social interaction, despite the divisions which exist between people.
[2] A reference to the supra-individual dimension of the constitution of the objects of experience in the philosophy of knowledge of Immanuel Kant (1724–1804). For him, individual subjects come to know the world of the senses by filtering experience through universal categories such as cause and effect, space and time, which are held to be built into our perception *a priori*, that is, prior to experience. Any unity or order in the world does not reside in the nature of objects,

but is imposed by the categories. These are said to possess a necessary, 'transcendental' status and as such are the preconditions of all possible experience.

[3] In the moral philosophy of Kant the supreme moral principle which can be used as a test of moral rightness. He formulated it technically as 'Act only on that maxim through which you can at the same time will that it should become a universal law.' Another, looser, formulation enjoins people to treat others always as ends and never merely as means.

[4] *The Critique of Judgement* (Kant 1790). The first part of this volume is entitled 'Critique of Aesthetic Judgement' and includes sections on the beautiful, the sublime, fine arts and genius. The second part is entitled 'Critique of Teleological Judgement'.

[5] These are technical terms in Kant's epistemology. The knowledge we derive of the world of the senses via the *a priori* categories (see note [2] above) is held to be only knowledge of a phenomenon, or an appearance. The noumenon, or *Ding-an-sich* (thing-in-itself), is deemed to be unknowable, that is, not in itself an object of possible experience.

[6] See note [1].

[7] In the writings of Jürgen Habermas (1984: 19–22) the process whereby in practical (i.e. moral) discourse controversial validity claims as to the rightness of the moral norms of action can also be, like other validity claims in other discourses, subject to rational reflection. Habermas writes: 'In regard to these basic questions of ethics I am myself inclined . . . to a cognitivist position, according to which practical questions can in principle be settled by way of argumentation' (ibid.: 19).

Part II

REVOLUTION

5

THE REVOLUTIONS OF 1989 IN EAST-CENTRAL EUROPE AND THE IDEA OF REVOLUTION

Krishan Kumar

The events of 1989 in the East-Central European belt of satellite communist regimes was a most fitting finale for the twentieth century, bound to be recorded in history as the age of revolutions. They changed the political map of the globe, affecting even parts ostensibly distant from the scene of the upheaval in ways which are still far from being fully grasped. They are also certain to be scrutinized for the updating they offer to our orthodox views of how revolutions come about and how they are conducted in a new socio-cultural context.

(Bauman 1992a: 156)

ANNUS MIRABILIS

It is evident that what Zhou Enlai is alleged to have said about the consequences of the French Revolution, that 'it is too early to say', applies *a fortiori* to the revolutions of 1989 in East-Central Europe. But no one has felt inhibited by this, and rightly so. It has seemed clear to the majority of observers that, whatever the precise and particular outcomes, the events of 1989 have a 'world-historical' significance. 'No politically literate person in the world', says Daniel Chirot, 'can doubt that 1989, like 1789, will be remembered as one of those decisive years in which decades of slow political and economic change and development culminated in a series of unexpected, dramatic events that suddenly redefined the world' (1991a: ix). It became common to say

127

that 1989 was 'an earthquake in world politics', a 'year of wonders', an *annus mirabilis*.[1]

It was, of course, first and foremost a year of wonders for the Eastern Europeans themselves. For Janusz Ziółkowski, sociologist, Solidarity supporter and, since 1989, Polish senator, the momentousness of the events must sweep aside any doubts that what had occurred was truly a revolution. He added that '[b]y revolution I mean the overthrow of the existing political, economic and social order' (1990: 40). Ziółkowski is responding to the views of those, such as Timothy Garton Ash, who question the use of the term revolution – 'a word so closely associated with violence' – when the changes were carried through by means that were 'almost entirely non-violent'. Romania, Garton Ash concedes, clearly experienced revolution: blood was spilled. But Poland, Hungary, Bulgaria and even Czechoslovakia and East Germany are more cases of what he calls 'refolution': 'a mixture of popular protest and élite negotiation', reforms from above in response to revolutionary mass pressure from below. But there was, he admits, in all cases not just a change of government but a profound 'change of life'. Moreover, the 'astonishing speed' with which the change came, the 'sudden and sweeping end to an *ancien régime*', may indeed 'justify the use of the word "revolution" ' (Garton Ash 1990: 14, 20, 139; see also Arato 1990: 27; Dahrendorf 1990: 5, 74, 103; di Palma 1991: 50; Weitman 1992: 12).

What is being raised here are classic questions in the study of revolution. Is violence a central criterion, as liberals have commonly held; or is it merely incidental, as most Marxists have argued? Is what matters the speed and depth of change, rather than its forcible accomplishment? And if so, how might we gauge the depth of change? We generally look first at changes within society; but here the problem of time, of how long it takes for change actually to show itself at different levels of society, is acute. Zhou Enlai's quip returns to harass us.

But we need to remember that the great revolutions of the past have struck most contemporaries – as opposed to later academic students of revolution – more from the point of view of their external impact than of their effects on their own society. The English Revolution of the seventeenth century was ambiguous in this respect, though there is no doubting its contribution to radical thought in the American colonies. But since the American and

French revolutions of the eighteenth century no one has questioned the international significance of revolution. It was largely in pointing to this that Hegel, Tocqueville and Marx made their great contributions to the study of revolution.[2]

The 1989 revolutions have irresistibly sounded this note. It has been impossible not to think of 1989 in terms of its impact on the world as a whole. And, while the question of long-term effects on this scale poses difficulties even greater than those that apply to changes within society, the immediate effect has been clearer and more dramatic. The course of world history seems so obviously changed, despite deep uncertainties as to the ultimate outcome. George Schöpflin emphasizes the largely European dimension:

> [Nineteen eighty-nine] was the year when Europe grew up and shook off the legacy of the Great European Civil War of 1914–45 and began to redefine itself in its own terms and against the now declining superpowers which had exercised tutelage over it for so long.
> (1990: 3; see also Garton Ash 1990: 156; Halliday 1990: 9)

But to most observers the really important change was in the contest of ideologies, and the world conflicts that flowed from it. What 1989 meant was the end of the communist challenge and, with it, the elimination of one of the two principal contenders for world hegemony. We could no longer speak of Three Worlds – 'the very concept of a Third World presupposes two others' – only of One World, the world of liberal capitalist society (Dahrendorf 1990: 22; see also Jowitt 1991: 82). For some, such as Francis Fukuyama, this outcome amounted to no less than 'the end of history'. It vindicated Hegel's contention that, with the French Revolution and the announcement of the principles of the modern liberal state, the dialectic of conflicting ideologies in history had reached an end and been resolved (Fukuyama 1992). There had been attempts since then to upset this fundamental settlement, but all had ultimately failed.

Ken Jowitt, on the contrary, has argued that 'the Leninist extinction' – the 'mass extinction of Leninist regimes' in 1989–91 – will produce not stability but an entirely new world 'disorder'. The liberal capitalist West may have won; but its victory opens the way not, as Fukuyama and others would have it, to the end of fundamental political and ideological conflicts but to the start of a period of new conflicts and international turmoil. In the new environment Western civilization will be forced to re-examine its own premises, based on the three revolutions – British, American and French – that brought liberal capitalist democracy into being; it will face constant challenges both from within and from without.

> In the immediate future, the Leninist Extinction is likely to dramatically, and in some instances traumatically, challenge and undermine the national boundaries and political identi- ties of Third World nations, Western nations, and the charac- ter of the Western world itself, as well as create obvious and serious obstacles to stable and viable élite and regime replacements in the Soviet Union, Eastern Europe, and Asia.
>
> (Jowitt 1991: 83; see also Jowitt 1992b: 306–31)

This is an international context in which revolution, far from having exhausted its appeal with the 1989 events (see, e.g., Eberle 1990: 207), appears likely to flourish. For some indeed the striking thing about 1989 is that it has renewed the whole idea of revolu- tion, after a period in which it seemed to have lost its force and relevance. In the West and the industrial world generally, revolu- tion has for most of the twentieth century been in abeyance (Kumar 1988). The work of the revolution seemed to be over, the myth of revolution pernicious. Nineteen eighty-nine, the year of the Eastern European revolutions, was also the year of the bicentenary of the great French Revolution of 1789. In the West it occasioned an outpouring of 'revisionist' works on the Revolu- tion, questioning its historic meaning and significance and point- ing to the disastrous consequences that flowed from it (see, e.g., Schama 1989). The Revolution was over – not just in France but throughout the Western world.

In 1989 the torch of revolution passed once more, as it had in 1917, to the East. If the West, sunk in the torpor of affluence, had lost the taste for revolution, in the East it still seemed to have the capacity to inspire popular feeling and mass action. The events of 1989, said Fred Halliday,

> have restated, in a dramatic form, the most neglected facet of political life, ... namely the capacity of the mass of the population to take sudden, rapid and novel political action

after long periods of what appears to be indifference. In their speed and import and the uncertainties they unleash, they can only be compared to a war, in which all established expectations and plans are swept aside.

(1990: 4; cf. also Cumings 1991: 101; Habermas 1991: 29–30; Kuran 1991: 36; Weitman 1992: 13)

And not just revolution, the form, but democracy, the content of the modern revolution, seems to have gained fresh life from 1989. Most obviously this is seen in the rediscovery of the idea of civil society, as a tradition that can regenerate the concepts and practices of democracy today (Cohen and Arato 1992; Kumar 1993). More generally, the realization that democracy can still move men and women to take to the streets and risk their lives has re-opened the debate about the forms and meaning of democracy, east and west, north and south (Held 1993). Slavoj Žižek argues that 1989 reminded the West in particular of the democratic promise of their own societies; this is the chief source of the enthusiasm with which the West greeted the events of that year.

[W]hat fascinates the Western gaze is the *re-invention of democracy*. It is as if democracy, which in the West shows increasing signs of decay and crisis, lost in bureaucratic routine and publicity-style election campaigns, is being rediscovered in Eastern Europe in all its freshness and novelty. The function of this fascination is thus purely ideological: in Eastern Europe the West looks for its own lost origins, for the authentic experience of 'democratic invention'.

(1990: 50)

Revolution and democracy; 1789 and the revolutionary tradition; the 'end of history' and new beginnings – all this returns us, as Zygmunt Bauman says, to 'the age of revolutions'. But *pace* Bauman this must take us back well beyond our own century. In fact the revolutions of the twentieth century, notably the communist revolutions of 1917 and 1949, are for obvious reasons peculiarly unhelpful as points of departure (though for equally obvious reasons they remain important as points of reference). We need to go further back. The age of revolution is two hundred, perhaps even three hundred, years old. Not only does 1989 connect up with 1789 and 1848 but it also does so with 1776 and 1688. What Václav Havel called 'the chain of spectacular trans-formations' that took place in 1989 reaches back deep into the past.

What are the connections? What kind of challenge do the 1989 revolutions pose to 'our orthodox views of how revolutions come about'? What is the 'new socio-cultural context' in which they occur, and how does that affect their character? What kind of 'updating' may be necessary in understanding them?

THE 1989 COLLAPSE AND THEORIES OF REVOLUTION

Some commentators on 1989 have simply reached for their Crane Brinton. Brinton's *Anatomy of Revolution* (first published in 1938) drew upon the 'classic' revolutions of 1640, 1776, 1789 and 1917 to set out a 'shopping list' of general causes of revolution: a downturn in a generally advancing economy, a government in financial difficulties, the 'desertion of the intellectuals', the 'loss of confidence among many members of the ruling class' and the 'conversion of many members of that class to the belief that their privileges are unjust or harmful to society'. Brinton cautioned that 'some, if not most of these signs may be found in almost any modern society at any time', and that the extension of his 'tentative uniformities' to other revolutions must be undertaken 'with caution and humility' (1965: 7, 68). This has not prevented students of revolution from using his list as the key to revolutions at all times and places. Usually the 'structural strains' identified by Brinton are coupled with some set of 'triggers' or 'precipitants' – a bad harvest, a bungled use of force by the government – that explain the actual onset of revolution at a particular time (see, e.g., Smelser 1963).

It has not proved difficult to find most of these factors at work in the 1989 revolutions (Schöpflin 1990; Eisenstadt 1992: 21–2; Bozóki 1992: 170–2). A particular favourite is the 'desertion of the intellectuals' in Eastern Europe and their uncovering and denunciation of what Daniel Chirot calls 'the utter moral rot' at the heart of their societies (1991b: 20; see also di Palma 1991; and Coser, this volume). Teodor Shanin similarly argues that the concept of a 'moral economy' is necessary to make sense of 1989: 'It was mass indignation and not mass hunger which made

radicals ... go on the offensive, drew masses of people into protest and broke the resolve of the rulers to hang on, come what
may' (1990: 71; see also Holmes 1993). Nor is it hard to find
plausible 'precipitating factors' that brought matters to a head in
1989: popular candidates are Hungary's decision to open its borders with Austria, and General Jaruzelski's calling of the Round
Table conference with Solidarity.

No one can doubt the importance of a factor such as the loss
of legitimacy in bringing about revolution. But this very example
illustrates what is wrong with the Brinton-like approach to 1989.
For had not communist rule in Eastern Europe (outside Russia)
always been regarded as more or less illegitimate – not just by
the subject populations but even, one might reasonably suppose,
by many of the rulers themselves? Communist regimes throughout Eastern Europe had either been directly imposed by Russian
arms or were sustained by them (the Balkan states to some extent
excepted). Eastern European societies after 1945, as so often
before in their history, were in the nature of conquest societies.
Their rulers were satraps, like the provincial governors of the
ancient Persian monarchy. The legitimacy of these rulers was in
question from the very earliest days of communist rule. This is
clear from the fact that, despite the enormous risks involved and
the many chilling examples of what failure might mean, their rule
was repeatedly challenged by movements of mass protest and
rebellion – in 1953, 1956, 1968, 1970, 1976, 1980–1. The question
must be, why did the movements of 1989 succeed when all the
earlier ones failed? It clearly cannot do to explain this by pointing
to a loss of legitimacy of the ruling groups. Their illegitimate
character was a constant throughout the period of communist
rule.[3]

Other popular theories of the causes of revolution do not fare
much better when confronted with 1989. Take James Davies'
'inverted J-curve' theory. This argues that 'revolutions are most
likely to occur when a prolonged period of objective economic
and social development is followed by a short period of sharp
reversal', thus frustrating expectations of a steadily increasing
level of 'need satisfaction' (Davies 1962: 6). With some qualification, owing partly to the ambiguity of the concept of 'need
satisfaction', the theory holds up quite well for the classic revolutions of 1640, 1766, 1789 and 1917.

But 1989? The theory may work for some of the earlier Eastern

European rebellions, especially the long Polish sequence that began in 1956 (but it was precisely the message of the last attempt, Poland's 'self-limiting revolution' of 1981, that revolution in the full sense was impossible against the organized communist state, which was here to stay for the foreseeable future).[4] In these cases it applies at best to unsuccessful efforts to reform or topple communist rule. But it can scarcely be persuasive in the case of 1989, when communist rule actually was overthrown. For what has been the common coin of observations on the Eastern European economies before 1989 is to note their stagnation, their slow strangulation under the grip of increasingly inefficient and irresponsible centralized control (Hungary being the main exception – and fittingly the country where the communists were displaced, contrary to the theory's expectation, with the least disturbance). Not, then, the outrage of frustrated populations accustomed to steadily increasing standards of living, and fearful of losing them, but stoical resignation in the face of a long-drawn-out deterioration in their conditions of life characterizes the attitudes of most Eastern Europeans on the eve of 1989.[5]

But Davies does nevertheless give us a lead, if we expand his theory to include political as well as economic change, and if we expand our horizons to consider the Eastern European societies within the context of the Soviet empire as a whole. This last is critical. It points to the main weakness of most of the usual theories of revolution, and in particular the reason for their failure in the face of 1989.

Most conventional theories of revolution, Marxist as well as liberal, focus on factors internal to society. It is the conflict of classes, or mass discontent, or struggles within the ruling class, that bring on revolution. This emphasis seemed satisfactory enough for most of the revolutions from the seventeenth to the nineteenth centuries. Increasingly, however, it has become clear that they leave out an important part of the story. The pressures that have brought about revolution have been at least in part the result of external, international factors (see, e.g., Skocpol 1979). This was true even for England's 'Great Rebellion' of 1640, when fears of collusion between a Catholic-inclined king and the Catholic powers of continental Europe fuelled revolutionary passions. It is truer still for the American and French revolutions of the eighteenth century, which can scarcely be understood without reference to the rivalry and struggle for hegemony between Britain and France. With the Russian Revolution of 1917 we are squarely within the domain of world revolution. Neither the causes of the Russian Revolution nor its outcome can be separated from the international context. With every succeeding revolution of the twentieth century – China, Vietnam, Cuba – the importance of factors external to the society has grown. Revolution in our time has taken on the character of an 'international civil war' (Neumann 1949).

The revolutions of 1989 confirm this picture. The situation of Eastern Europe since 1945 is, as is well known, the result of superpower agreements, notably those reached at Tehran (1943) and at Yalta and Potsdam (1945). Eastern Europe was ceded to the Soviet 'sphere of influence'. Since 1945 its position as part of the Soviet bloc determined its fate. Every effort to change its condition in any essential respect was suppressed by the actual or threatened use of Soviet force. From 1985 onwards that situation changed dramatically. The USSR under Gorbachev, realizing that it could no longer compete successfully with the United States and the West, in either the military or the economic sphere, began to reform. One consequence of the new thinking was to let Eastern Europe go (the 'Sinatra doctrine' replaced the Brezhnev doctrine).

The 'Gorbachev factor' was therefore the essential external ('geopolitical') element that made the 1989 revolutions possible – made them, one might almost say, necessary.[6] Without the support of Soviet troops the regimes of Eastern Europe tumbled one by one. The speed astonished everyone, participants as well as observers, but in retrospect it is not so surprising (Kuran 1991). All the internal elements for revolution – alienated intellectuals, revisionist Marxism, delegitimized élites, disaffected populations – had been there for a long time, almost as long as the regimes themselves. By themselves, given the unwillingness of the West to interfere in the internal affairs of another superpower, they could do nothing – or, rather, their expression in fitful movements of revolt led nowhere. They were the sealed-in elements in a steel cauldron. Once Gorbachev had taken the lid off, their combined force easily swept the party-state away.

Bronisław Geremek, one of Solidarity's leading theoreticians in the 1980s, wrote after the events of 1989: 'De Tocqueville's famous aphorism that for a bad government the most dangerous moment arrives when it starts to introduce reforms seems to be fully applicable to the situation in Central Europe.' He further notes that Tocqueville also said, in *The Old Regime and the Revolution* (1856): 'Patiently endured so long as it seemed beyond redress a grievance comes to appear intolerable once the possibility of removing it crosses men's minds' (Geremek 1990: 99). Tocqueville's analysis anticipates Davies' formulation (as Davies of course acknowledges), with the critical difference that in the case of the Eastern Europeans (unlike France or Russia before their respective revolutions) the reforming government was not their own, in most cases, but that of the external power that had for so long made them 'patiently endure' their grievances without hope of redress. Now, since 1985, a reforming government, that of Mikhail Gorbachev in the Soviet Union, not only showed that communism could be changed, thereby raising hopes and expectations throughout the sphere of Soviet influence, but more or less guaranteed that a movement for change would not be put down by force (and, even more, actually was active in stimulating change throughout the region). This is the principal difference between 1989 and 1956 or 1968, when Khrushchev's denunciation of Stalin and the 'thaw' that followed it established the essential conditions for the rebellions and radical reforms of those years in Hungary, Poland and Czechoslovakia – but without affecting the resolve of the Soviet government to stay firmly in control. It is also the difference between 1989 and 1980–1 in Poland, when, as Geremek observes, 'comprehensive economic and political reforms proved impossible because they were not accompanied by favourable international circumstances' (1990: 106).

It has struck many commentators on 1989 that, if they are looking for a classical theorist of revolution as a helpful guide, then Tocqueville is their man (see, e.g., Garton Ash 1990: 141; Pye 1990: 6; Kuran 1991: 24; Jowitt 1992a: 213 n. 20; Weitman 1992: 14). It is not just that Tocqueville seizes, with unparalleled insight, on the general forces that undermine governments; it is also because he is the incomparable analyst of the particular revolutions of 1789 and 1848 (and understood, better than anyone at the time, the principles of the revolution of 1776 in America). In the eyes of participants as much as observers, 1989 connects up with the revolutionary inheritance of the West. Its meaning therefore has to be sought, at least in part, by seeing where it stands in the revolutionary tradition.

THE EVENTS OF 1989 AND THE REVOLUTIONARY TRADITION

The revolutions of 1989 can be seen to stand – to use Robert Redfield's terms – within a 'great tradition' and a 'little tradition' of revolution. The 'little tradition' is the sequence of risings and attempted reforms within the communist world, from the East German rising of 1953 to the Polish Solidarity movement of 1980–1. Like all traditions, it has its symbolic heroes and specially charged events. Poland is the brave warrior who refuses to accept defeat. It expresses the steady current of opposition throughout, swelling to a flood in the 1980s. The Hungarian Rising of 1956 and the Czech Spring of 1968 symbolize heroic but tragic endeavour. They teach bitter lessons; but they are also an inspiration to future generations. The greatest shame lies in not having tried.[7]

In the perspective of the 'little tradition', the 1989 revolutions are the culmination of these efforts. The movements of 1989, the various Civic and Democratic Forums, helped each other; their leaders were in touch with each other; the success of one was the signal for renewed efforts on the part of others, so that there appeared to be an inexorable logic to the exhilarating chain of events that began with Hungary and Poland in early 1989 and was crowned by the spectacular overthrow of Ceauşescu in December of that year.

The 'great tradition' is the European or Western revolutionary tradition stretching from the English revolutions of the seventeenth century to the Russian Revolution of 1917, and its twentieth-century successors in the non-European world. Marx's category of 'bourgeois revolutions' links many of these revolutions; but it is Tocqueville who makes us most aware that the sequence of revolutions – including the so-called 'communist' revolutions – have a common theme. That theme is democracy. Reflecting in particular on the American Revolution of 1776 and the French Revolution of 1789, Tocqueville is convinced that they are part of a general 'European revolution' which is sweeping the world. The ideology of that revolution is democracy (Tocqueville 1835). Each particular revolution expresses different facets of the world-wide movement towards democracy; each can be scrutinized for what it shows of the varying forces in conflict. Every revolution therefore has a particular and a general aspect;

differing according to the circumstances of time and place, they are nevertheless members of the same family.

The relation of the 1989 revolutions to the little tradition, the specifically Eastern European tradition of revolt,[8] is relatively straightforward. Essentially it concerns the contribution of the dissidents. In retrospect at least there is a clear movement among them from attempts to reform the system, to establish 'socialism with a human face', to the conviction that the system cannot be reformed but must be rejected altogether (although not necessarily by a head-on collision with the state). There is a satisfyingly evolutionary and 'progressive' quality to this movement that sits well with many conventional views of how revolution comes about. The fact that these views are, in this as in most other cases, mistaken should not lead us to ignore the importance of dissident thought and action in keeping alive the spirit of revolt within these societies. The dissidents, most of whom were intellectuals, did not overthrow communism, not even when they combined with the workers in Solidarity. But, like the *philosophes* of the Enlightenment, they were the gadflies of the *ancien régime*, the critics and tormentors whose constant undermining of the pretensions of their rulers is probably a necessary ingredient in all revolutions.

The relation of the 1989 revolutions to the great tradition, the centuries-old European revolution, is not so simple. The kinship was claimed again and again – not least in the declaration that the revolutions represented 'the return to Europe' (Kumar 1992b). For some, such as Ewa Kowalska, a young Slovak historian, the events of 1989 were

> the culmination of the slow and continuous 'general revolution' of the western world, of the process that began economically and politically with the English and French revolutions and that is coming to an end spiritually and nationally with the upheavals of central Europe.
>
> (quoted in Darnton 1991: 17)

The desire to link up with the Western revolutionary inheritance has been a common theme of nearly all accounts, from both East and West, of the 1989 revolutions (see, e.g., Prins 1990).

But there is an emphatic rejection of one part of that inheritance – that represented by the Russian Revolution of 1917, and its particular successors. Eastern Europeans as much as Western liberals deny the validity of Lenin's well-known assertion that the Russian Revolution 'merely recommences the French Revolution'. For them the Russian Revolution was, if not a cynical repudiation of it, at the very least a massive deviation from the mainstream of the European revolutionary tradition.[9] Now that revolution has revealed its bankruptcy, the falsity of its claim to continue and complete the French Revolution. The Bolsheviks, said François Furet, 'thought that with 1917 they had buried 1789. Here, at the end of our century, we see that the opposite is happening. It is 1917 that is being buried in the name of 1789' (1990: 5).

So the first aspect of the problematic relation of 1989 to the Western revolutionary tradition is its selectivity, its refusal to accept that the model of the communist revolution belongs to that tradition. This is in effect to reject Marxism and its whole account of the role of revolution in modern world history.[10] No surprise here; but we should be aware of the peculiarity of the claim being made in the name of 1989. It is to appeal to a highly truncated version of the revolutionary tradition – a version that denies the legitimacy of revolution to bring about economic and social equality (or 'social' along with 'political' and 'legal' citizenship). The communist revolutions of the twentieth century stand condemned for precisely that, for what are seen as the disastrous political consequences of their stated objective of achieving a classless society.

The rejection of one part of the revolutionary inheritance is closely linked to another peculiarity of the 1989 revolutions: their unwillingness to announce anything new, their self-consciously backward-looking nature. Virtually every commentator has remarked on this. Jürgen Habermas has called the 1989 revolutions 'rectifying revolutions', or 'revolutions of recuperation'. They seek to remedy, to recover, to restore, not to discover new principles of state and society. Habermas notes their 'total lack of ideas that are either innovative or orientated towards the future'. In his view, 1989 'presents itself as a revolution that is to some degree flowing backwards, one that clears the ground in order to catch up with developments previously missed out on'. Eastern European societies wish to re-start their history, in the first place by going back to the political traditions of the interwar period that were cut short by Nazism and communism. At a deeper historical level they also wish to 'connect up constitutionally with the inheritance of the bourgeois revolutions, and socially and politically with the styles of commerce and life associated with developed capitalism' (Habermas 1991: 26–7; see also Dahrendorf 1990: 23; Garton Ash 1990: 154; Blackburn 1991: 237; Enzensberger 1991: 20).

Backward-looking revolutions are not new – in fact most revolutionaries, according to Barrington Moore, like most generals 'march into the future facing resolutely backward' (1972: 168–9). But since the French Revolution, at least, what Hannah Arendt called 'the pathos of novelty' has been a distinguishing characteristic of almost all revolutions. To be a revolutionary – itself a new type – was to blaze a new path, to aim to start everything *de novo*. In turning their backs on the new, the revolutions of 1989 bid fair to return us to the pre-modern sense of revolution, as a return or a restoration (see Arendt 1963: 21– 40).[11]

We shall consider in a moment what the significance might be of this unexpected turn in the ideology of revolution. But firstly we should ask: if the revolutions of 1989 look backwards, what precisely are they looking back to? What aspects of the revolutionary tradition matter to them? What can we learn about the 1989 revolutions by comparing them with the various revolutions of the past that go to make up the revolutionary inheritance? We know that 1917 is no starting point, except negatively. But it has been the common practice of most commentaries on 1989 to look to one or more of the other great revolutions for the light they might throw on its meaning.

The year of the Great French Revolution, 1789, is a natural reference point. It is the year most commonly referred to by most Eastern European participants (including Russian reformers), and by many Western commentators as well. It is almost impossible to avoid 1789. Rightly or wrongly it has long been regarded as the symbolic starting point of the whole modern revolutionary tradition. Since that tradition is about the struggle for democracy, and since the 1989 revolutions were in the first place about democracy and human rights, it has seemed well-nigh inevitable that homage should be paid to the revolution that issued the Declaration of the Rights of Man and the Citizen and carried out the first real experiments in democracy in the modern world (see, e.g., Furet 1981: 79; 1990: 5; Sakwa 1990: 377).

But there is another reason why 1789 is a popular parallel. It symbolizes mass action, and for many theorists, as we have seen, this is part of the significance of 1989. The 1989 revolutions, on this view, have put back on the agenda the possibility of political change directed by the people. They demonstrated, says Habermas,

> precisely the sort of spontaneous mass action that once provided so many revolutionary theorists with a model, but which has recently been presumed to be dead. . . . It was mass anger . . . that was directed at the apparatuses of state security, just as it had once been directed at the Bastille. The destruction of the Party's monopoly on state power could similarly be seen to resemble the execution of Louis XVI.
>
> (1991: 27, 29–30; see also Bozóki 1992: 176)

I have discussed elsewhere the limitations of this view of the 1989 revolutions. The importance of mass action – even in Romania – has generally been exaggerated, to the neglect of the importance of manoeuvrings among the Communist Party élites, including those of the Soviet Union.[12] But 1789 is problematic for other reasons as well. It connotes, beyond democracy and citizenship, Jacobinism, the Terror, plebiscitary dictatorship. It evokes ideological fanaticism of the kind that was the principal target of the 1989 revolutions. It is the classic example of the revolution that, conceived in freedom, gives rise to tyranny and totalitarianism. It is in this, as in several other respects, the precursor and parent of 1917. Eastern Europeans do not reject 1789 as they do 1917. Its contribution to democratic theory and practice is seen as incalculable. But, enamoured as they are of the liberal varieties of democracy, 1789 is bound to appear in their eyes highly equivocal.

Another popular parallel is 1848. The reasons are obvious. The 1848 revolutions took place, to a good extent, in the very region of East-Central Europe that is also the heart of the 1989 revolutions. They were the first European revolutions to raise seriously the questions of nationalism and ethnicity that have come to dominate the politics of the region in the post-1989 era. Like 1989, 1848 was also a 'revolution of the intellectuals', in Lewis Namier's well-known phrase. These were, moreover, intellectuals who were mostly liberals. They were acutely aware of the dangers of democratic despotism and anxious to secure the rights of individuals through constitutions and the rule of law. In all these

141

ways 1848 offers the 'obvious parallel' to 1989 (Berlin 1990: 148; see also Trevor-Roper 1989: 14; Garton Ash 1990: 134–49; Howard 1990: 3; Ziółkowski 1990: 41–2; Osiatyński 1991: 823–4).

Indeed, 1848 does have many things to offer. Foremost among them might be the fact that many of the very same groups that contended in 1848 – Czechs, Slovaks, Poles, Hungarians, Ruthenes, Rumans, Slovenes, Croats, Serbs – are once more resuming historic struggles, the sources of which were first revealed in 1848. And, as in 1848, there is the brooding presence of the two giants on their flanks – Germany and Russia. But the parallel also has problems. Not just nationalism but also socialism was released by 1848. The 'social question', first raised in the French Revolution, returned to haunt the liberals of 1848. This was the central point made by both Tocqueville and Marx in their incisive analyses of 1848. The 1848 revolutions were buried not just by nationalist conflicts but by the class conflicts that erupted in the June Days in Paris and the workers' risings in Berlin and Vienna.

These comments might, if anything, serve to underline rather than question the parallel between 1848 and 1989. Is it not the theme of every journalistic commentary on Central Europe – and Russia – today that the societies of the region might succumb to the forces of nationalism and social unrest? And yet there is an important difference between the situations in 1848 and 1989. The men and women of 1989 have lived through a social experiment, the system of state socialism, the very premise of which has been the primacy of the 'social question'. Unlike the liberals of 1848 they do not confront the demands of the socialists as political innocents. Trotsky once wrote caustically of the bourgeoisie of 1848 as being 'shabbily wise' with the experience of the French bourgeoisie during the French Revolution. Shabbily or not, we can say that the bourgeoisie of 1989 is wise with the experience of 1848 and 1917. Their whole concern is not to let the democratic revolution be 'blown off-course' by the urgent pressures for social and economic well-being. Hence their fervent and almost desperate espousal of strict liberal doctrines of the relation between state and society. For their part socialists and communists in the region know that they cannot press their demands in the old way. They, too, have to speak the language of liberal constitutionalism, or risk being excluded from political society. None of these things of course guarantees success. Nationalism and social distress may very well undermine the

142

precarious stability of current democratic regimes in East-Central Europe. It is an old and powerful combination. But we can at least say that no one is more conscious of the danger than the liberals of 1989.

And what of 1776 – and 1688 and 1640? What of the Anglo-Saxon revolutions? The literature on 1989 is noticeably thin on references to these revolutions, by comparison with later ones. But are there not good grounds for tracing the filiation of 1989 from these important ancestors? Not only is there the interesting parallel that all these Anglo-Saxon revolutions, like those of 1989, claimed to be doing nothing new, but merely to be returning to an earlier, purer state of affairs, or restoring a constitutional agreement that had been wantonly disturbed by an 'innovative' monarch. More important is the fact that, far more than the French, these revolutions were predominantly constitutional, and concerned above all else with a political settlement that would guarantee liberal freedoms. If the 1989 revolutions are about democracy, constitutions, citizenship, the rule of law, the protection of individual rights and the creation of a pluralist civil society, then it is hardly possible to think of more suitable parallels than the English and American revolutions.

Some commentators have certainly been aware of this. Ralf Dahrendorf, for instance, has argued that in trying to understand the predicament of the Eastern Europeans in 1989 we should go back to *The Federalist Papers* and the writings of Alexander Hamilton and James Madison on civil society and the rule of law ('As a manual of liberal democracy, *The Federalist Papers* are unsurpassed'). He also recommends Edmund Burke, 'the great Whig who ... had supported the American Revolution' (Dahrendorf 1990: 26–7).

Andrew Arato, searching for a concept of revolution to fit the events and ideology of 1989, also turns initially at least to America.

> Generally speaking ... if one is to speak of any revolution in the East perhaps it should be a 'conservative' one, in the spirit of Hannah Arendt's analysis of the American revolution where organized society (the state legislatures) came to represent the *pouvoir constituant*, rather than atomized individuals in a juridical state of nature, as in the views of Sieyès anticipating the French reality.

He is dissatisfied with this since in the case of the 1989 revolutions the constituent power was composed 'not of legitimate provincial legislatures but illegitimate communist parliaments and entirely self-appointed round tables' (Arato 1990: 30).

This seems unnecessarily cautious and restrictive. In no revolution, not even the American, is there such a halo of legitimacy surrounding the actors that their opponents cannot plausibly accuse them of unlawful and reckless innovation. Moreover, what in this context has struck all observers about 1989 was the relative orderliness of the overthrow of the party-state and the movement to some sort of parliamentary democracy. In many cases it was leading elements in the Party who themselves negotiated the transition. Except in Romania, there was remarkably little violence. So the manner of change, and many of the arguments used to justify it, have revealing similarities in the cases of both 1989 and 1776, not to mention 1688 and even 1640.

But the more important thing, once more, is the content of the revolution. Here the claims of the English and American revolutions are particularly compelling. No one can doubt, for instance, that the concept of 'civil society' has been central in the thinking of the Eastern European dissidents who prepared the way for 1989. It can almost be said to have set the political agenda for the 1989 revolutions. Adam Seligman has shown that, if we wish to get the fullest and most far-sighted discussion of the concept the best places to look are England and, especially, America in the seventeenth and eighteenth centuries. Here were worked out the moral foundations and the political and social requisites for a functioning civil society.

Seligman argues that in the case of one society, eighteenth-century republican America, the ideal of civil society did find a real political and social expression. He also shows how fragile was its base, and how, not just in America but also in Europe, the foundations of civil society were steadily eroded throughout the nineteenth and twentieth centuries. Seligman is not optimistic about the prospects for civil society in Eastern Europe (1992; see also Keane 1988a: 31–68; 1988b: 35–71).

This is the real value of considering the revolutions of 1989 in the perspective of past revolutions. Comparisons can be frivolous as well as odious; but they can also be instructive. Revolutions in the West have a history. The revolutions of 1989 belong to that history. In deeds as well as words, the peoples of Eastern

Europe have expressed the desire to 're-join' the West, after a period of enforced exclusion. Their actions have been inspired by Western examples; their intentions have been proclaimed in terms drawn almost entirely from the vocabulary of the Western revolutionary tradition. It would be strange indeed if that tradition had nothing to teach them, or us, in our efforts to understand them.

THE 1989 REVOLUTIONS: CONTINUITY AND DISCONTINUITY

We have been concerned so far with the ways in which 1989 connects up with previous revolutions, and the revolutionary inheritance in general. There are continuities of ideology, clearly, and to some extent of practice. But in what ways might the revolutions of 1989 represent something new? Have they, as Zygmunt Bauman says, been conducted in a 'new socio-cultural context', and, if so, with what effect?

One important novelty, much commented on, is the role of television and the electronic media generally. The 1989 revolutions were, says Garton Ash (1990: 94), 'tele-revolutions', as must be all revolutions at the end of the twentieth century. Every student has remarked on the importance of the print media – books, pamphlets and newspapers – in all the great revolutions from England in 1640 to Russia in 1917. Now, with radio, television, cable, satellites, computers, videocassette recorders, photocopiers and fax machines, there has been a qualitative leap in the expansion of the technology of information and communication. The media are now 'global, instantaneous, simultaneous and total' in their effect. This, suggests Deirdre Boden, makes the 1989 revolutions 'like no others in human history'. The rulers of Eastern Europe were confronted by populations educated, informed and entertained by the mass media of the West. There was simply no way in which they could seal off the flow of images and sounds flooding from outside. Especially in the key months from June to December 1989 there was a 'chain reaction' triggered by the media images of events in China, Poland, East Germany and other socialist countries. From the Baltic States to Bulgaria, the socialist countries were ringed by a belt of territories that insistently beamed images of protest and revolt into the living-rooms of the people of Eastern Europe (Boden 1992: 328–9; see also

145

Eberle 1990: 199; Pye 1990: 8–9; Rustow 1990: 79–80; Cumings 1991: 112–13).

Notoriously difficult as it is to assess the effects of the mass media, there can be no doubting their importance in the making of 1989. What they point to, moreover, is another feature of the 1989 revolutions that emphasizes their novelty: their place in global patterns of change. Again, it is clear that there was a global aspect to many earlier revolutions (see, for the example of 1789, Wallerstein 1989). Once more, however, the great increase in the range and intensity of globalization seems to indicate something new. The 1989 revolutions are impossible to understand without reference to some major currents of change in the world as a whole.

Economically, there is the emergence of a global economy – more clearly than ever before dominated by the major capitalist powers – whose pressures on the stagnant economies of Eastern Europe were unquestionably one of the principal sources of change in the region. 'Socialism in one country', never, as social-ism, had much chance of success; industrial development under state socialist auspices, in relative isolation from the dynamic capitalist world economy, proved in the end equally bankrupt. What is now occurring is 'the incorporation [of Eastern European societies] as subordinate elements within the economic, cultural and military/strategic networks of the international capitalist system' (Panitch and Miliband 1992: 2; see also Hill 1992; Lavigne 1992).

Politically, the 1989 revolutions seem to belong to an equally marked 'global revolution' of democracy (Pye 1990; Rustow 1990). In the 1970s and 1980s, dictatorships gave way to demo-cracies, of various kinds, in almost every continent of the world. It seemed obvious to consider the 1989 revolutions as 'a sub-category of a more generic phenomenon of transition from auth-oritarian rule' (Bova 1991: 113).[13]

The results of this comparison have yielded some genuinely interesting parallels and similarities – the importance of reforming élites, for one thing, and, less obvious, the role of religious oppo-sition (for 'the resistance church' in Eastern Europe, see Weigel 1992). But, as compared with the global economic pressures, it is less easy to discern at more than a superficial level a common pattern of 'transition to democracy' across the globe. Partly this is because the political sphere is always more marked by particular features of history and culture. But more importantly there is a fundamental difference between the political changes in Eastern Europe and those in the rest of the world. Only in Eastern Europe did democracy have to emerge from totalitarian societies, where economic, political and cultural power were fused in a single centre, to the exclusion of virtually all elements of pluralism. Nowhere else was there such a total politicization of society. The 'transition to democracy' in Eastern Europe has features for which, as several scholars have pointed out, we simply have no parallels in either past or present experience. Not only do the sources of change differ in important respects from other transitions; the outcome of the change must be less easy to anticipate, and less secure, than elsewhere.[14]

The economic and political developments of the last part of the twentieth century have led to a strong revival of modernization theory – indeed, as Lucien Pye sees it, 'a vindication of modernization theory' (1990: 7). This provides yet another way to understand the 1989 revolutions (di Palma 1991: 52–3, 73–4; Ekiert 1991: 291–3; Janos 1991; Eisenstadt 1992; Fukuyama 1992; Müller 1992). Here again there is a mixture of old and new. In one variety of the theory, much favoured by certain Sovietologists until recently, modernization theory accounted precisely for the stability of the Soviet system, and its likely persistence for a long time to come. State socialism and liberal capitalism were seen as alternative routes to modernity. There would be a degree of convergence between them, but both had their peculiar characteristics and both were able, in a literal as well as a more metaphorical sense, to deliver the goods (Janos 1991: 88–93).

Such an approach might appear to share in the collapse of state socialism, but it does not take very much modification to make modernization theory serviceable once more (see, e.g., Bauman 1992a: 169–70). The new emphasis falls on the later stages of modernization, observable in late twentieth-century Western societies. Soviet-type societies may have been capable of achieving the earlier levels of modernization – mass literacy, urbanization and industrialization of the basic, Fordist, kind. But they have proved incapable of moving into the age of the 'information society', 'post-Fordist' practices in work and organization, and trans-national patterns of production, trade and finance. Nor are they in any way capable of responding to the new levels and types of consumption fed by these developments, though,

147

dangerously, their populations are made only too aware of them. The dynamics of modernization have undermined the stability of the Soviet-style system. The party-state has reached the limits of its ability to modernize. The old theorists were right: modernity, as the latest stages show, ultimately requires pluralism and a developed civil society, if not active democracy. Gorbachev understood this clearly; hence his desperate efforts to reform (Lewin 1989). The reforms were not sufficiently far-reaching and, in any case, opened the way to the collapse of communism throughout Eastern Europe.

There is a general plausibility to this picture that makes its appeal understandable. The problem is how far it explains the revolutions of 1989. Modernization theory has always moved at such a high level of abstraction as to fit any phenomenon it cares to deal with. It can explain both the persistence of the Soviet system and, with the merest modification, its dissolution. Such generosity in a theory is suspicious. In the case of the 1989 revolutions, it might account for some of the very general pressures on Eastern European regimes. But it cannot account for the timing or the manner of their going. Theories of revolution drawn from the armoury of structural-functionalism always contain the same weakness. They point to 'strains' and 'dysfunctions' in the system, but cannot explain why or when those strains become insupportable. There is, as we have seen, no difficulty in finding 'strains' in Eastern European societies. Many of these go back for decades. The populations of those societies had accommodated themselves in various ways to the system. Their efforts to change it had proved unavailing. What now made it possible not just to try again but to succeed? We need to understand the dynamics of mobilization and political transformation.

If not, or not only, modernity, what of 'post-modernity'? To what extent might the 1989 revolutions reflect not revolution's past but its future in a new, post-modern world? Zygmunt Bauman has suggested that the downfall of communism signifies the failure not just of a particular variety of modern society but of the modernizing project *per se*. Communism displayed, even more than capitalism, the Enlightenment ambition to construct a perfect, rationally ordered system of society.

Indeed it was under communist, not capitalist, auspices that the audacious dream of modernity, freed from obstacles by

148

the merciless and seemingly omnipotent state, was pushed to its radical limits: grand designs, unlimited social engineering, huge and bulky technology, total transformation of nature.

The 1989 revolutions, says Bauman, represent the failure and end of that dream.

What the affluent west is in fact celebrating today is the official passing away of its own past; the last farewell to the modern dream and modern arrogance.... With communism, the ghost of modernity has been exorcized.

(Bauman 1992a: 179–80; see also 166–7)

The sense of an ending, perhaps opening the way to something new, is to be found in a number of other comments on the 1989 revolutions. Shmuel Eisenstadt notes that, compared with past revolutions, there was in 1989 'no totalistic, utopian vision rooted in eschatological expectations of a new type of society.... There was no new revolutionary International; only a plethora of discussion groups, seminars, and the like.... Accordingly, the future is much more open' (1992: 25–7). Habermas has protested, in the name of 'the still unfinished project of modernity', against the 'post-modernist critique' that interprets the events of 1989 as a 'revolution to end the epoch of revolutions'. In this view, which Habermas contests, the 1989 revolutions represent a revolt against reason. They champion the claims of 'a self-empowering subjectivity' against the Enlightenment dream of power and control based on objective knowledge (Habermas 1991: 29). The 1989 revolutions here take their place as not the least manifestation of that 'death of grand narratives' that has been seen as the hallmark of our condition of post-modernity. No more can we believe in Truth, Progress, History, Reason, Revolution. What we are left with instead is irony, pragmatism and the quiet pursuit of private purposes (see, e.g., Rorty 1989).

Bauman, as we have seen, is sympathetic to this view. What for him has increasingly characterized the modern world, pushing it into the era of post-modernity, is the obsession with private choice and consumerism. It was the denial of this that was the undoing of communism, and the driving force behind the 1989 revolutions.

[W]hat eventually brought communism down was not the envious comparison with the productive successes of capital-

149

ist neighbours, but the enticing and alluring spectacle of lavish consumption enjoyed under capitalist auspices. It was the post-modern, narcissistic culture of self-enhancement, self-enjoyment, instant gratification and life defined in terms of consumer styles that finally exposed the obsoleteness of the 'steel-per-head' philosophy ... [I]t was the overwhelming desire to share (and to share immediately) in the delights of the post-modern world ... that mobilized the massive dissent against communist oppression and inefficiency.

(Bauman 1992a: 171; see also 222–5)

We might all share Bauman's disquiet at this situation, if this is indeed our common condition; and we might wish to endorse the hope of his erstwhile compatriot, Czesław Miłosz, reflecting on the changes of 1989, that 'the turmoil in these countries has not been a temporary phase, a passage to an ordinary society of earners and consumers, but rather the birth of a new form of human interaction, of a non-utopian style and vision' (1990: 165). Once more we have to fall back on the verdict, 'it is too early to say', though the signs are not propitious. 'Normalization' seems to be precisely what the citizens of the new democracies crave, and in the circumstances of the time one can hardly blame them.

But the meaning of 1989 is, after all, not so very clear. The very terms of modernity and post-modernity are still being hotly debated, and even if we were to characterize the 1989 revolutions as 'post-modernist' it is by no means necessarily to consign them to the sphere of rampant consumerism. That would in any case make nonsense of some of their most obvious features. The language of the 1989 revolutions was the language of rights, democracy and freedom. These are concepts whose meaning, as with all concepts, is historical. In different revolutions they have spelled different things. In the present case they may well, and justifiably, include the claims of private choice and private life. But that does not exhaust their current meaning. When, for instance, Eastern Europeans appeal to the idea of civil society, they are invoking a democratic inheritance with possibilities going beyond anything yet achieved in either West or East (Arato 1990). Those possibilities remain to be realized, but they are part of the revolutionary tradition to which the 1989 revolutions are heir.

The 1989 revolutions partake both of the old and the new. The novelties must be given their due. But the 'backward-looking' character of the revolutions is also abundantly clear, as is their connection with the democratic legacy of the great revolutions of the West. This, far from suggesting that the epoch of revolutions is over, actually points to quite a different possibility. For are we not, in the West as much as in the East, still trying to fulfil the promise of the democratic revolution? Does the democratic revolution not have, as Tocqueville argued, the character of a permanent revolution? Can such a revolution be halted by post-modernist fiat?

NOTES

1 See Dahrendorf (1990: 5); Garton Ash (1990: 156); Halliday (1990: 5); Pye (1990: 56); Schöpflin (1990: 3). And cf. Ellen Rice: '. . . 1989 may prove to be one of the great Years of Revolution in history' (1991: x).
2 Among later students of revolution who have emphasized the international aspect the most prominent have been Sorel (1885), Acton (1906) and Palmer (1970). See also Skocpol (1979).
3 See Geremek (1990: 93–4); and cf. his observation (ibid.: 108): 'In an extended time perspective, the successive crises [of Eastern European politics] may be viewed as the spasms of an organism seeking to reject an alien body.' On the insufficiency of the concept of legitimacy to explain regime change in general, see Przeworski (1986); Bova (1991: 122–3). 'What matters for the stability of any regime is not the legitimacy of this particular system of domination but the presence or absence of preferable alternatives' (Przeworski 1986: 51–2). One might also add, 'possible' alternatives.
4 The significance of Poland's role in the overthrow of communism has been everywhere remarked. For some commentators, the effective beginning of the 1989 revolutions was the election of a Polish Pope in 1978 – the mass enthusiasm for which, especially after the Pope's visit to Poland in 1979, led to the formation of Solidarity. See Garton Ash (1989: 42–54; 1990: 133–4). Leszek Kołakowski puts this in the grander perspective of post-1830 'Polish messianism', the idea of Poland as 'the Christ of nations' whose suffering and crucifixion would redeem mankind. Noting Poland's prominence in opposing communism throughout the twentieth century, he argues that 'its pioneering role in the slow decomposition of Sovietism cannot be denied' (Kołakowski 1992: 50–1). See also Geremek (1990).
5 On the economies of Eastern Europe in the 1970s and 1980s, see Vanous (1982); Nove (1983); and Lavigne (1992). [See also Bottomore in this volume – Eds.] It could be argued that 'rising expectations' were fuelled by the 'demonstration effect' of Western consumerism, as witnessed on the television screens of Eastern Europeans. But such

an effect had been in evidence for decades without leading to the overthrow of communism. Once the system collapsed, of course, the pent-up desire for Western-style goods was given full rein. But it did not cause the revolutions of 1989: like the loss of legitimacy of the rulers, it was constant more or less throughout the whole period of communist rule.

A further economic argument has been that the revolutions were caused by the increasing articulation of Eastern European economies with the capitalist economies of the West. This, it is claimed, explains in particular the sequence of revolutions in 1989, with the more articulated (Hungary, Poland and East Germany) being the first to go, and the least articulated (Czechoslovakia, Bulgaria and Romania) the last. See Hill (1992). This is unconvincing, not only for its reliance on the very shaky economic statistics of Eastern Europe but for its economic determinism, which fits 1989 even less well than it does earlier revolutions. Generally Bronisław Geremek's verdict seems right:

Political crises tend to break out in Eastern bloc countries in all kinds of economic conditions. The timing of events in Poland and Hungary in 1956 and those of 1968 in Czechoslovakia and Poland, can hardly be explained in economic terms alone.

(1990: 107)

This applies *a fortiori* to 1989.

6 For the evidence on this, including the role of the Soviet Union in fostering change in the region, see Kumar (1992a: 322–34, 345–9). Most of the accounts of the 1989 revolutions refer to Gorbachev's role or the 'Moscow factor', though disagreeing on the relative weight to give it. Those who regard it as indispensable, perhaps even 'decisive', include Garton Ash (1990: 140–1); Halliday (1990: 19); Grilli di Cortona (1991: 323–4); Hirst (1991: 229); Osiatyński (1991: 838, 843–4). For a dissenting voice see Tony Judt, in Judt et al. (1990: 171).

7 Hence this *cri de coeur* of a Bulgarian student activist after the revolution: 'We don't have the Hungarian 1956, the Czech 1968, the Polish 1980 – nothing to show that the older generation had tried to change the system, nothing to wipe out the shame from their faces' (quoted in Kovacheva 1992: 53).

8 The 'Eastern European tradition of revolt' is not of course restricted only to the anti-Soviet risings of the post-1945 period. There is a history of revolt going back to the eighteenth century, which includes not just the revolutions in – and against – Russia, but the various revolts against Ottoman rule. There are also some important continuities between the older and newer kinds of revolt, especially regarding the role of intellectuals in them. For some brief remarks, see Seton-Watson (1972); see also Bauman (1987c).

9 There has of course always been an argument to the effect that the Russian Revolution was not really 'European' at all, but reflected the peculiar, part-Asiatic, development of Russia. This despite the

admitted fact that the revolution was carried out under the auspices of a clearly Western ideology, Marxism. For the view that the revolution of 1917 is better regarded as part of the Western inheritance, and Russia part of Europe, see Kumar (1992b).

10 Eastern Europeans do not have much truck with those accounts that try to save Marxism by giving a Trotskyist account of both 1917 and 1989 – see, e.g., Callinicos (1991). On the irrelevance of the attempts by socialists to 'save' socialism in this way, see Frank (1990).

11 There is also restoration of course in a more obvious sense: 'The revolution has also involved a restoration: in Poland, the Czech and Slovak Republic, and Hungary, property confiscated forty-five years ago is being returned to the heirs of the original owners' (Osiatyński 1991: 824).

12 See on this Kumar (1992a: 317–24). In addition to the literature referred to there, in support of this view, see, on the Czech case, Rady (1993), and, on the Romanian case, Deák (1992). The issue is debated in most of the contributions to Banac (1992).

13 The model for this kind of comparative politics are the studies of 'transitions from authoritarian rule' in southern Europe and South America. See especially O'Donnell et al. (1986). For applications to Eastern Europe, see Bova (1991); Karl and Schmitter (1991); Bozóki (1992); Linz and Stephan (1992). See also Przeworski (1991a) and Misztal (1992).

14 In a sceptical note on what he calls the 'facile concept' of the 'transition to democracy', Ken Jowitt observes: 'Economic and social development places democracy on a nation's political agenda; but irreversible breakthrough to democracy depends on quite different sociocultural and institutional factors.' In his view the 'Leninist legacy' in Eastern Europe separates the region radically from other 'transitions to democracy' in other parts of the world. See Jowitt (1991: 90; 1992b: 284–305).

It is clear that the main dividing line is between those who regard the communist regimes as essentially totalitarian, and those who think that, particularly since the 1960s, they were closer to authoritarian regimes and therefore contained elements of pluralism. For the latter group, comparisons between Eastern Europe and other transitions from authoritarian rule in southern Europe, South America and south-east Asia are not only legitimate but illuminating; for the former group, not. For other examples of those who, like Jowitt, think that the comparisons are specious and misleading, see Ekiert (1991: 287–9); Grilli di Cortona (1991: 324–5, 328).

6

PROBLEMS AND PROSPECTS OF A SOCIALIST ECONOMY IN EUROPE

Tom Bottomore

The year 1989, the bicentenary of the French Revolution, was a symbolically appropriate one for revolutionary upheavals. But the revolutions in Eastern Europe differed in many respects from their predecessors' in 1789, or 1848, or especially 1917. Indeed, according to many commentators, they were revolutions against socialism, and this phenomenon had, or would have, important consequences for the socialist movement in Europe as a whole. This initial judgement, which was far from being universally accepted, in any case needs to be re-examined in the light of more recent experience, and in relation to the expectations that were prevalent before the revolutions.

In the summer of 1989, when I was completing my book on *The Socialist Economy* (Bottomore 1990), a part of which was concerned with the state socialist societies, I (like other observers) did not anticipate the dramatic changes in the Eastern European societies which occurred at the end of the year. The growing popular opposition in these countries seemed to me, in mid-1989, ultimately irresistible in the conditions created by the reforms and the new policies in the Soviet Union, and I argued that over the next few years multi-party political systems would be established, as had already begun to happen in several countries, which would make possible wide-ranging public debate about economic and social policies, and a fundamental reconstruction of the political system and the administration. In some cases, I considered, this process was likely to produce coalition governments, over shorter or longer periods, representing more adequately the diversity of opinions and interests that has long been concealed or suppressed. In such governments the role of the previously dominant communist parties would be drastically reduced, but I thought that the revived socialist parties and allied groups might be strong enough to ensure the continuance of the broadly socialist policies in a democratic system.

There can be no doubt that the vigour of the popular movements which developed so rapidly in the second half of 1989 came above all from their opposition to the political dictatorship of the communist parties, expressed in the demands for a democratic regime which would put an end to the totalitarian control of every aspect of social life, and re-establish fundamental rights of citizenship. Such demands embraced in principle all those issues concerning civil, political and social rights (but with an emphasis on the first two) which form an essential part of the historical tradition of democratic socialism, and from this point of view it was not unreasonable to suppose that the re-emerging socialist parties, and perhaps even in some cases thoroughly reformed successors to the old communist parties, inspired by such ideas, for example, as those of the Prague Spring of 1968, would have a major role in the new governments, at least in some countries.

However, the political demands also necessarily raised questions about the structure of the economy, since the system of collective ownership and central planning had been a creation of the communist dictatorships and was sustained by the party apparatus and the bureaucracy. Moreover, the increasing difficulties of these planned economies had already engendered ideas and practices to restructure the economic system, notably in Hungary from 1968, but also in the controversies about, and changes in, the Yugoslav self-management system, and from the mid-1980s in ever-broadening discussions in the Soviet Union. These debates and reforms led to a rapidly growing interest in 'market socialism', though it should be said that this was, and is, very diversely conceived. During the past decade indeed discussion of a socialist economy has concentrated particularly on this issue of planning and markets, which I also took as one of the main themes of my book.

In mid-1989 it was not clear what the economic consequences of a successful restoration of democracy by the opposition movements would be, but I envisaged changes of a slower and more cumulative nature than those which actually occurred soon after-wards. It certainly seemed possible – and here perhaps I was unduly influenced by the examples of the Hungarian Rising of 1956 and the Prague Spring of 1968 – that many of the Eastern European countries would move towards a democratic socialist system, though I also noted that there would be powerful forces, especially in Poland and Hungary, working for a restoration of capitalism. In this analysis two factors, I now think, were under-estimated. The first was the extent of the economic frustrations in societies which had experienced a lengthy period of relative stagnation, greatly affected it is true by the world economic recessions of the 1970s and 1980s. The second – far more import-ant – was the degree to which the detestation of the communist dictatorships had ramified into a hostility towards socialism as such, with which these dictatorships were identified. There was also a third factor, to which I did give some attention in discussing the possible orientations of new political movements and parties; namely, the revival of strong nationalist sentiments and move-ments, already evident at that time in Yugoslavia and the Soviet Union, but subsequently becoming much more prominent throughout Central and Eastern Europe.

The actual course of events in 1990 did result in the formation of coalition governments, which were predominantly conservative in several countries (while in others the conservative forces were very strong), and these governments embarked upon projects for a more or less rapid restoration of capitalism, though in forms which ranged from some kind of social market economy to a full-blown free market economy in the British style (which seems to me a singularly unfortunate model to emulate). Almost every-where, therefore, an extensive privatization of publicly owned enterprises was either envisaged or already beginning.

At the same time the apparatus of central planning was being 'deconstructed', though again in different degrees and at a differ-ent pace in individual countries. So the idea of 'socialism with markets', which had been developing at least since the 1960s – involving on one side greater autonomy for publicly owned enterprises, including such forms as the Yugoslav self-manage-ment system, operating in a regulated market environment, and on the other side a change from detailed central planning of quantitative outputs of both consumer and producer goods to indirect 'indicative planning' by means of financial and fiscal regulators – suffered an eclipse.

The changes in Eastern Europe have undoubtedly had profound consequences for the whole European socialist movement, and also, in unanticipated ways, for the people of those countries. Let us first consider the effects on the socialist movement generally. The collapse of the socialist system in most of the region, and the increasing turmoil in the Soviet Union and Yugoslavia, reinforced the 'conventional wisdom' or 'folklore' that has come to dominate the Western media and public opinion during the past decade, according to which publicly owned enterprises are necessarily inefficient and central planning a total failure. It follows that the only economic system capable of delivering high standards of living is a market-driven, private enterprise economy, moderated only by some degree of welfare provision and some minimal overall regulation by the state. This is the ideal expounded by Mises some seventy years ago, by Hayek and such bodies as the Adam Smith Institute more recently.

Like all folklore, however, this is unreliable, insecurely founded and sometimes self-contradictory. In practice many publicly owned enterprises have been efficient and technologically innovative, in a number of Western capitalist countries as well as in the socialist countries (as I described in my book). Equally, central planning has been highly effective in many different contexts, not only in war economies or in periods of rapid industrialization, but also in other situations; for example, in the post-war development of Japan and several Western European countries. Indeed, it may be argued more generally, as Tinbergen has done, that economic planning in Western Europe

has succeeded in avoiding the main inconsistency in unplanned economies of the pre-1914 type, namely, the underutilization of productive capacity as a consequence of business cycles and of structural disequilibria. It is highly probable that the disappearance of the business cycle after World War Two has been obtained with the aid of macroeconomic planning of the type described in this article.

(1968: 109)

More recently, of course, the business cycle has reappeared in Western capitalism, but this may well be connected with the movement away from planning; and Tinbergen's general argu-

157

ment seems to be strengthened if we consider the counter-example of those two countries – the United States and Britain – in which, by comparison with Western Europe, the economy is least planned, with the lowest level of public ownership, and at the same time shows the most marked signs of economic decline over the past decade.

I therefore maintain the view expressed in my book that one should not accept uncritically the current folklore about public ownership and planning; which does not mean, of course, that an equally uncritical folklore about the unalloyed virtues of such ownership and planning, whatever the forms that they may take, should be accepted. In parenthesis I should say that as I worked on my book it became more and more apparent that one great deficiency in the economic and sociological literature on economic systems was the paucity of systematic and comprehensive studies of the historical experience of planning and of the management and administration of publicly owned enterprises in their various forms; and in particular, of rigorous comparisons between planned and unplanned economies, private and public enterprises. The pursuit of such studies is evidently a matter of great importance for European socialism, because planning and public ownership have constituted the core of socialist thought and practice (in both democratic and dictatorial forms, though in very different ways), in the sense that they have been seen as the principal means of achieving greater economic and social equality, and over the longer term that kind of community of equals which used to be described as a 'classless society'.

Here, however, I want to concentrate on the economic questions. It has frequently been said that central planning is most effective in those situations in which a society has a single overriding aim to achieve – in a war economy or the drive for industrialization – but that its effectiveness diminishes considerably in an advanced industrial society in which there are a multiplicity of diverse and competing needs or wants to be satisfied, and continuous rapid technological innovation. This, however, seems to me dubious, considering the experience of post-war planning in (say) France or Japan, and it is in part a question of the kind of planning and of the socio-cultural context in which it takes place. In Eastern Europe the failures of planning from the late 1960s seem to me to have had their source primarily in the political system; that is, in the dictatorship of the communist parties which created attitudes both in the dominant élite and in the subordinate population that were inimical to effective planning and efficient production (resulting, for instance, in widespread corruption). From this standpoint it would be worthwhile perhaps to substitute, at least in part, for the familiar distinction between 'imperative' and 'indicative' planning one between 'dictatorial' and 'democratic' planning, and to devote more thought to the possible forms of such democratic socialist planning, various aspects of which were extensively discussed in the 1930s and 1940s (see especially Durbin 1949) and again more recently by Nove (1983).

Two other issues, however, arise in connection with planning. One is the role of the bureaucracy and the degree to which it may impede innovation and growth. I have discussed this at some length in my book, and here I shall only remark that I accept broadly Schumpeter's view that bureaucratic management as such is not a major problem; but with the important qualification that the bureaucracy of a party which monopolizes political power is quite another phenomenon, and that in such a political regime bureaucracy at the level of the enterprise may indeed be an obstacle to the rapid introduction of new technology and increasing productivity. The second issue, widely debated for the past two decades, concerns the relation between planning and markets. Here I take the view that the socialism of the future will unquestionably be socialism with markets. That, however, is only the first vague formulation of a complex, controversial proposition, from which innumerable questions and diverse answers emerge. What will these markets be like? How will they be regulated, and by what means? Through what mechanisms will they be related to planning? To what extent should planning be curtailed as well as becoming more indicative and more democratic? To such questions I can give only a brief and tentative answer here.

There should be markets for labour (with appropriate means, through education and training, to ensure that the need for qualified personnel in every sphere is broadly met, and with an essential socialist emphasis on full employment), and for consumer goods (again with some appropriate regulation, by fiscal and other means, to ensure that the basic needs of the whole population are given priority over luxury consumption). It may also be that some kind of market for capital and producer goods should develop, though this is a much more complicated question, and in my view investment should remain largely a matter for the community as a whole, through publicly owned investment and other banks, the state, and regional or local authorities.

Finally, there is the overarching question of how to relate planning to markets, and here I can only repeat the conclusion reached in my book, namely that it raises immensely complex problems for the resolution of which no master blueprint exists (a view also taken by Brus and Laski 1989), but that this does not mean the problems are ultimately insoluble if we make proper use of the historical experience of planning in different types of modern society and proceed by a process of trial and error.

This is part of my general argument that a major effort of thought is required in order to develop new conceptions of the functioning of a socialist economy; which also involves reconsidering the place of social ownership as the other core element, alongside planning, in the socialist idea of a new economic and social order. Again it is part of the current folklore of capitalism that an economy can only be flourishing and dynamic if it is more or less completely dominated by markets and by private enterprise, but this doctrine is quite unsubstantiated and there is indeed much evidence against it (e.g. the case of Britain), not to speak of its total neglect of all the adverse social and cultural consequences of such *laissez-faire* arrangements (which include unemployment, extremes of wealth and poverty, and large-scale environmental damage). Moreover, it is by no means demonstrated that over the longer term an economic system of this kind will even be more efficient, in some of the many possible meanings of 'efficiency'; and it may indeed be more useful to consider this question from the wider standpoint of the 'optimal' organization of production, and to take seriously Marx's conception of socialist production as a process in which the producers 'regulate their interchange with nature rationally ... and accomplish their task with the least expenditure of energy and under such conditions as are proper and worthy for human beings' (1894: 820).

For socialists, at all events, social ownership has always had a crucial importance as a means of giving wage-earners greater control over their working lives, and in a broad sense over the whole labour process, thus increasing the extent of democratic participation in determining the whole form of social life, and by the same means restricting and reducing the domination of society by a capitalist class. From this starting point, however, we must

160

go on to examine some of the questions that can be raised about the operation and performance of publicly owned enterprises, but I want to preface my comments by reiterating the view I expressed in relation to the problem of planning; namely, that in Eastern Europe, with the partial exception of Yugoslavia, the failings of public enterprises – which were not, however, universal – stemmed primarily from political causes, from the subordination of the population to a self-perpetuating ruling group. Eastern Europe as a whole, therefore, was a special case, which no Western socialist would have wanted to take as a model for a socialist economy or society. But there remain many general questions to be answered, about the extent of public ownership, the internal organization and degree of autonomy of public enterprises, the possible defects of bureaucratic management with respect to innovation, and the kind of incentives that would stimulate high productivity. Having examined these and related issues in my book I will here simply summarize the main conclusions at which I arrived.

First, from a socialist perspective, I consider essential the social ownership of major financial institutions, of large-scale enterprises in the basic sectors of production, and of infrastructural services such as transport and telecommunications; in addition to which the state and other public agencies should continue to be responsible for, and to improve steadily, the provision of a wide range of social services, including health and education. But secondly, this is far from suggesting that the whole economy should be publicly owned; and as democratic socialists of diverse schools (from the Fabians, Kautsky and the Austro-Marxists up to the recent advocates of a socialist market economy) have always argued, there would be a very substantial sphere of private production by individuals, families and small- or medium-sized enterprises. Moreover, public ownership itself does not imply the creation of one giant corporation in each sector, but rather the existence of several large organizations (in the case of banks, for example) which may compete with each other. Thirdly, publicly owned enterprises and services should have a high degree of autonomy, within the framework of a general plan, in respect of the organization of production, investment, recruitment of employees and regulations with suppliers and customers, all of which implies market relations of various kinds and also, I think, some form of self-management.

It also needs to be emphasized that the forms of social ownership may themselves be extremely varied, as Kautsky (1902: 166) argued long ago when he wrote that

> the greatest diversity and possibility of change will rule. . . . The most manifold forms of property in the means of production . . . can exist beside each other in a socialist society, the most diverse forms of industrial organization . . . of remuneration of labour . . . of circulation of products.
>   [Also quoted in Bottomore 1990: 17 – Eds.]

Even in those sectors where very large enterprises are essential it does not follow, and is indeed undesirable, that there should be huge monopolistic state corporations; and we need to consider instead, as I have suggested, the development of enterprises which compete with each other in a regulated market and within a general system of planning. It seems to me also possible to envisage, in the context of such diverse forms of ownership, the development of enterprises in which there is mixed public and private ownership through various types of shareholding. All of which is no doubt very complex, and certainly not to be achieved through any sudden transformation. It is something that can only be constructed gradually over a long period of time, as Otto Bauer very sensibly argued in his exposition of the process which he called a 'slow revolution'. [See Bottomore and Goode 1978: 26, 39, 288 – Eds.]

This conception of a socialist economy as one in which social ownership and planning still have an essential and positive role is not only defensible in theory against the current folklore; many of its elements already exist in practice, to some extent, in Western European countries and seem likely to develop further as the economic recession deepens. In mid-1989 I thought that this process would be aided by the changes in Eastern Europe, to the extent that these societies, on the basis of already extensive social ownership and planning, moved towards a democratic socialist system. But events took a different course, and the socialist movement in these countries has been obliged to start again from the beginning, in the most unfavourable conditions, where the legacy of communism has made possible an initial powerful reaction in favour of the restoration of capitalism, in some cases conceived in extreme *laissez-faire* forms.

However, the implementation of the new economic policies so

far has brought much disillusionment, and it now seems possible that the revival of socialism will be more rapid than appeared likely in 1990. The first consequences of the policies pursued in much of Eastern Europe can be characterized very broadly as follows:

1 The economy has contracted in all the countries concerned, in some cases dramatically.
2 This substantial deterioration is marked by a number of specific features:
   (a) the emergence for the first time in most of these societies of large-scale unemployment, which has continued to increase;
   (b) a sharp fall in living standards for a large part of the population;
   (c) the appearance of a very marked division between rich and poor, more pronounced in some countries than in others. Furthermore, the new rich do not, for the most part, seem to be engaged in production but in trade and speculation (including various black markets). In that sense the emerging capitalism is a kind of casino capitalism, with some resemblance to that in Britain, while the 'real economy' continues to deteriorate;
   (d) the loss of important social rights; first, obviously, the right to employment, but also such things as low-cost housing and transport, and notably some rights which particularly concern women, such as access to family planning (including abortion), long-term paid maternity leave and child care facilities.

This economic decline, and the specific economic policies that were initiated by conservative groups aiming to restore capitalism, have also had wider consequences. The societies are increasingly divided, and the popular movements which made the revolutions have themselves split into conflicting groups. There is increasing social conflict, which is assuming the character of incipient class conflict, as well as savage conflicts between nationalities.

A second feature of the changes, however, is that the projects to privatize the economy have generally made rather slow progress. They were initiated by those groups which simply wanted to restore capitalism, strongly encouraged by the governments of some leading capitalist countries and by the World Bank and the

International Monetary Fund, and supported at first by a majority of the population, whose experience of what was called 'real socialism' had made them hostile to any idea of socialism at all, and who also hoped, as did the new dominant groups, that embarking on the free enterprise route would attract substantial Western aid (which has largely failed to materialize). In short, many people expected an economic miracle. But the reality is very different. Privatization, in conditions of rapid economic decline, encounters formidable obstacles, among which is the emerging internal opposition from those large groups in the population which suffer the greatest hardship from current policies.

In a few countries, however, the question of restructuring the economy was approached more cautiously, and I think more rationally. Czechoslovakia provided one example, but it is in Russia that the strongest resistance to any wholesale dismantling of the socialist economy has appeared. Here, as elsewhere, there were powerful conservative groups which wanted to proceed as quickly as possible with the creation of a capitalist free-market economy in one form or another; but after several years of controversy and elaboration of diverse projects, it seems clear that there will be no immediate large-scale abandonment of social ownership in major sectors of the economy, and the planning system, rather than being dismantled or reformed, appears simply to be in disarray (or chaos).

What I conceived as an alternative course, which might have been followed in all the countries of Eastern Europe with great benefit to their populations, would have involved concentrating economic policy on improving production in the large socially owned enterprises, once the stranglehold of the Communist Party apparatus had been eliminated, and at the same time encouraging the development of private businesses in those fields – retail trade, services, small- and medium-sized manufacturing concerns – where they were most likely to have an immediate effect on the supply of goods, especially final consumer goods. The first of the two elements I have mentioned in a policy of this kind would involve radical changes in the organization and management of production – greater autonomy for enterprises, proper accounting procedures, public scrutiny of the performance of such enterprises, a different relationship between the banks and industrial producers, and so on – and such measures will be indispensable wherever this alternative policy is embarked on.

If such a policy is in the end adopted in Russia it will undoubtedly have an important long-term influence on the development of other Eastern European countries, and it may also influence the socialist movement and socialist governments in Western Europe, perhaps making them somewhat less reticent and defensive about public ownership and planning in their policies for restructuring the capitalist economies, and more responsive to the idea of socialism with markets. They might then come to support more actively alternative, more distinctively socialist policies in Europe as a whole, and of this there are already some indications in the European Parliament. All these changes, however, are likely to be slow, and we can hardly expect the new face of Europe to be visible before the end of this decade – even then perhaps still indistinctly.

NOTES

Author's Note: Some sections of this essay, which was originally written in autumn 1990, have been revised to take account of the passage of time, but the substance and argument remain unchanged.

Editors' Note: Tom Bottomore had clearly based this chapter on an article with the same title which he had published in *Rethinking Marxism*, 4, 3 (Fall 1991). It is, however, substantially different from that piece, representing his later thoughts on the implementation of the new economic policies in Eastern Europe from 1990 onwards. He was continually assessing and reassessing the significance of the events in Eastern Europe as they unfolded and produced a number of overlapping studies. At the time of his sudden death in December 1992 he was just beginning what he had promised us would be a substantial rewrite of the present manuscript for this volume, including a revised title, 'The Future of European Socialism'. His notes indicate that its opening sentence was to read: 'My essay has nothing to do with modernity or so-called postmodernity, but very much to do with some of Zygmunt Bauman's writings, especially on socialism.' In view of the fact that this new study had barely begun, we have retained the author's original title as more appropriate to the text published here. We are grateful to William Outhwaite for locating those notes as well as a later version in Professor Bottomore's papers, and to Katherine Bottomore for releasing them to us.

7

THE SOCIAL ROLE OF EASTERN EUROPEAN INTELLECTUALS RECONSIDERED

Lewis A. Coser

Analysis of the roles of modern intellectuals has been a major concern of the sociology of knowledge ever since the seminal writings of Karl Mannheim. Mannheim argued that in the modern world the clash of contending doctrines and ideologies has built a tower of Babel so that it is no longer possible for the spokespersons of antagonistic classes and strata to find common ground. If the intellectual arena is dominated by spokespersons for differing interests, truly objective thought becomes impossible. Given this desperate situation, Mannheim argued, only disinterested intellectuals, detached from the concerns of all interest-dominated groups, would be able to develop truly independent modes of thought. In a world dominated by what has been called a dialogue of the deaf, only *free-floating*, i.e. detached, intellectuals would be capable of advancing objective modes of thought through translation of one structure of ideas into another, and through attaining knowledge no longer contaminated by the advocacy of special interests.

According to Mannheim, intellectuals, whether in the East or in the West, were often subservient to the dominant classes, yet a significant portion of them were able to take advantage of their peripheral location in the class scheme of things to voice criticism and to formulate independent thought. To a greater or lesser degree, Mannheim argued, intellectuals have the ability to develop unfettered thought. Given the alienated condition in which they necessarily find themselves, they have a chance to reach a realm of objective truth that is unattainable for those who are the spokespersons of the diverse interests that compete for power in the political and ideological arena.

The widespread international discussion among sociologists of the idea of a free-floating stratum of intellectuals did not lead to a clear-cut endorsement or rejection of the Mannheim thesis. Yet most Western sociologists dealing with Soviet Russia and its satellites seem to have agreed that the bulk of intellectuals in this arena were clubbed to endorse the dominant Stalinist ideology.

When we speak of the intelligentsia in Central and Eastern Europe we must always keep in mind that they differ in significant degrees from their counterparts in the West. As Zygmunt Bauman has put it, this social formation has, since its inception,

> the tendency to view the relation between the political state and civil society as one of conflict and competition rather than of consensus and mutual support. There also remains the remarkably elevated status of the intellectual profession and of the educated intellectual élite in general. Their fore-fathers, after all, enjoyed a virtual monopoly of spiritual leadership ... for a long period in national history they played the role of a substitute for the absent national state.
>
> (1987c: 172)

Given this historic role of intellectuals in the East, it stands to reason that they have not been willing to play a subordinate role in recent years when revolutionary or near-revolutionary events toppled the Stalinist and Stalinoid powers that be.

The exhilarating days of revolt among huge masses of dissatisfied people, though occurring only a year or two ago, lie already in the past, and, with 'normalcy' and material as well as psychic deprivations marking public and private life, one might have expected the intellectuals to be disappointed and disillusioned so that they would flee from the political arena or choose instead the path of accommodation and compromise with the powers that be. This has, however, not been the case. In Poland, the Kurońs and Michniks have again begun to play roles to which they became accustomed in the past. They are again the critics and the gadflies of the regime. But Lech Wałęsa, no intellectual he, sits in the seat of power, while his one-time advisers have again been pushed into peripheral positions. Václav Havel seemed for a time to be the only major figure who had been able to maintain a stance of intellectual dominance and a position of

167

large-scale power. One could until recently hope that Czechoslovakia, which managed after the First World War to be led by a man, Masaryk, who became a major statesman without abandoning his status as an intellectual, would manage once again to be an exception in Eastern and Central Europe. This is not very likely in any of the other countries I shall discuss.

When we assess prospective positions of intellectuals in the East in the next few years it might be helpful to have recourse to a fruitful conceptualization of the American political economist Albert Hirschman (1970). He suggests that those who are dissatisfied with a given course of action in the political and social field, those who dissent from the course of action that the powerholders have chosen, have basically two options: they can choose the course he calls *Voice*, or the one he calls *Exit*. They can specify their grievances, propose remedies and suggest changed goals as well as changed means, and they can maintain the option of *Voice* for a fairly long period. But when they speak to the deaf, when they make no inroads on policies they consider noxious, nay disastrous, they will finally choose the option of *Exit* or, to borrow from Lenin's image, they will vote with their feet.

It is impossible in the present moment to estimate the proportion of intellectuals who might choose these divergent courses in the time to come. But one has the impression that a sizeable number will choose *Exit* – as it is now increasingly possible to do – in case their *Voice* is not being heard.

Some Eastern European intellectuals may have thought for a brief moment that, as happened to some extent in the Weimar Republic, the former outsiders would become insiders. But this has not generally been the case, even though one can, of course, point to some exceptions. The outsiders of yesteryear are still mostly on the outside. Far from becoming part of the ruling élite, they have largely maintained the tradition of their predecessors in the nineteenth century in saying 'No' to those in power.

Yet, many of the observers of the fate of intellectuals in the years before the recent momentous events in the East asserted for a long time that modern Eastern European intellectuals had sold their independence for a mess of pottage.

In addition, intellectuals in the Soviet realm, it was asserted, were not only handmaidens of the powers that be, but had become part of the dominant élite. György Konrád and Iván Szelényi (1979) argued forcefully and apparently convincingly that intellectuals in the Soviet sphere were relatively distinct from the state and party bureaucracy until relatively recently but that they were now in the process of amalgamation with the ruling political and managerial élite. 'Since the sixties, it seems to us', they wrote, 'the distinction between bureaucracy and the intellectuals has become more and more open to question . . . the differences between intellectuals and bureaucrats are gradually disappearing' (1979: xiv).

Konrád and Szelényi, having been born and educated in Hungary, and being themselves *free-floating intellectuals*, asserted that the bulk of the Hungarian intelligentsia, of which they were a part, had made their separate peace with the powers that be. They concluded in the mid-1970s, when their book was written, that it was next to impossible to maintain or build up an independent, intellectual stance in the Soviet sphere. Szelényi emigrated and Konrád joined the inner emigration. 'The Eastern European intellectuals', they say, 'relatively early on conceived the intention to strive for something like state power' (ibid.: 85). Whereas Western European intellectuals, they argued, sell their cultural wares on the open market of ideas, Eastern European intellectuals, given the absence of such a market, at first consolidated their position in the political and socially dominating state bureaucracy and later on embarked on the road to power for themselves.

Konrád and Szelényi's thesis builds upon the writings of a number of earlier observers of the Soviet scene who had already argued that Eastern European intellectuals had attained state and societal power in the Soviet system. Following in the steps of Max Nomad, and of James Burnham, Milovan Djilas and Alvin Gouldner, they argued that the universal class to which the future belonged was not the proletariat but a new class, or a new stratum, encompassing both the technical intelligentsia and the humanistic intellectuals. There were disagreements among these writers and many others as to whether one could call the new intellectuals a class or a stratum, whether one deals here with a state capitalist or state socialist formation, etc. But what all these analysts had in common was the assertion that the bulk of Soviet intellectuals had made their peace with the regime and had in fact become a vital part of it.

We have witnessed the bankruptcy of this set of ideas. Professors and students, members of the learned professions, scientists and humanistic scholars and religious leaders were in the forefront of the groundswell of opposition and revolt that swept the Soviet Union and its satellites in the late 1980s. Why was this the case? Only very tentative suggestions can be offered at this point.

For the purpose of this chapter, intellectuals may be defined as men and women who live for ideas rather than off ideas, and who play creative roles in the world of symbols. There were several reasons for their recent revolt 'before the Fall'. They are of a general nature. Academic intellectuals have had access to sources of information denied ordinary citizens and have been in communication with foreign academics. They have had long and unusual contact with unorthodox ideas because of their exceptional access to foreign lines of information. Moreover, this privileged access to foreign ideas has fostered among many of them a sense of relative deprivation. In contrast to them, the majority of the population was successfully insulated from foreign ideas and hence could not compare its lot with that of its foreign counterpart abroad. The intellectual discontent, on the other hand, was animated by the constant comparisons of 'how bad it is with us and how good with them'.

Until the communist collapse, few ordinary citizens but a fair number of intellectuals could travel abroad. Actual experience with the style of life of their Western counterparts here again fostered a sense of relative deprivation. As intellectuals developed discontent through comparison with the Western world, it was also mainly they who had access to native clandestine publications. It seems to be by and large the case that most of these publications were written and read by intellectuals.

Intellectuals not only profited from contacts abroad and from exposure to internal dissenting publications, but also were the major group that maintained continuity with the past. Two points are salient in this respect. It was mainly, though not only, intellectuals who could buy books both in second-hand book stores or in new editions. When the latter became quickly sold out, the use of the libraries was easier for intellectuals than for ordinary citizens. Intellectuals were mainly responsible for keeping alive ideas and values of the past. They, and they alone, could keep up a dialogue with a whole gamut of writings of the past instead of limiting themselves to the array of writings that were officially sponsored and propagated. A second point is perhaps even more important. The Marxist tradition is largely anchored in the world of ideas that may be roughly called 'enlightened'. This differed markedly from other totalitarian societies.

Nazi ideology rejected the liberal past of Germany *in toto* and, in the name of racial criteria, rejected the Enlightenment as a period of history which they alleged was both decadent and contemptible. In contrast, the Soviet ideologists of the Stalin period and after clung to ideas rooted in the Enlightenment in a way the Nazis could not. Enlightenment thinkers such as Diderot or Rousseau were approached with sympathy and admiration by Soviet spokespersons in a way that would be inconceivable among Nazi thinkers. To be sure, they were considered 'bourgeois thinkers' and hence had to be approached with caution, but they could not be silenced if for no other reason than that they had been very much part of the world of ideas of Marx and Engels. What is more, the major guiding ideals of the Enlightenment still served, at least in part, as ideological guideposts for the Marxist–Leninist picture of the world of the future. It was understood that actual conditions were not yet in tune with Enlightenment standards, so that the latter remained a promise for what was to come once the communist society would be achieved. As the Israeli political scientist Shlomo Avineri put it,

> there always existed a gap between the emancipatory promise of Communism and the actuality of 'real-existing socialism'. The Stalinist Constitution of 1936 was replete with paragraphs which were part and parcel of the European Enlightenment – the reality was something quite different. Hence hypocrisy – or The Lie, as Havel has called it – became the operative principle of communist regimes.
>
> (1991: 443)

What I have just said about members of the creative stratum of intellectuals applies also to the world of students, at least of those among them who aspired to become intellectuals in the future. In particular, students are a relatively mobile element, socially speaking, and they were in the Soviet Union and in Central Europe before the collapse. As distinct from persons whose livelihood is tied to regular attendance to quotidian tasks within bureaucratically organized structures, students are relatively dispensable. They can leave their university for a week or two without dire consequences. A particular course of lectures is

not likely to be much perturbed if some students have a somewhat irregular attendance. The instructor may indeed be indispensable but part of his or her audience is not.

Students have more leisure than most adult citizens to read
outside their field. They can attend demonstrations or dissenting
gatherings. They are not as tied to a specialized realm of learning
as are their professors. They can read the great writers of the
past without too much guilt about neglecting their specialized
fields of study. Even if they have made their choice about fields
of study at a relatively early stage in their university careers, they
can still 'shop around' in the world of ideas. Students are also
prone to adopting idealistic views, especially because they are not
caught as yet in the bureaucratic university machine. They tend
to be more flexible and critical in their orientation than their
elders.

The fact that students occupy special positions during their
years of study does not mean, however, that they will develop
into a 'universal class', as Herbert Marcuse and many of his co-
thinkers in the West expected. In the late 1960s and early 1970s,
in the United States as well as in Western Europe, each cohort
of students may have aspired to social vanguard positions, but
after a number of years the bulk of the student élites are likely
to find a niche in bureaucratic society. Only a small portion of
them are likely to grow into principled opponents of the powers
that be. And as in the West, so *a fortiori* in the East, the bulk of
students, even if – as in the late 1980s – they are still opposed to
the present state of affairs, are not in their majority to grow into
principled intellectual opponents of the governing élites. In fact,
many key state officials or managerial élite members of newly
formed private enterprises are likely to be recruited from articulate and well-trained former students, be it in engineering, finance
or public administration.

What I have said about free-floating intellectuals and students
applies to many academics as well, and, at least in part, to some
independent professionals such as medical doctors, or lawyers.
Before the communist collapse, like intellectuals and academics,
such persons may have had access to foreign publications, at least
in their own field, and they often received permission to attend
conferences or meetings of their Western colleagues abroad. They
may hence have formed markedly negative ideas about the standards and skills of their Soviet colleagues when measured against

foreign achievements. They would also have tended to admire the technical and technological resources of their foreign colleagues as compared with those of their own.

I finally come to a category of intellectuals that has been in the forefront of dissent, and was so in the Soviet Union and also in Central Europe in the 1980s: creative artists, be they writers devoted to *belles-lettres*, or musicians, playwrights or painters. I need hardly repeat here what I have already said about the importance for these men and women of contacts with their counterparts in the outside world. It is important for them to be published abroad to gain an audience among esteemed counterparts in the West. In fact, such an audience abroad compensates to some extent for the absence of an audience at home. During Stalin's reign and again during the Brezhnev interlude, the censor was perceived as the deadly enemy of creative writers. Things were not very different in regard to controlled concert audiences or theatrical performances. If you were prevented by the censorship from finding an audience for your writings at home you were drawn to an audience on the outside or in clandestine publications. But if you cannot exhibit your pictures or cannot have your music performed, you are in an even more desperate situation than the writer who may have access to alternative publishers. Only a very determined playwright is likely to continue writing for a theatre that does not exist, at least at home.

This limited and preliminary survey of some of the reasons why writers and artists may be specially disaffected from regime thinking will have to suffice. I now return to the broader question of why it was that outside observers, be they academics or journalists, failed to discern repressed rebelliousness among intellectuals during the period of communist rule. One of the facts that led to such disastrous misjudgement was that disaffection was indeed hardly observable; for on the surface it seemed that most intellectuals had adjusted to the expectations of those in power. Few in the West could see the seeds beneath the snow, and most, by and large, remained deaf to the stirrings among intellectuals, except, of course, when these dissenters began to publish and discuss their works *sub rosa*. But even in this case, those who published clandestinely were a small minority. The Poles had a better chance at this than other iron curtain countries. The Polish church became a refuge for independent oppositional thinkers and the

Polish oppositional intelligentsia had access to smuggled copies of genuine Polish thought through the Paris-based magazine *Kultura*.

I do not think that it was the doctrinal message of the Polish Catholic hierarchy that made it into a major pillar of anti-communist thought. It is worth remembering in this connection that liberal-left elements among the Lutheran clergy in what was then East Germany pursued similar anti-regime pathways despite the evident fact that doctrinally East German Protestants and Polish Catholics had precious little in common. It was not church doctrine but rather a similar structural position that allowed these dissimilar religious authorities to play key supporting roles in Poland and East Germany. In both cases, members of the clergy managed to give shelter to clandestine dissident thought and anti-regime gatherings. It would have been almost as difficult for the East German regime brutally to suppress the Lutheran clergy as it was for its Polish counterpart to wage open warfare against Catholic clerics. The Lutheran clergy, even though by no means as hierarchically structured as the Polish church, still had enough resources to appear as a saving remnant to important segments of, especially, the student youth of East Germany. That all this could have happened in a Lutheran church which, since the days of its founders, had been more respectful towards secular authority than other Protestant denominations was indeed a kind of minor miracle. In any case, it is well to remember that clerical intellectuals, whom secular analysts tend to forget, may in fact play central roles in at least the earlier stage of anti-totalitarian revolutions.

The emergence of a popular opinion and audience in the East is intimately connected with the emergence of the structures of a civil society uncontrolled, or at least inefficiently controlled, by the agencies of the state. In both cases one can now discern in retrospect the emergence of people who 'think otherwise' and who have now gained access to a much wider horizon than was possible in the past. It should be mentioned in this respect that the new knowledge that can be spread to any audience and that can be reached by intellectuals is by no means limited to political or economic topics. The Russian sociologist Igor Kon was, in the 1980s, engaged in building up a whole set of publications (now complete) that aimed at the sexual enlightenment of vast strata that until shortly before had not been permitted to discuss sexual matters that were well known to Western high-school students.

One should not forget that many of the facets of the revolt of the intellectuals in the last ten years were simply not detectable with the usual seismometers. As to the inability of the bulk of 'Kremlin watchers' among Western journalists and public commentators on Soviet affairs to predict what has happened, let me say, if only in parenthesis, that this was due not only to the inherent difficulty of spotting changing tides, but also to the intellectual biases of those in the West who were supposed to be in the know. In particular, the analyses that came from the (misnamed) 'intelligence community' were subject to so strong an ideological bias that they became systematically unable to discern novel developments in the Gorbachev era and earlier. Rigidly held ideological positions so distorted the critical capacities of professional Kremlin watchers and their academic and bureaucratic camp followers that they developed what Thorstein Veblen called an 'unfit fitness' to understand what was brewing in the Soviet Union and in the Eastern European satellites. Their seismometers systematically distorted their ability to see the signs of the breakdown to come.

The extreme rapidity with which all types of intellectuals voiced their thoughts once the censorship became attenuated and once they had regained a modicum of freedom, is astonishing. In any case, when one looks at the former Soviet Union and most of its erstwhile satellites, what one can observe, looking back, are the slow and hesitant ways in which non-intellectual strata take up ideas first enunciated among intellectuals.

It is important to note that what has been happening in the East in the last decade is the re-emergence of an audience for intellectuals. For the first time in many years there has developed a public opinion, that is, a relatively unfettered public concerned with unconventional plays, films, novels and essays that have appeared on the public scene. To the degree that such an audience is in the process of formation, independent writers, playwrights, painters and musicians are spurred on since they feel that they have resonance in the educated strata of the society.

Yet all of this does not imply that the present situation makes things easy for intellectuals in the former Soviet sphere. A hiatus of almost eighty years in the development of unfettered thought must surely have serious consequences for present generations of

LEWIS A. COSER

intellectuals and of intellectual publics, and the ravages that
Stalinist-armed ideologues have caused in the intellectual life in
the East cannot be remedied from one day to the next.

A Soviet historian speaking to a Western colleague in the mid-
1970s said: 'The most difficult of a historian's tasks is to predict
the past' (quoted in Lewis 1975: 69). This brilliant paradox illumi-
nated a central difficulty in the life of intellectual strata in the
former Soviet sphere. By the late 1980s, there was growing uncertainty. Analytically speaking, the Party's dominant position on
the intellectual scene has come to an end. A variety of intellectual
tendencies are given a freedom that they have not enjoyed since
the early 1920s. But a veritable tower of Babel has led to a
confusion of tongues that can disorientate, if only for a transitional period, even the best of intellectuals. I earlier had
occasion to hear the complaints of recently arrived Soviet immi-
grants to the United States that it was difficult to find one's
bearings in a culture in which so many divergent points of view
were presented to the public without any guidance on how to
find the truth in the welter of opinions. In the late 1980s, something similar was visible. Analytically, it would seem that ordinary
Soviet citizens and perhaps also intellectuals seemed to ask for
guidance, even though they prided themselves on the new-found
freedom to form an opinion. The historian who only a few years
previously had to affirm, say, that Bukharin was an agent of the
imperialist bourgeoisie at this juncture learned that Bukharin was
among the most brilliant of the founding fathers of the Soviet
Union. But could he or she really be sure that Bukharin would
not again be dethroned tomorrow? One felt that it could not
have been much fun to have been a historian in the contemporary
Soviet Union, and it is understandable that some of them were
happier when the Party had the truth by the tail.

One felt also that what is true in the world of history is the
case in many other domains of higher learning. Just imagine
the poor economist brought up on the verities of *Das Kapital*
who is expected to handle the intellectual heritage of that arch-
enemy of the proletarian vision, Lord Keynes, or, worse still, the
free enterprise verities that are now being dispensed by the latter-
day descendants of Adam Smith, or of the Harvard contingent
of unfettered market doctrine.

I recall observing that, given such difficulties and tensions, one
would expect that a sizeable number of intellectuals, unable to

further endure the contradictory messages under which they had to operate, and also given their inability to raise their *Voice* in a systematic manner, would choose the *Exit* option if and when it became available. It is interesting to note that Soviet Jewish intellectuals, who suffered, of course, from oppression not only because they were Jews but also because a majority of them were intellectuals and professionals, continued to leave for Israel even though that country was a far from ideal haven.

In an opinion poll among students in Moscow and Leningrad in July 1991 (reported in the *New York Times*, 14 July 1991) 40 per cent of them said 'that they were prepared to leave the country if it became possible'. It could, however, have been said at this time that there was one other alternative course of action that sizeable numbers of Eastern European intellectuals might have chosen to follow when the two others discussed above did not happen to be realistically available.

> Frustrated and embittered by the orthodoxy of the Soviet world of scholarship [writes Esther Fein, a perceptive Moscow correspondent of the *New York Times*, in the edition of 26 June 1991], many of Aleksei Titkov's young colleagues took to drink. Others emigrated, most grew lazy and bored. The most despondent killed themselves. Mr Titkov, a 31-year-old political historian, said he could not take any of these paths. . . . Afraid of becoming a victim of the rigid system, he and a number of like-minded colleagues are funding their own independent research institutes.

Mr Titkov was chairman of the Epoch Centre of Humanitarian Studies, one of a hundred independent research centres that had emerged during 1990 outside the official Academy of Sciences. Such centres were usually self-financed by young academics exploiting opportunities to study social, and to some extent natural, sciences that were forbidden territory before the Gorbachev reforms. These young persons were apparently given encouragement by at least some of their elders in the official Academy. (It is worth noting, by the way, that 250 members of the Academy went abroad on long-term contracts in 1990 compared with 50 in 1989.) It seems to have been the case that official scientists were very worried about these recent trends and favoured all sorts of concessions to the young rebellious scientists in order for them not to leave the Soviet Union. 'I did not want to deal with politics or with the Communist Party', said Aleksei Yurasowski, the 44-year-old editor of the journal *Istoriya SSSR* [*History of the USSR*], who had chosen his specialty, Russian feudalism in pre-Mongolian times, with this end in view, but had in 1991 joined other unorthodox scholars. Most of the institutes were financed by a combination of personal investment, some state money, and profits from commercial ventures like book publishing. 'These new organizations are able to carry out their work... by exploiting one of the greatest weaknesses of the Soviet economy; [members] are paid for state jobs that require little or no output or attendance' (ibid.).

I have no way of knowing whether the above description referred to a restricted or to a relatively widespread development among young scientists. It seems in any case another possible outcome of the *Exit* option when exit from the official organization leads to a sort of inner emigration that strives to compete with the official world of scholarship, perhaps leading to a situation of dual power in the world of ideas.

I might emphasize that I have tried to develop the rudiments of a Weberian typology concerning intellectual strategies in the East in the era of *glasnost*. It stands to reason, of course, that in concrete reality there will be mixed types. What is more, I am fully aware that one other possible course of action for intellectuals is to succumb to the lure of power and to join anti-intellectual positions within the hierarchy of the *nomenklatura*. I stand opposed to the views of Szelényi and others that intellectuals will, as a whole, join the powers that be. Still, it has been my general view that I would not at all be astonished to see some of them doing just that. Once an intellectual does not mean that one will always be one. It is indeed the case that there have already arisen tendencies among oppositional dissenting intellectuals in the East to see themselves as anointed élites destined to lead the people into a future of bliss, even against their own wishes. Given the enormous cultural differences between the élite and the masses, such messianic hopes did exist, to be sure, not only among nineteenth-century anarchists but also among the Bolsheviks. Granting all that, I would argue, nevertheless, that the bulk of intellectuals resisted these appeals. In the past the attempt under Stalin and his successors to co-opt intellectuals and innovators never succeeded. Bauman was profoundly right when he wrote: 'The party has neither eliminated nor "devoured"

the intelligentsia. The two exist side by side, as structurally separate social categories, whatever their personal or functional connections' (1987c: 178). A lot of major events have happened since
Bauman wrote this, but I believe that this analysis is still correct
today. The Party has lost its monopoly of power and been weakened to a degree that neither Bauman nor anybody expected,
but the intellectuals continue to be a 'separate social category'.
The structural setting is, as it was, such that there must be conflict
between the intellectual and the – albeit now discredited – Party
(ibid.: 79).

It may have been noticed that I have scrupulously refrained
from calling intellectuals or bureaucrats, be it in the East or the
West, a social class. I deem it essential for the emergence of a
class that its members be linked through a consciousness of kind
and through frequent associations among each other. But such
common consciousness did not and could not emerge among
intellectuals in the East. A remark by Michael Mann on the
Roman peasantry in volume I of his *The Sources of Social Power*
serves us well here.

> 'Extensive classes' can exist only if interaction exists. Thus
> to the extent that Rome was built up of a number of vir-
> tually self-sufficient production units, it could contain *many*
> local, small, similar 'classes' of direct producers, but not a
> societal-wide producing class capable of enforcing its own
> interests. The masses were trapped within the more exten-
> sive 'organization charts' of their rulers, 'organizationally
> *outflanked*'.
>
> (1986: 264)

This was almost completely the case for intellectuals in the Soviet
realm until the late 1980s. They could not develop a consciousness
of kind or a self-consciousness as a separate class. They were
largely unable to build bonds among each other except in restricted and always endangered private circles. This is why, despite
the predisposing factors that I mentioned in the early parts of
this chapter, they emerged as an important force only with the
breakdown of the Soviet camp.

Intellectuals could not develop a united front during the Stalin
regime and after. They were dispersed both geographically and
structurally. Perhaps with the exception of some relatively small
circles mainly in the big cities, they had no contact with one

another and possessed no media of communication that might have allowed them to take part in a fruitful exchange of ideas. Academic intellectuals had few contacts with extra-academic colleagues. Within the academy there were almost insurmountable obstacles to even initiating contact between disciplines. The Party controlled nearly all media of communication and until almost the breakdown of much of the system there was no way of transcending the immediate circle of personal friends. To be sure just as in Nazi Germany, personal bonds of friendship between actual or potential dissidents provided at least some shelter from an otherwise all-pervasive Party control, but it was impossible to move from the restricted context of personal friendship to action on the public scene. The various official organizations of writers, artists and the like served only as distribution centres for patronage, bribery or hardly camouflaged occasions for co-optation. They served to ensure privileges to the obedient and were largely closed to dissenters. Lecture tours, permission to make foreign trips, luxury accommodations in vacationland, as well as alluring book contracts, were the coin in which the conformists were paid. We all know about the brave, heroic dissenters who helped prepare some of the ground for the late efflorescence of unfettered thought. But to believe that intellectuals as a whole were in the process of forming a unified ruling class borders on the fantastic.

In this connection, the importance of generational differences between the various cohorts of professionals, the various technical and bureaucratic strata, but also among intellectuals has assumed saliency in the last fifteen years. The younger generation tends to be considerably more educated than previous cohorts; it has developed proficiencies in various occupational positions which are clearly much superior to those of preceding generations. Younger thinkers grew up in the post-Stalinist period in which, first, at least some, and, later, all of the controls of Stalin's days had been lifted. Most of the dissenters of the recent past are young or at least early middle-aged, whereas the bulk of the conformists are considerably older. The young know that they are indispensable, and they possess a sense of personal worth that contrasts with the social insecurity, the fear of demotion, of their parents' generation. The older generation may upon occasion raise their *Voice* in communist regimes but, as we have seen, the young men and women of recent years dream of *Exit* or withdrawal.

The first generation or two of Soviet communists were ideologically attracted to the Party; the present young, on the other hand, have largely escaped from the Party ideological controls of former years, and are still in search of a new *Weltanschauung*.

Alvin Gouldner (1979) and Daniel Bell (1974) and a number of other observers have tried to show that the intellectuals of East and West have reached a position in the modern world that is based on their indispensability. Hence, so they argue, the bulk of intellectuals everywhere have exploited this indispensable position in order to have access to the ruling bureaucratic strata and have hence lost the rebelliousness that may have characterized them at some point in the past. But this thesis of indispensability is highly dubious. If indispensability were indeed always a source of power and influence, sanitation work and baby-sitters would possess a great deal of power since they are indeed indispensable in modern society.

There is, however, a defensible sense in the recent assertion about the indispensability of intellectuals in former state socialist societies. As long as these societies were in the process of construction, as long as they had to build the foundations of their power, they needed the support of a great number of mental technicians and of practitioners of Kuhnian 'normal science', that is, of persons who could be entrusted with the major specialized tasks that had to be performed as they made their transition from agrarian, pre-capitalist societies into fully fledged technological and industrial societies. Such mental technicians and 'normal scientists' operated often in rather crude and insensitive ways; they were largely unable to think creatively, and they were given to stereotypical types of thinking. But they were the best that Soviet societies were able to mobilize in their struggle to transform backward societies into modern industrial powers.

At the point at which these regimes achieved the building of a relatively modern technological society and faced the need to reach out for equal status with the leading Western societies, they faced major obstacles. The breakthrough to modern post-industrial society could no longer be accomplished by a workforce that was adequate at solving previous problems but had not really begun to think creatively. A more sophisticated type of thinking was needed, and such thinking was hard to find in the ranks of the obedient. Hence the Gorbachev regime made major efforts to attract intellectuals and this meant major concessions to their interests. This accounts for the gradual loosening up of censorship restrictions, the rehabilitation of many previously banned writers, and many other efforts to convince intellectuals that they were no longer the stepchildren of the regime. Whether this strategy will be ultimately crowned with success is too early to tell, but I have strong doubts. Intellectuals in the former Soviet Union and in the rest of the erstwhile Eastern bloc clearly rejoiced when it became apparent that the anti-intellectual strategies of previous regimes had finally been discarded. They seem to have felt that this new friendliness to the intellectual élite was more than a temporary gesture. It was clear, for example, that the regime could hardly have undone its lifting of the censorship of many Western and Eastern writers, from Orwell to Pasternak. Once readers have become acquainted with the thought of such 'subversive' writers it is difficult to undo the damage. Once an intellectual has been rehabilitated it is hardly possible to ban him or her a second time.

One final observation on the role of intellectuals in the former Eastern bloc seems in order. Members of classes are always intent upon transmitting their privileged position to their children. Indeed, one of the most potent motivations for consolidating positions among the rich and powerful is to ensure the inheritance of their privileges by their children. There can be no ruling class without inheritance. But it is indeed one of the salient characteristics of Eastern European regimes of yesterday that powerful bureaucrats have no means of transmitting their positions of power and influence to their children. To be sure, they can use their connections to place their children in prestigious academic institutions, or they can engage private tutors, but these are evidently only stopgaps while authentic inheritance is unavailable. Given this state of affairs, the rulers are not an authentic class but rather a formation like the medieval clergy which performed many of the functions of a ruling class but which could not transmit its powers since its members were celibate.

Let me put it another way. Dominating and ruling strata in a Soviet-type system will find ways of transferring their cultural capital to the offspring but they have no way of transmitting wealth or power. They may succeed in assuring that their children will be among the educated but they cannot be sure that their children will be of high rank in the bureaucracy, and they surely cannot assure positions among intellectuals for their children.

This being the case, one has to conclude that there are ruling strata but no ruling classes in Soviet-type societies and, in addition, that intellectuals are surely not a class. Paradoxically, intellectuals may have more class features now than in the past since they can transmit their cultural capital at a time when this type of capital is a scarce and valued commodity.

No matter which camp has been most persuasive in the debates about the power of intellectuals, the events of 1989 and after have refuted the thesis of the intellectuals as the new ruling class more powerfully than any polemics. From Romania to Bulgaria, from East Germany to Poland, intellectuals, far from backing the various Stalinoid regimes in which they had a fairly good position in comparison to other strata, have been in the vanguard of the mass movements that toppled these regimes. Many intellectuals, it turns out, have become not the ideological defenders of these regimes but their determined adversaries. Far from having capitulated to the people in power, far from having attempted to seize power for themselves, they have been in the forefront of the masses of people who demonstrated on Wenceslas Square or in the streets of Berlin or Moscow.

It turns out that intellectuals are not inclined to sever their ties to the tradition of the Enlightenment, and that they believe and have convinced large masses of their compatriots that the pen is mightier than the sword. They are the salt of the earth.

8

A NEW MIDDLE CLASS?

Edmund Mokrzycki

THE COMING OF THE MIDDLE CLASS

The biblical tone in the subheading is not accidental. In Poland and other countries of Central and Eastern Europe, the middle class is often considered in eschatological terms. Polish neo-liberals, for example, are convinced that the real renewal of Polish society will come with the development of the middle class – a 'new middle class' – which will originate from various sectors of the post-socialist society, in a process of natural selection, activated by free market mechanisms. On the other hand, Polish neo-liberalism is also empirical and pragmatic. It is said that the new middle class is experiencing a painful delivery, lacking local capital and strong traditions and in an atmosphere of growing social resistance to liberal reforms. The conclusion is that its birth has to be protected and expedited. The proper economic and institutional conditions have to be established for this new class to develop rapidly and efforts have to be made to change social consciousness, warped by decades of communist propaganda, which has been especially hostile towards the middle class.

Creating a social class, even planning to expedite its birth, departs from orthodox liberal views. But it should be remembered that in all of contemporary Europe, liberal principles are undergoing a spontaneous re-interpretation through adaptation to local conditions. The idea of transformation itself is closer to the traditions of revolutionary creativism than liberal *laissez-faire*. In Eastern Europe the former idea has undergone an important evolution since 1992, from thinking in the categories of a 'Velvet Revolution' to thinking in categories of real revolution in the sociological sense, that is, deep and rapid social restructuring

(Arato 1994). As long as it was believed – as did the authors of the Polish shock therapy – that lifting communist restrictions *per se* would activate pro-market and pro-democratic forces, it was possible to hold that the programme of Eastern European 'transformations' has nothing to do with revolution, but is, if anything, a sort of counterrevolution using chiefly macro-economic means.

With time, however, a completely different view of the situation emerged. In none of the post-communist countries has the opening of the economy and liquidation of the communist system of power led to radical changes in social thinking, attitudes and behaviours. 'Natural market forces', if they exist at all, seem to run much deeper in these societies than had been previously thought. The disassembly of the socialist system of central distribution is meeting with an increasingly strong and well-organized resistance. Structural reasons for resistance (but not social ones) have appeared since the time when the reforms were first implemented. The strongest and best-organized resistance is not where the greatest poverty is and not even where the greatest decline in real income has occurred. It is where the decline in real income is only one of the indicators of social degradation. The class of industrial workers, which, in Poland, had been a class 'in-itself-and-for-itself' for several years, is now obviously fighting not only to raise wages, but also to survive in its present form. The Polish peasantry, a class which has survived in its pre-war form thanks to the convoluted agricultural policies of the socialist state, is also fighting for survival, condemned to extinction under conditions of open competition with European agriculture. Under the guise of socially neutral macro-economic decisions, the reforms have activated the powerful processes of a rapid and radical macro-social reconstruction.

The motor of this deep, if not spectacular, revolution is the state. It is acting in the interests of all of society, or, strictly speaking, of society as a whole, following abstract ideological assumptions and not, as is usually the case in revolutions, specific social forces activated by group interests. In short, this is a revolution without a social subject and without a revolutionary ideology; an enforced revolution in which the 'top' is isolated, because the rest of the society, while endorsing the abstract and far-reaching goals of the revolution, does not generally accept the specific, intermediate measures.

The situation is one of a reforming state versus a reformed

society; a 'transformation' steered by the government which meets with a growing social resistance; and the absence of a crystallized social force whose current interests are in agreement with the line of the reforms and which would constitute a natural political base for the reformers. This is the context in which many, not just the neo-liberals, look forward to the coming of a middle class and believe this event can be precipitated. Is this a rational attitude? Let us first look at the concept of the middle class.

WHAT IS THE MIDDLE CLASS?

The standard answer is that it is a class occupying the central space in a stratified society. But the definition is empty until the rules of social stratification are presented, and there are as many rules as there are theories of stratification. In a word, the concept of the middle class is relative to a social theory. What is more, in practice the middle class is a historical concept which refers to modern capitalist societies. The term can be used in a general sense and it is used as such by some (e.g. Kurczewska 1992b). However, in this case ideas connected specifically with the historical concept are transferred into the general idea of a middle class, in a way that does not always make sense.

The career of the idea of a middle class originated with the theoretical and ideological dispute initiated by Marx's and Engels' *Communist Manifesto*. They stated that the further development of capitalism would lead to the polarization of capitalist society, that is, to the disappearance of intermediary groups between the bourgeoisie and the workers. In 1848, the year of the publication of the *Manifesto*, these groups consisted of the petit bourgeoisie and affluent artisans. Marx and Engels believed that these groups would disappear and their representatives would either rise to become part of the bourgeoisie or would be pauperized and fall back into the working class. This proved to be an erroneous prognosis. Not only did no such polarization occur, but also the space between the bourgeoisie and the workers started being filled with a growing number of new groups, later assigned the common label of the 'new middle class'. This 'new middle class' category encompasses representatives of professionals, managers, upper- and middle-class officials, teachers and specialists of all kinds.

In the context of this essay, there is no need to wonder if the new middle class is a middle class in the same sense as the petit bourgeoisie. Of course it is not, but that is not important. The new middle class is a middle class not because of its similarity to the petit bourgeoisie but because of its place in modern capitalism. The roles have been reversed. The importance of the petit bourgeoisie is systematically declining. If it continues to be considered an important part of the modern middle class, it is partly for historical reasons. It is also because, in certain respects (e.g. income but not lifestyle, education, or role played in production), it is still close to the dynamically developing new middle class, which is characterized by skills and knowledge rather than by the ownership of any means of production. This is a symptomatic shift, for it reflects the basis of the development of modern capitalism.

Sociologists are surprisingly unanimous in their view of the middle class as the foundation of the economic, social and political order in modern capitalism. If the middle class is really the core of a modern society and decides the direction and dynamics of its development, it is not just thanks to the shop- and hotel-keepers. It is largely because of the enormous and constantly growing group of increasingly better paid, better educated and efficient managers, technicians, administration employees, scientists, specialists of various kinds and other hired employees with the highest qualifications. Frequent estimates place the middle class in the most developed societies at over 50 per cent of the population. The petit bourgeoisie constitutes a marginal percentage of this figure and is increasingly distinct from the rest of the middle class. In its system of values, its political behaviour and, importantly, its attitude towards the new market policies, it is shifting closer to the lower classes. In short, assuming that the middle class is in fact the mainstay of the market and democracy, it is not because of the small owners. Election results in a number of European countries where xenophobic nationalism emerged as a real political option (e.g. France and Austria) suggest quite the opposite. (I have purposely omitted examples from the Weimar Republic.) It is also to be noted that whatever the case may be with the petit bourgeoisie, the new middle class is first of all the *product* of the capitalist system. It is only with this in mind that one can consider its role as a secondary reinforcement of the system.

EDMUND MOKRZYCKI

A NEW MIDDLE CLASS IN POST-COMMUNIST EASTERN EUROPE

The 'new middle class' that Eastern Europe is waiting for is not a middle class in the above sense. 'New' means only that it is being reborn and 'middle class' refers to 'small private owners'. This justifies the demand to stimulate the development of the 'middle class' and even to create it. Privatization and reprivatization programmes serve this end. It is commonly believed that these programmes – in both the Polish and the Czech versions – provide workers with a unique chance to change social status overnight, i.e. to move into the 'middle class'. The development of the middle class is often treated as the most important goal and as such it serves as a context in which to evaluate such phenomena as *nomenklatura* companies (to which I will return later). Hopes are placed in the spontaneous development of small independent traders. It is believed that this form of trade is a business school of sorts and is also a source of local capital.

On the one hand, the Eastern European neo-liberal concept of the middle class goes back to the *Communist Manifesto* terminology: the middle class is conceived in terms of its relationship to the means of production. On the other hand, the term 'middle' in this context does not indicate a social space between some upper and lower classes; rather, it refers to all those who, in one way or another, have acquired means of production and supposedly constitute an embryo of the future 'capitalist' society.[1] It is significant that in Poland, where private farming survived, the peasants, who constitute a quarter of the population, are hardly mentioned in discussions of the middle class, even though they are definitely to be included in the category of small private owners. Neither are the intelligentsia, who, largely because of their similarity to the Western knowledge class, could be the subject of interest of ideological enthusiasts of the middle class. The question is: why?

AN IDEOLOGICAL *GESTALT*-SWITCH

The answer lies in neo-liberal ideology. Neo-liberalism turns away from the ideological order so characteristic of liberal doctrines, by prioritizing not the principles of individual freedom and social self-regulation, but the model of a capitalist economy which

188

epitomized these principles when the doctrine was being crystallized. Returning to its pragmatic base, neo-liberalism finds it unavoidable to cut off its own philosophical roots. A revolutionary creativism and an acceptance of a strong, dominating (and aggressive should the need arise) state authority is the direct result of this ideological *Gestalt*-switch. In the case of Eastern European neo-liberalism, the *Gestalt*-switch goes even further because of the extraordinary circumstances in which neo-liberal thought is being applied in this region. The neo-liberal revolution in Eastern Europe must go incomparably deeper than Margaret Thatcher's correction of capitalism in Britain. It is, in fact, a completely different enterprise – not so much a drive to revive old roots and remove abnormal growths as a need to plant a new tree in uncertain ground.

This sense of building a capitalist economy from the basics, as well as a modern, liberal and democratic society, is one of the most important tenets of neo-liberal thought in post-communist Eastern Europe. This facilitates understanding why the 'new middle class' is, for the Eastern European neo-liberals, the key to the future and why it is identified with the category of new owners and new entrepreneurs – new 'capitalists' if you will. The new middle class is not a class of a new society, fitted in somewhere between the other classes. Rather, it is a new society *tout court*, emerging from the social legacy of the past, both communist and pre-communist. That is why, on this view, peasants, even the wealthiest among them, and the intelligentsia have no place in the middle class, nor do they collectively approximate this class.

THE DECLINE OF THE INTELLIGENTSIA

One side-effect of the neo-liberal reforms is a violent process of disintegration and decline of the intelligentsia in general and the intellectuals in particular. This process is taking place all over Eastern Europe, although not to the same degree. In Hungary, it has taken the gentlest form, mainly because of the opportunities which 'goulash communism' created for the development of a modern knowledge class. Poland is hardest hit in this respect, with the traditional Eastern European intelligentsia undergoing a real shock therapy in order to adapt. As a result, some intellectual professions are simply disappearing, at a rate which would have been difficult to imagine just a few years back. Polish science and academic learning, which until recently represented an average European standard, now exist as pauperized institutions pushed on to the margin and abandoned by the best of the academic and administrative cadres. Some of the professors go abroad, others change profession, whilst the majority takes up additional and often non-academic occupations, quickly losing their academic qualifications. In many departments there are few teachers under 40 years old, the younger generation having not entered academia at all.

The development of science and university education has its own inner logic. Demography alone suggests that in Poland these fields are already lost. It is anticipated that in a few years, assuming an economic revival takes place in the meantime, there will be a mass exodus of the more affluent young Poles to universities in Western Europe and North America. Polish university standards will fall drastically and so will the standing of Polish diplomas. Small private schools, which have already started developing, will remain a marginal phenomenon for years to come, educating in strictly specialist, market-orientated fields.

These side-effects of the reforms have to be considered for two reasons. Firstly, we are dealing with the sudden disappearance of this part of the Polish intelligentsia, which the Western concept of a knowledge class covers relatively well. Secondly, it is this part which is responsible for the social reproduction of the whole class. The decline of the academic intellectuals will thus lead to important structural changes on a much wider scale than so far anticipated.

THE DISMANTLING OF COMMUNISM AND THE DISASSEMBLING OF HISTORY

A general problem is that the Eastern European reforms are usually perceived as the dismantling of communism and a 'return to Europe'. This view is, however, a disassembly of the social history of the region preceding communism, because the two overlap in the social and economic dimensions. The legacy of communism cannot easily be separated from its historical context. The 'return to Europe' is a wonderful ideological metaphor, which, however, falsifies the essence of the matter.

Seen in a historical perspective, the neo-liberal reforms are one more modernizing leap forward in Eastern Europe's timeless bid to catch up with Western Europe. Each previous attempt at the modernization of Eastern Europe, beginning with the grand Westernization implemented by Peter the Great and ending in the socialist experiment, resulted in the revolutionary destruction of a part of the social tissue. This is once again the case. Of necessity, the reforms strike at institutions and group interests created under real socialism (Mokrzycki 1992). But they also strike at institutions and group interests of much longer standing in the country. A side-effect of reform is the gradual disappearance of the basis of great social groups formed in the specific Eastern European historical context.

The present situation of the Polish intelligentsia is a case in point. It can be seen as the drama of a declining class and the drama of a society which will have to bear the costs of reconstructing an educated class. But the situation can also be considered as an unavoidable adaptation process which will transform the anachronistic, overdeveloped and inefficient Eastern European educated élite into a modern knowledge class or, at least, the germ of such a class. It is worth noting at this point that real socialism, although repressive in respect to the traditional Polish intelligentsia, did create conditions for this class to retain its unique élitist character, regardless of the civilizational changes occurring around it. This was mainly due to socialism's cult of learning and the soft financing it provided.

Another example which is interesting for its clarity is the present situation of the peasant class in Poland. The ideological tenets of real socialism condemned this group to extinction by transforming it into a farm-workers' class, but economic arguments saved them from such a fate. Consequently, the Polish peasant class survived, but was forced to be the most exploited part of the planned economic system. Administrative restrictions on the sale and inheritance of farm property; the setting of prices for agricultural products and machines; the state economic monopoly in respect to agriculture; and the corruption and arrogance of local authorities – were all disadvantageous from the point of view of the peasants. These constraints created conditions in which not only the economic, but also the civilizational, development of the peasant class was frozen at a point corresponding to their condition at the turn of the previous century in Western Europe. The fall of the planned economy has revealed the surprising fact that without the niche created by repressive socialism, the Polish peasant has little chance of survival.

In the latter case, the drama unfolds not only collectively in terms of a class, but also in the individual sphere. In contrast to the professionally mobile academic intelligentsia, peasants have few possibilities for changing occupations, being restricted mainly by low educational standards and meagre housing opportunities, i.e. the shortage of apartments. It is in these categories, not, I believe, in the academics' moral and intellectual superiority enabling them to understand the need for painful reform, that one should search for the reasons behind the difference in reactions to group degradation demonstrated by the academic community and the peasants. The staff of academic institutions usually apply individual strategies of escape from the consequences of academic decline. But the peasant who is deprived of such possibilities reacts with group pressure in a sometimes repugnant form. Economists generally agree that under present Polish conditions these pressures only prolong the agony of the traditional peasant economy.

THE 'NEW MIDDLE CLASS' AND THE FACTS

Let us return to the Eastern European idea of a new middle class as the beginning of a new society. The ideological sense of this idea is clear: the 'new middle class' is a middle class not because of its position in an existing structure of an existing society, but because of its role in creating the new society of tomorrow. In this ideological context one should not ask what attributes make this group a middle class, but rather which of its attributes will help it become the moving social force in the market- and democracy-orientated transformations.

To remain with the Polish example, the private sector in Poland is developing dynamically indeed. Between 1989 and 1992 its participation in global employment grew from 12 per cent to 56.6 per cent; in global production from 7.4 per cent to 45.3 per cent, excluding the grey and black economies which are estimated at some 20 per cent. There are, however, no reliable data on the size and inner structure of the new middle class (not to mention definitional problems).[2] In mid-1992 there were 1.5 million private businesses registered in Poland. However, there is no way to be sure if they were all 'for real', just as there is no way to find out how many unregistered firms were operating successfully. One should also keep in mind the instability prevalent in this sector. There is a large group of people on the sector borderline who often, and with ease, change over from 'owner' to 'employee' or to 'unemployed' (often fictional unemployment in these cases).

Sociological materials seem to confirm the common assumption that the new middle class is extremely diverse. For instance, according to CBOS poll centre data, the average income per person in the households of private entrepreneurs was 2.318 million zlotys. This group outdistanced all the other professional categories (the next group – managers and intellectuals – achieved 1.469 million zlotys), but it also demonstrated the greatest inner differentiation (CBOS 1992).

The social genealogy of the new middle class is unknown. What is clear is that it comprises representatives of all the social classes and layers existing in real socialism – from peasants to intellectuals – in unknown proportions. Three groups making up this new middle class deserve special attention: (1) the 'private initiative' of socialist times; (2) the socialist, Solidarity and post-Solidarity *nomenklatura*; and (3) the declassed intellectuals.

(1) *Private initiative*. It is a common misconception that this sector was the Trojan horse of capitalism in the socialist fortress. In reality, it was an integral part of the socialist economy, just like the Lenin Steelworks or the state farms. The first weeks of reform demonstrated the complete dependence of this sector on the central distribution of goods, especially through its symbiotic relationship with state industry and trade. Market instruments, as far as they have been activated by reforms, turned out to be destructive rather than healing for this sector.

Nor is it true that the socialist 'private initiative' constituted an area in which the capitalistic spirit, in the Weberian sense, prevailed. It was rather the place where the mentality and capabilities characteristic of the small economic underground and the grey economy were formed. The last two years have shown that these features have not disappeared under the new conditions. The 'private initiative' of old did not become a core for the new middle class to build around. The processes of a 'positive disintegration' prompted by the 'transformation' shock have touched it to no less a degree than other professional groups. Few members of this group were able to adapt to new conditions

193

and enter the heterogeneous stream feeding into the new middle class.

(2) *Nomenklatura.* Another important element is constituted by the numerous groups who are nevertheless extremely effective in the accumulation of capital. This is the 'old and new *nomenklatura*' as it is called, since its members come from the sphere of the communist, as well as Solidarity and post-Solidarity, establishments. The speed at which this group operates and the exceptional efficiency of its undertakings are connected with the capable use of legal loopholes, ties with local and central authorities and corruption. This community blends over a considerable social space into the power élites, creating, together with them, what could be called a post-communist *upper* class. From the sociological point of view, these groups have little to do with the 'private initiative' of old and do not resemble any of the more important parts of the Western middle class.

These groups are active on the political scene, posing as representatives of the middle class. Their energy, an instrumental approach to politics and a good knowledge of the post-socialist economy at the intersection of the public and private sectors gives these groups an exceptional advantage in the struggle for the division of state property. This is most probably the Polish upper class *in statu nascendi.*

(3) *The 'declassed' intelligentsia.* Owing to education, professional capabilities, international contacts and their ease in adapting to changing conditions, this part of the new middle class has the greatest chance of forming the basis of the future middle class in the Western sense. A further unavoidable degradation of the traditional group of intellectuals will only expedite the already intensive process of supplying people with top qualifications to the private sector (see Domański n.d.). In view of the decline of public schooling, science, culture, health-care, etc., it is only a question of time before these fields are taken over by small private service centres. These centres will not be able to replace the government in aiding, for example, the development of science or education, but they will bring over to their side the rest of the talented staff.

A CLASS OR AN IDEOLOGICAL ARTEFACT?

The thesis I am leading up to is that the 'new middle class' constitutes a heterogeneous formation. It is, after all, not just a question of social genealogy. The differentiated genealogy has its continuation in things like the differences in education, professional opportunities, community ties and the opportunities for mobilization in defence of group interests. In Poland, there are also cultural differences coming to the fore. They create a social gap between the uneducated shop-owner and the former university professor, even if the latter is also a shop-owner (although he or she is more likely to be a partner in a consulting firm).

Of course, even the greatest differentiation of the new middle class does not exclude the thesis that it is a social class *in statu nascendi*. However, sociological research and public opinion polls indicate that caution is in order. The new middle class has its own profile in just a few aspects: income (with the above reservation), attitude towards economic reform in general and a behavioural syndrome which may be described as life optimism. In other aspects, the new class is more of a statistical category, whose theoretical sense is an open question.

There are no grounds to consider that this class is particularly prone to liberal ideological choices. Polls on people's attitudes on matters such as democracy, privatization, unemployment and the welfare state indicate that on what can be considered a liberalism scale private entrepreneurs score above the average, but always below the intellectuals. Among the characteristics which, in almost all the surveys, are systematically correlated positively with support for liberal reforms, higher education takes first place, young age is second and residence in a big city third (CBOS 1992; Kolerska-Bobińska n.d.; see also Demoskop reports).

In Poland, education is unquestionably the most important correlate of preferences and ideological choices. It refers primarily to a broadly understood liberalism, particularly its operationalized version, which lies at the root of Polish reforms. Jan Jerschina and Jarosław Górniak, in their research into social consciousness in Poland, report that:

> One of the most important results of our research is that the division between those who received a liberal (in four years of secondary school) and higher education, versus those with elementary and vocational education, is the strongest

factor which affects attitudes towards a free market society, individualism and collectivism, reprivatization and privatization, political reforms and democratic values. One may say on the basis of this empirical experience that we have to deal with two different educational classes in Poland.

(1992)

THE INTELLIGENTSIA AND THE MIDDLE CLASS

The paradoxical conclusion is that the Eastern European new middle class is still more an ideological artefact than a reality. Expecting strong social support for reforms (the market and democracy) from this group is based on weak doctrinal assumptions and is quite illusory at present. Real social support comes from a totally different side – the declining, traditional intelligentsia which, in the light of these doctrinal assumptions, should demonstrate a completely different ideological orientation.

There are different ways of explaining this paradoxical situation. The explanation, widely suggested by the media, in terms of the intelligentsia's intellectual and moral virtues, which compares the intellectuals' patience with the aggressive demands of other groups, is rather naive. The connection between ideology and interest is one of the most persistent rules of all social order. Events in Poland since the introduction of Balcerowicz's plan[3] in January 1990 confirm this truth with clinical precision. It was to be expected that at the moment the micro-economic consequences of macro-economic decisions touched Solidarity's political base, the ideological 're-education' of this base would be accelerated (cf. Mokrzycki 1990) and Solidarity itself would make a complete 180 degree turn, while retaining anti-socialist slogans. A similar ideological turn was made by the peasants much more quickly and with less ideological effort. This is explained by the unprecedented brutality with which the new economic principles struck at the vital interests of this group and by the lack of close connections with the new political élite.

The case of the intelligentsia keeps on returning in this discussion, not without cause. It would seem that the neo-liberals looking for the middle class in Central Europe have excessively narrowed down the field of observation. Their thinking seems to be based on the quiet assumption that in rejecting a 'third road' and choosing the 'first', capitalistic one, Central Europe is of necessity repeating the capitalistic cycle of development. Under this assumption the growing group of private owners is given *ex definitione* the status of a class. Under this assumption it is also obvious that it is this class which is the leading social force in the process of creating, reinforcing and developing capitalistic relations and democratic institutions. Under this assumption the knowledge class is not important: its tasks and role in the social structure will appear later, in the context of a modern developed capitalism.

The problem is that Central Europe has no chance of choosing the historical context and so it has no opportunity of achieving modern capitalism in accordance with the logic of its historical development. The context is given and it is a contemporary one, in which the small private owner is a figure of secondary importance. The new middle class in the Western sense of the term comes to the forefront and the most important role in the contemporary context is played by the knowledge class. Liberal reforms in Central Europe, to the extent that they are effective, inscribe themselves into this contemporary context. And on the other hand, the success of these reforms is clearly dependent on their correlation with the tendencies of contemporary capitalism.

The intellectuals of Central Europe seem to be reading this tendency properly. Here lies the key to understanding their patience in the face of violent economic and social degradation and their political support, not only for reforms in general, but also for particular programmes such as privatization, which lead to disadvantageous changes in the job market as far as this group is concerned. Ideology, knowledge and social involvement unquestionably have a part to play in the intellectuals' attitude towards reforms. But it is doubtful that their attitude would be the same were it not for the fact that education, a potential professional mobility and the capability to adapt to new conditions give individual intellectuals a good position to start from in the new system. It is because of this that the traditional professions of the intelligentsia, in contrast to the peasants' or workers' occupations, are an undefended social space, to use Thomas Heller's concept. The representatives of the future middle class will come from this undefended social space, that is, if the whole 'transformation' manoeuvre continues, more or less successfully. This transformation of a class into a class has already begun and is quite obvious to those concerned.

EDMUND MOKRZYCKI

CONCLUSIONS

The strict relation between liberal economic reform and the formation of a middle class is undisputed. What is doubtful is the Eastern European neo-liberals' ideas about this relation, conceptions which have already taken root in the common thinking of the region. Firstly, considering the middle class today in terms of the *Communist Manifesto*, regardless of where, is an anachronism. A middle class understood in this way (the old middle class as it is sometimes called) has lost its importance with the development of contemporary capitalism and it is improbable that it will regain it, thanks to the Eastern European revolution – even if this revolution will lead us to 'one immense "South"' instead of to Europe, as Adam Przeworski (1991a: 17) recently suggested.

Secondly, it is a misunderstanding, resulting from the mixing up of correlate and cause, that the middle class is being promoted and stimulated in its development in order to support market reforms. The middle class, in all its meanings, even as the petit bourgeoisie, is just as much a creator of the market as its product.

Thirdly, the very idea of creating a class can be understood only in terms of a paradigm which was in force in Eastern Europe until recently. And yet the idea appears as a serious element of our theoretical, practical and even ethical thinking, beginning with the debate about *nomenklatura* companies and ending with the Mass Privatization Programme. As Przeworski astutely observed: 'Perhaps revolutions are shaped by the very systems against which they are directed' (1991b: 14). The sociology of knowledge offers an explanation why this is so.

Fourthly, the owners 'class' in Central Europe (disregarding countries of the former USSR) shows no sociological characteristics of a class, not to mention a class capable of a grassroots support for reforms. It is a class which is deprived of an inner bond, external contacts, an ideological platform and political representation (if one disregards the numerous armchair parties which attempt to speak for this category). It is a 'class' which is unable to articulate its interests and does not show any particular preferences for liberal values.

Finally, theoretical assumptions, the experiences of other countries and empirical data from Central Europe all suggest another approach to the study of the emerging new middle class. Educated people will remain in the centre of this study one way or another,

198

regardless of whether Central Europe will finally find its way into Europe or the South; and regardless of whether the capitalism here will be affluent or poor, although in each of these extreme cases the role of educated people would be different and would lead to different consequences in terms of social structure.

Krzysztof Zagórski states that 'the sociological meaning of the new middle class in the most developed "post-industrial" and "post-modern" societies (if the latter exist at all) is approaching the Eastern European, traditional definition of intelligentsia' (1991: 75). In the macro-sociological dimension the similarities are illusory. It is the social context which determines, on the one hand, what the intelligentsia was and still is in Eastern Europe and, on the other, what the middle class is in Western countries. In the micro-sociological dimension, the similarity is striking, particularly when one compares the intelligentsia with the knowledge class (Kurczewska 1992a). This does not mean that (assuming an optimistic, European scenario) the intelligentsia, a product of Eastern European backwardness, can actually take the initiative and serve as the new middle class, as Henryk Domański (1991) seems to be suggesting.

What one can conclude from this is that in the process of the immense macro-structural changes that have already begun in Central Europe, and which will intensify, assuming the European scenario, the unavoidable crisis of the anachronistic intelligentsia and the equally unavoidable development of the modern middle class along with the knowledge class will activate powerful micro-sociological mechanisms of adaptation, leading to the transformation of the former of these classes into the latter.

NOTES

1 'In the current parliament there are about a hundred representatives of the middle class' (Szemplińska 1993). The context suggests that the journalist counted only those deputies who were considered articulators of the interests of 'business' in the Sejm, whatever the term may otherwise mean at the current stage of reforms.

2 Zdzisław Zagórski (n.d.) has tried to estimate the number and composition of the emerging middle class. Considering it as a class of small owners (but without the peasants), he sets its number at 8 per cent of the population as at late September 1991. However, these estimates are based on very risky methodological assumptions and quoting them without detailed commentary would hardly be purposeful.

3 Radical measures of economic liberalization instituted by the Polish

government on 1 January 1990, the architect of which was the Finance Minister, Leszek Balcerowicz, originally an academic economist, partly Harvard educated. On that date, in Poland, a complete and sudden switch to a market economy was instituted, including the liberalization of all prices at a stroke and the removal of all foreign trade restrictions, state licences and regulations governing small businesses. At the same time, the zloty was made freely convertible on the internal market and the state's monopoly of money-changing was abolished, making legal the private trade in foreign currency. See Millar (1994), from which this information was taken [Eds].

9

DEMOCRACY VERSUS A NEW AUTHORITARIANISM IN EASTERN EUROPE

Jerzy J. Wiatr

The collapse of communist regimes in Eastern Europe has been met with high expectations concerning both the quality and the durability of the new democratic systems which – with remarkable ease and speed – replaced the ageing communist dictatorships. A few years after the 'Fall of Nations', however, there are growing fears that Eastern Europe may deviate from the road to democracy and end, at least for a period of time, under a version of authoritarianism.

The reasons for such fear are much less connected with the possibility of communist counter-reformation than with the possibility of new (non-communist) authoritarianism emerging within the fragile structures of the new democracies.

Communist parties have disappeared (or reformed themselves into non-communist, left-wing parties) everywhere in Eastern Europe. Their influence varies from country to country, but even the most successful ones (like the Lithuanian Democratic Labour Party, formerly the Communist Party of Lithuania, which won an absolute majority of the parliamentary seats in the 1992 election) do not attempt to abolish democratic regimes but instead work within the framework of the new democracy. Russia and some other post-Soviet republics (e.g. Belarus, Kazakhstan, perhaps even Ukraine) may still face a possibility of a communist come-back, due to much deeper roots of the communist regime and the enormous difficulties in transforming the societies in which communist regimes lasted longer and had deeper consequences for the life of the society.[1] However, even in Russia the main challenge to democracy seems to come from the Right, that is, from the nationalistic forces devoted to the restoration of the old power and glory of the Russian empire. In the other Eastern European societies doubts about the stability of new democracies result mostly from the intensity of social conflicts, the low effectiveness of democratic structures and the rise of nationalistic authoritarian movements.

Put in the simplest way, democracy is a political system which permits political articulation of conflicting interests and their resolution through an orderly political process based on free elections. Free and competitive elections constitute the cornerstone of democracy not only because they allow the selection of leaders by the people whom the leaders govern, but also because they offer ways in which social conflicts can be mediated in an orderly manner and managed in the political sphere. Democratic stability can, therefore, be seen as the state of affairs under which conflicts are managed within and only by the democratic political process, i.e. elections and their impact on the formation of executive authorities of the state. In societies characterized by high intensity of social conflicts, this may lead to fragmented legislatures and unstable executive branches of government. Neither of these two situations, however, equals system instability. A democratic system is stable as long as its rules are observed, even if cabinets change and legislatures are divided into many parties. What mostly concerns observers of East-Central European post-communist politics is not the fragmentation *per se* but the possibility that the young democracies may be unable effectively to deal with intense social conflicts and, consequently, will be replaced by some version of authoritarianism.

There are three principal areas of conflict in East-Central Europe. First, the transformation of the economy, combined with the collapse of the COMECON international system of commerce, has produced recession and a sharp decline in the standard of living, unemployment and a general feeling of frustration. It has also produced a sharp differentiation of economic interests. The emerging pattern of income inequalities creates the feeling that the new privileged class benefits from the change of the system which makes the life of the majority of the population increasingly hard. The second source of conflicts is ethnicity. Compared to the post-Soviet and post-Yugoslav republics, Central European states are somehow less affected by this problem but they are not free of it. Czechoslovakia has achieved what, it is to be hoped, will be a civilized, peaceful divorce, with growing awareness of the importance of ethnic cleavages, particularly in Slovakia (Jackson 1992).[2] Hungary and Poland are, in relative terms, ethnically homogeneous but both have manifested ethnic tensions, as well as experienced the exploitation of ethnic slogans (including anti-semitism) in their recent electoral campaigns of 1990 and 1991 (cf. Engelberg 1990; Schöpflin 1991). Thirdly, the collapse of communism has cleared the way for conflicts of values between those who opt for a liberal, secular state, as well as for the guarantees of individual freedoms, and those who want the state to uphold the moral and religious values of the dominant religion. Poland has emerged as the main battlefield of this conflict, with strong pressure for the adoption of strict anti-abortion legislation, re-introduction of religious instruction and prayer in the public schools, adoption of the religious institution of the military oath, and so forth. While Poland seems to be an extreme case in this respect, the other Central European countries – particularly Hungary and Slovakia – may face similar problems in the future.

ECONOMY AND DEMOCRACY

Of the three areas of conflict listed above, the economy has had the most visible impact on the stability of new democratic regimes, at least for the time being. The collapse of the communist regimes was conditioned more by their failure to satisfy the economic aspirations of their populations than by any other factor. Élites rebelled (where they did so) against the lack of freedom but the masses were mobilized by the economic inefficiency of the old system and by the stagnation (or even decline) of their standard of living. The change of the regime was perceived as leading to rapid improvements in the economy, because it was believed that the key reason for the hardships experienced by East-Central European societies was their inefficient economic systems of 'command', i.e. centrally planned production, and also because it was hoped that the change of regime would result in substantial economic assistance coming from the West. Intellectuals and political leaders of the democratic opposition tended to underestimate the seriousness of the economic crisis. In some instances they offered over-optimistic predictions of the future.[3] In addition, during the early stage of democratic transformation, economic alternatives were not explicitly stated. Ellen Comisso observed correctly that (in Hungary) 'the fact that economic issues received so little attention in the campaign was both a cause and a consequence of the under-organization of explicitly economic interests' (1991: 128). It was also true in Poland and in Czechoslovakia during the first elections of the transition, 1989 and 1990, respectively. The failure of the democratic opposition to deal realistically with the question of economic choices was largely the result of its lack of practical experience as well as of its idealistic expectation that the departure from the old regime would make the solution of economic problems easy. This was not going to happen.

Three years after the change of governments and regimes in the region, East-Central Europe, plagued by enormous socio-economic problems, sees no prospect of their effective resolution in the near future. On the one hand, there is deep recession, much sharper than anticipated and resulting in high unemployment, a declining standard of living and the crisis of state finances (leading in turn to the collapse of public services, education, health care, etc.). On the other hand, growing economic inequalities produce resentment and tensions. This is to a large extent due to the fact that East-Central European societies have experienced a relatively egalitarian structure of income distribution and functioned under the protection of a welfare state, which, however inefficient, made them believe that their basic needs were, and had to be, protected by the state. Previous social upheavals – particularly in Poland (1956, 1970, 1980–1, 1988) – were mostly conditioned by the inability of the state to live up to its social commitments, not by a rejection of the very concept of the social welfare state, committed to the principles of social justice (Kolerska-Bobińska 1988). Studies of social values demonstrate a relatively egalitarian orientation among Eastern Europeans despite their fascination with the Western type of free market economy. The privileges of the political élite figured prominently among the issues raised by the critics of the communist regime. People expected more – not less – equality and justice from the new democratic governments. It may be true that such a combination of egalitarian social values and economic expectations is not realistic, but the impact of the value systems on the present attitudes and reactions towards the economic reforms cannot be ignored.

The choice of economic reform strategy has deep consequences for the effects of the reforms as well as for their evaluation by the public. Departing from the command economy of the old regime, post-communist countries face the problem of choosing not only the direction but also the speed with which they are going to change. The choice of a radical or 'shock' strategy implies (1) a rapid decline of consumption, and (2) its early recovery. The success of such a strategy depends on the ability of the reformist government to maintain public support for the 'bitter pill' reforms for a period of time long enough to reach the beginning of the recovery.[4] The radical strategy carries the risk of a popular explosion strong enough to paralyse or overthrow the reformist government before the positive effects of the reforms materialize. In East-Central Europe the pressure for adopting radical strategies comes both from outside (the World Bank and other international agencies) and from inside (the impatience of both the public and the leaders with gradualism, reflecting, to large extent, their dissatisfaction with the unsatisfactory results of the reformist policies of late communist governments). Poland in particular chose the radical strategy and can, therefore, be considered a good experimental field for studying the effects of such a strategy and its impact on the society.

Three years after the 'zero hour' of the Polish reform launched on 1 January 1990, it is virtually impossible to formulate a comprehensive and fair judgement of its effects. Its advocates point to such achievements as a balanced consumer market and convertibility of the currency. Its critics list deep recession, high unemployment, a growing budgetary deficit and a declining standard of living as proofs of its failure. From the present point of view, it is less important to formulate a definitive judgement about the achievements and failures of this strategy than to assess its consequences for the Polish public and Polish politics.

There is strong evidence that the public response to the socioeconomic change of the last three years has become increasingly negative. The original support – based on the popularity of the Solidarity movement and on hopes that the change of regime would open opportunities for the rapid solution of the protracted crisis – has evaporated. Tadeusz Mazowiecki's humiliating defeat in the first round of the presidential election, in November 1990, signalled this trend very clearly. So do the survey data. The Centre for Social Opinion Research (CBOS) found that Poles' evaluation of their personal economic situation has steadily declined; in the July 1992 survey of the adult population 46 per cent of all respondents declared that their income was much too low, and 37 per cent said that it was too low to meet needs.[5] In the same survey respondents were asked under which of the latest Polish prime ministers their life was easiest. Thirty per cent named Mieczysław Rakowski (1988–9), the last head of government of the old regime; 22 per cent, Tadeusz Mazowiecki (1989–90); 6 per cent, Jan Krzysztof Bielecki (1991); and only 3 per cent, Jan Olszewski (1991–2); 24 per cent declared that things were always the same and 15 per cent opted for the 'difficult to say' response. Asked about the future, 76 per cent of respondents predicted that the standard of living would continue to decline.

The level of economic dissatisfaction in Poland is alarming. It is true that the transformation of the economy from the centralized, 'command' type to the market-orientated had to entail social costs, but the blow to the living conditions of the population could and should have been reduced by a more socially responsible public policy. Adam Przeworski made this point clear when he compared Poland and Hungary and concluded that the former 'embarked on the transition to the market economy without having even a programme for protecting individuals from the vicissitudes of the market economy' (1991d). With the national budget falling victim to the unsuccessful monetarist policy, the social expenditures suffered the heaviest blows, particularly education, culture and the health service.

In terms of social interests the Polish economic strategy must be seen as radically increasing income inequalities. This, combined with the reduction of the protective social programme which in the past helped the poor to avoid the harshest consequences of the economic crisis, produces social tensions. The poorer strata would have been able to swallow the 'bitter pill' if (1) they had received a degree of social protection from the state, and/or (2) they had seen the burdens of the crisis put justly on the shoulders of everybody. Neither of these happened in Poland. Consequently, the pattern of the Polish economic transformation tends to generate more intense social and economic conflicts than is the case in Hungary or in Czechoslovakia. In addition, the historically proven militancy of Polish labour made things even more difficult for the Solidarity-based governments. Poland can serve as a warning example to countries which undertake the transition to a market economy. Such transition will be seriously jeopardized if it is not combined with a comprehensive social policy aimed at the reduction of social costs and social injustice.

NATIONALISMS

The state of the economy has resulted in disillusion and labour unrest, but – at least for the time being – has not brought the collapse of the new democratic order. It is ethnic conflict which destroyed the peace and stability of the post-Yugoslav republics and resulted in the most cruel war on European territory since 1945. The lesson of Yugoslavia, even if extreme, should be taken seriously since to some degree the Yugoslav drama reflects universal problems of nationality in Eastern Europe.

These problems were not created by the communist regimes but rather inherited by them from the past. Yugoslavia in the pre-communist years lived through a period of authoritarian Serbian hegemonic rule (1918–40), followed by the bloody warfare between Serbs and Croats during the German–Italian occupation. One can blame the communist regime for not having been able to do away with such a heritage but one must also admit that the forty-five years of the 'Titoist' regime constituted the most stable and relatively harmonious period in the relations between the Yugoslav nationalities.[6]

Elsewhere in Eastern Europe it was mostly the same story with local variations. History has left the region with borders which do not correspond to the ethnic and religious divisions. When Western Europe experienced the process of nation-building, in the Eastern part of the continent nationalities lived within multi-ethnic empires, unable to establish the states which would, broadly speaking, correspond to national identities. When the empires collapsed in the early twentieth century – as the result of the First World War – the principle of national self-determination was adopted as the doctrinal basis for the resolution of the national issue. Even then, however, the delimitation of borders presented the state-builders with enormous problems. Under the terms of the Treaty of Trianon (1920), millions of ethnic Hungarians were left outside the borders of Hungary (in Romania, Yugoslavia and Czechoslovakia), leaving a strong basis for the resurrection of the Hungarian nationalistic appeal. Today, the question of the Hungarian minorities outside Hungarian borders is being raised by the right-wing nationalists. An ethnically mixed population in Silesia made the delimitation of the Polish–German and Polish–Czechoslovak borders so complicated that the eventual decisions of the victorious powers concerning the division of disputed territories between Poland, Germany and Czechoslovakia were preceded there by Polish uprisings in the Polish–German borderland and by Czechoslovak military action in the summer of 1920. Bulgaria and Yugoslavia quarrelled over the identity of the Macedonian part of the Yugoslav kingdom, the quarrel continuing well after both states had become communist. And the Soviet Union itself became the largest multi-ethnic empire of the twentieth century, inheriting all the national conlicts of imperial Russia – and adding some new ones.

If history is the main factor in explaining the intensity of ethnic conflicts in Eastern Europe today, the question can be raised why such conflicts were relatively dormant under communist rule. Some answer it by pointing to the strength of state repression. There is no doubt that the communist state was repressive and that manifestations of ethnic aspirations were frequently put down by force. To my way of thinking, however, force alone is not an adequate explanation. Firstly, there were other repressive regimes which proved unable to control mass dissatisfaction regardless of how brutally they were responding to it. Iran of 1979 or Afghanistan during the Soviet intervention of 1980 can serve as examples. Secondly, the repressiveness of the communist regimes declined over time and in some cases the level was not fundamentally different from that of moderately authoritarian regimes elsewhere. Yugoslavia under the late Titoist regime can serve as illustration. Therefore, while not denying the existence of political repression, one must look for some other explanation of the moderateness of ethnic conflicts under the Eastern European communist regimes. To my way of thinking, as long as the communist ideology retained some of its legitimating appeal, it helped to produce relative calm in the relations between nationalities. With the gradual disappearance of the communist legitimacy (part of which was the idea of internationalist co-operation of various nationalities) the old prejudices and hatreds came to the fore, sometimes deliberately exploited by politicians in search of popular appeal (cf. Woodward 1992).

Both post-Yugoslav and post-Soviet republics face grave dangers due to the intensity of ethnic conflicts and the lack of a workable formula which could serve as an acceptable basis for nation-building and the resolution of conflicts between nationalities living within a state. Other post-communist societies are, to various degrees, also challenged by ethnic problems. More dangerous than the conflicts themselves is the fact that they give impetus to the authoritarian movements which combine nationalism with populist socio-economic demands. Such movements still operate within the framework of democracy. There has been no attempt to overthrow the post-communist democratic government by force. At least not yet. But the main danger should not be underestimated. With the growing popular dissatisfaction one cannot exclude the scenario under which a new authoritarian regime would be established by the electoral victory of a nationalist party. It is, therefore, important to watch the direction in which political sentiments change in the post-communist states.

RELIGIOUS FUNDAMENTALISM

While economic unrest and ethnic tensions seem to constitute common problems for all post-communist states, religious fundamentalism is more visible in Roman Catholic countries than elsewhere. Poland – and to some degree Hungary – faces the re-emergence of aggressively fundamentalist religious politics which aims at the transformation of the legal order in a direction congruent with the teaching of the Roman Catholic church. Prayers and religious instruction in public schools, the religious formula of the military oath and – particularly – the prohibition of abortion are the most characteristic manifestations of such politics. Poland is the most strongly affected post-communist country in this respect, due probably to the traditional high position of the Catholic church and the influence of the Polish-born Pope John Paul II.

Abortion is the hottest of these issues for two reasons. Firstly, it profoundly affects the lives of most families. Secondly, on this issue the conflict between the majority of the population and the policy promoted by the church (and the Christian-Nationalist Party in the Sejm) is the strongest. In some other cases the public is supportive of the position of the church, particularly in matters of symbolic importance. So, for instance, 48 per cent of the CBOS sample favours religious instruction in schools on a voluntary basis, and 24 per cent opt for making it mandatory; only 24 per cent declared that it should be taken away from public schools.

On the abortion issue, however, public opinion is clearly on a collision course with the church. In March 1992 when the anti-abortion bill had already been presented to the Sejm a public opinion survey showed overwhelming support for a more liberal measure.[7]

Abortion – or, more generally, the nature of the state – has divided the Polish public very deeply. The essence of this conflict – unlike the economic ones – is a clash not of interests but of deeply internalized values. Those who opt for freedom of choice are not necessarily advocates of abortion but opponents of the way in which the Roman Catholic church dictates its norms to the state and deprives women of their right to privacy. Those who favour the 'pro-life' option follow their religious beliefs as well as supporting the institutional interests of the church. Since a compromise on this issue is particularly difficult, the abortion controversy is bound to inflict tensions.

While Poland is the front-line country as far as Catholic fundamentalism is concerned, there are signs that similar political trends are emerging elsewhere. In 1992, anti-abortion legislation was introduced in the Hungarian parliament, although the intensity of conflict seems to be somehow less than in Poland.

Religious fundamentalism operates within the framework of democratic institutions. It is, however, a danger to the survival and – even more – the quality of democracy for two main reasons. Firstly, it tends to polarize the society into two mutually hostile and uncompromising camps. Secondly, if new constitutions accept the principle of the privileged position of the Roman Catholic religion and the Roman Catholic church in the state, it would lead to the limitation of the rights of minorities and the abandoning of the principles of a liberal-democratic state.

WILL DEMOCRACY SURVIVE?

In the autumn of 1990, at what turned out to be the last Yugoslav–Polish political science seminar on social and political reforms, I presented a paper under the title 'Will Democracy Win in East-Central Europe?' (Wiatr 1992). My moderately pessimistic predictions focused on the danger of a 'new authoritarianism' resulting from economic instability, social frustration, ethnic conflicts and radicalization of the anti-communist Right, as well as from the heritage of the authoritarian political tradition. Five years later, these worries have not been put to rest. The tragic demise of Yugoslavia with the cruel ethnic war resulting from the élites' inability to seek and find compromise solutions reminds us of the fragility of the new democracies. Central Europe is in somewhat better shape and even the dissolution of the Czecho-Slovak federation does not seem to have led to the retreat from democracy in any of the successor republics. I am, however, increasingly concerned about the possibility of social upheavals, which can result from economic frustration and the feeling of the underprivileged that they had been given the 'bitter pill' while others have received the benefits. Strikes of coal-miners, teachers, medical personnel and other social groups in Poland created such a state of tension that it led to the parliamentary vote of no-confidence against Hanna Suchocka's cabinet and the eventual dissolution of the Sejm in May 1993. Even if Poland is considered to some degree atypical, because of the much greater militancy of its working class, based on years of previous, largely successful, experience, one should pay attention to the consequences of growing social conflicts for the stability and, indeed, the very survival of the new democratic regimes.

From various corners one now hears voices which despair of the viability of democracy in conditions of rapid change. The Polish sociologist Grzegorz Ekiert (1991) goes as far as to predict that to reconstruct the Eastern European economies in conditions of severe socio-economic dislocations, some form of 'coercive policy' will become necessary. There is a growing fascination with the example of the Asiatic 'tigers': authoritarian regimes which were able to produce rapid economic growth while keeping workers' demands under firm control.

I do not share this position for two, distinctly different, reasons. One is ideological. I believe that authoritarianism in the service of the interests of the rich and directed against the legitimate interests of the underprivileged would be the worst-case scenario for East-Central Europe. Having departed from the communist regimes, these countries deserve something better than to find themselves under an oppressive regime which – on top of everything else – would satisfy only the ambitions and interests of the new ruling class.

My other argument is analytical. I do not believe that a reform orientated authoritarian regime can be established and function in this region. The intellectual and professional élites would be too strongly alienated from such a regime to be ready to offer it their support. The armed forces, after their recent experience of depoliticizing and extrication from the control exercised by the Communist Party, would be hesitant in their attitude towards another non-democratic regime, particularly if it comes to power illegally. An authoritarian regime would also suffer from international isolation, since the European Community would not accept it as a *bona fide* member. Consequently, the more likely version of a new authoritarianism in East-Central Europe is, to my way of thinking, an anti-reform, populist and nationalistic one, which would combine verbal declarations of willingness to continue economic reforms with populist social politics and repressive measures taken against the 'enemies of the state': people with previous involvement in the communist regimes and advocates of political liberalism. The Polish social psychologist Krzysztof Korzeniowski (1992) has found that authoritarian predilections have been most strongly expressed by people who favoured the idea of a national-Catholic state and who are for the leadership of a 'strong man'. It is not inevitable, however, that things will go in this direction.

CONCLUSION

To avoid the switch towards authoritarianism, East-Central European states should adopt policies deliberately aimed at stabilization of the new democratic regimes. To my way of thinking, the following policies are of particular importance in this respect.

(1) Revising the strategy of economic transformation in such a way that the inevitable burdens are distributed in a socially more acceptable way, that is, more evenly and justly among all strata of the population. In particular, the most vulnerable sectors of the society (the old, the sick, the poor) should be given protection through special programmes. Unemployment should be actively curtailed by state-initiated public works and by other programmes aimed at creating jobs. The new rich should be taxed proportionally to their profits – without, however, destroying economic motivation – in a way which would make them contribute to the financing of the costs of transition in fair proportion to their means.

(2) A 'social accord' policy based on compromises between the government, the interest groups of the new capitalists and the

trade unions and peasant organizations. Such accords should be negotiated for several years and then be solidified by legally binding decisions of the parliaments. Schmitter's (1991) distinction between *corporatist, consociational, plebiscitary* and *electoralist* sub-types of democracy can offer an important and useful conceptual basis for projecting the type of democratic regime conducive to social peace in conditions of economic transformation. Consociational democracy, under which some basic interests are subjected to negotiated compromises rather than to the rule of an electoral majority, may be particularly helpful in defusing the political tensions which result from conflicting social interests. To my way of thinking, the Polish experiment of 1989 (Round Table negotiations and the coalition government of Tadeusz Mazowiecki) supports this thesis. It is true, as critics argue, that all pacts exclude some forces from the deal, but such exclusion, if kept within reasonable limits, may not do too much harm.

(3) Inclusion in the reform process of the left-wing parties with their roots in the reformist factions of the former ruling élites. Excluding reformist post-communist parties pushes them in the direction of populist militancy and weakens the moderately leftist forces from the former democratic opposition which, thus isolated (or rather self-isolated), cannot successfully oppose the Right Wing. Isolation of the post-communist Left makes compromises with organized labour less likely, particularly to the extent that these parties have their links with the trade unions. Divisions on the Left make the parties of the nationalistic and/or conservative Right artificially more powerful and, therefore, increase the danger of a new authoritarianism. Poland, after the parliamentary election of 1991, is a good example, since the isolation of the post-communist Left (the second strongest party in the Sejm) made it possible for the right-wing parties to dominate the first cabinet after the election.

(4) Building political institutions in a way conducive to the orderly representation of interests and their resolution. Parliamentary democracy – rather than presidentialism – and moderate proportional representation (with, say, a 5 per cent minimum of votes required for entering the Sejm) serve this purpose best. For reasons discussed at length by Arend Lijphart (1991), Juan Linz (1990a, 1990b), Fred Riggs (1988) and others, it is unlikely that a strong presidency will produce a political mechanism of interest

representation and conflict resolution; rather, it may suppress the expression of conflicting interests, at least for the time being.

Reflecting upon history should instruct us in our attempts to make democracy work in countries which have recently departed from the communist regimes. The history of Europe between the world wars is often pointed to as the crucial lesson. Among thousands of books written on this subject, Zygmunt Bauman's (1989) analysis of the Holocaust, particularly because of the emphasis on the interrelation between state and society, deserves particular attention. Today, it is more important to study potential dangers to young democracies than to applaud and describe their victory. The alternative to the success of young democracies – if this alternative were to be victorious – would make future generations of social scientists analyse the reasons and the consequences of the failure of democracy in post-communist Europe. Now, when it is still not too late, it is crucial to identify the key dangers and to think about strategies which would make democracy work.

NOTES

1 The *Los Angeles Times*, 23 August 1992, has reported the results of a poll conducted among residents of Moscow on their attitudes towards the abortive coup of 1991. Results showed a clear tendency to show greater leniency towards, and even approval of, the actions taken then by the communist hard-liners.

2 My visit to Bratislava in July 1992 (on the eve of the parliamentary vote for independence) confirmed my feeling that this 'marriage' cannot be saved – particularly if the only alternative to partition, offered by the politicians in Prague, is the status quo. This is not meant as a denial of the enormous problems independent Slovakia will face both economically and in terms of relations with its 600,000-strong Hungarian minority.

3 An interesting and remarkably honest interpretation of this phenomenon has been given by Poland's former Deputy Prime Minister and Finance Minister, Leszek Balcerowicz (1992).

4 This point is elaborated in depth in Przeworski (1991c).

5 *Nowa Europa* (Warsaw), 20 July 1992.

6 On the history of the Yugoslav national question, see in particular Shoup (1968) and Ramet (1984). Both authors, while critical of some specifics, considered the Titoist policy towards nationalities a success.

7 Data from the reports of the Centre for Social Opinion Research (CBOS), April 1992 and May 1992 (mimeographed).

ADDENDUM: CULTURE AND POWER IN THE WRITINGS OF ZYGMUNT BAUMAN

Ian Varcoe and Richard Kilminster

Zygmunt Bauman's many works speak for themselves; our aim here is not to summarize them. (A full bibliography of his writings is included in this volume.) As we wrote in the Introduction, he has not written a major, systematic treatise in sociology, nor has he attempted to found a school around a distinctive theoretical approach. With the exception of the three recent books on modernity (1987a, 1989, 1991), described by him as a trilogy, each of his books seems to be on a different topic. He may therefore seem to be a man of wide, but changing, interests who has resisted the pressure to specialize. This is indeed the case. Bauman is that rare specimen, the general sociologist. But to see him as an eclectic would be entirely to miss the truth. In fact, he has resolutely, and with remarkable consistency, pursued fundamental themes in sociology and social philosophy. He has had basic questions to ask. If he has not found an answer in a particular place, he has moved on to search elsewhere (Kilminster and Varcoe 1992: 207). This has given the impression of motility. But it is only a surface appearance. We believe that there are more continuities of theme and approach in Bauman's writings than meet the eye. These are interesting for what they reveal – together with shifts of emphasis and changes of view – of a mind at work, developing a body of ideas and shaping and re-shaping them in the light of changing circumstances and the movement of sociological discourse over more than two decades.

Our aim in this Addendum is to elucidate the two central themes of culture and power for the general reader. We will do this by indicating certain places in Bauman's texts where one can see his thought taking shape over time through the carrying forward and modifying of the two themes. For Bauman, culture and power are indissolubly linked and he pursues this dual-sided unity on different levels. At the deepest level, the burden of his work rests on an attempt to overcome the traditional structure/culture dualism, through a stress on their unity in practical activity, an insight he found in the young Marx and reinforced by Antonio Gramsci (ibid.: 206).

CULTURE

Bauman has tried to make the concept of culture central to sociological work on the ground that in it one can find the essential *problématique* of the discipline: that human life is simultaneously structured and structur*ing*.

> Specific cultural items-signs both express the existing social structure and create it; they are at the same time operative in achieving relative durability and its dynamic fluidity. So the two spurious, ill-famed 'contradictions' between 'thought' and 'reality' and between 'statics' and 'dynamics' are overcome at one stroke. The opinion of this author is that the two fallacies can be overcome either together or not at all.
>
> (1972a: 318)

The division between social structure and culture, which makes the latter a matter of values, is the basis of a positivistic sociology which gives structure an undue solidity and a determining quality, in the manner of a Durkheim (society *sui generis*) or a Parsons (central value system). Controversially, in his *Towards a Critical Sociology* of 1976, Bauman dubbed this whole approach the 'Durksonian' tradition (1976a: ch. 1), which, he argued, tacitly identified the anthropological need for 'a' society with 'the' particular society, thus presenting a given status quo as natural (ibid.: 18). It was not, therefore, the basis upon which a 'critical' sociology could be founded. Equally, he rejected a purely action-type approach such as that being proposed by phenomenologists and ethnomethodologists, on the ground that they had lost sight of the structuredness of social action, which alone would provide access to an understanding of power and inequality. Or, where they had grasped this reality (as in the case of Berger and Luckmann) (ibid.: 67ff), they only saw 'structuring' as happening within the realm of the reflective consciousness of individuals, thus reducing the critique of society to the critique of knowledge.

Bauman was interested in reconciling the two sides of the truth that he found in Marx, who, he says, was concerned with the central problem that human life never takes off from a base-line of freedom, but is always hemmed in by constraint, from the start. Yet human action is at the same time free, in the sense of willed or motivated. This life-long interest in culture stems from Bauman seeing this field as the one in which this fundamental insight can be best recognized conceptually. At the same time, the concept keeps us in touch with the level at which human life is habitually lived.

Culture is linked inextricably with power because some people are able to structure the world more than others; and they do so *for* others. These 'others' find that their world is structured for them and they are able to structure the world less than the 'structurers', who are the more powerful. Bauman has increasingly come to see modernity as a general structuring or ordering drive, with power implications. Latterly he has come to say that it is running up against its own inherent limits; it is a doomed project, because the urge to structure, or order, always creates new 'problems', or further untidiness (which he calls ambivalence). Even though both structure and structuring are involved in the human life process, it is quite clear that Bauman sees his sociology as being dedicated to recognizing as fully as possible the extent of *structuring*. Human life is active, conscious life – in the Marxian terminology, it is *praxis*. Thus: 'The continuous and unending structuring activity constitutes the core of human praxis, the human mode of being-in-the-world' (1973a: 56). Culture is structure. But it is, more fundamentally, *praxis*, that is, ordering in the quite neutral sense of reducing uncertainty. On the political or ethical level, Bauman himself is committed to extending human freedom. This is partly what he sees sociology as being 'for'.

In his English-language writings, this metatheory of culture is worked out on the socio-historical level initially in *Socialism: The Active Utopia* (1976b). There, socialism is seen as a changing vision of the good society, drawing action forward[1] into the future; and crucially serving as a measuring device, in the light of which the present flawed reality is judged wanting. Firstly, Bauman attacks the dualistic idea that culture is about values, as distinct from something else called structure. He finds this assumption to underlie both structural functionalism and its mirror-image critique, conflict theory. It is not, he says, a simple matter of whether everyone supports or shares in the central value system; or whether, on the contrary, it is structures which coerce people into compliance. Matters are far more complex than this. Secondly, Bauman's discussion of the problems facing socialism, understood as a horizon of expectations or demands, depends heavily on Gramsci's notion of the existing social order entering into and constituting everyday common sense. The status quo is a cultural reality and any future alternative to it will have to take a similarly cultural form.[2]

Both of these arguments follow closely from the conception of culture as *praxis* – as the communal, human way of ordering experience or constructing reality. Culture is not something added on to social relations,[3] which are somehow harder, tougher or more fundamental.[4] It is the very substance of shared social existence.[5] Culture is Janus-faced: 'It is, simultaneously, the objective foundation of the subjectively meaningful experience and the subjective "appropriation" of the otherwise inhumanly alien world' (1973a: 117). We can understand this the moment we reflect on the fact that the term culture, used conventionally, refers *both* to order and predictability *and* to creativity. In *Culture as Praxis* (1973a), Bauman had already suggested that the ordering function of culture takes on a peculiar state-assisted character in modern times. Later this was to be developed as the Gellnerian idea of a garden as opposed to a wild culture. In modern societies ambiguity becomes a problem, eliminating it a mission. Cultural crusades develop. This idea was later to be developed considerably by Bauman in *Modernity and the Holocaust* (1989) and *Modernity and Ambivalence* (1991). Here we need only note that in *Culture as Praxis* the Jews are mentioned in connection with this category of the ambiguous: or, as Sartre would have it, '*le visqueux*' (Bauman 1973a: 136–7).

POWER

Bauman's treatment of power is possibly his single most accomplished sociological analysis. It is linked to the central role he gives to culture; culture is interpreted more widely than it has customarily been in the British and American traditions. Structuring is the essence; it is the human capacity to order, to separate, to draw boundaries. Power is the way this happens between groups of people. This makes power as endemic as culture to the human situation. It 'works' by making the predictability of others' behaviour the prerogative of some groups as distinct from others. Or vice versa, some groups can make themselves relatively more unpredictable for others: this gives them more power.

To paraphrase Bauman: the degree of control that a group or an individual has over any given situation depends on how much of the other side's behaviour can be determined. To extend control in this way, the group must eliminate as much uncertainty from the other side's behaviour as possible. The other side must be deprived of the room for manoeuvre. Control increases as the other side's conduct becomes less and less unpredictable: it can be seen as repeatable, routine, governed by rules, and so on. This can be achieved in several ways. In the case of coercion, deviance from the pattern is rendered unlikely by the prospect of punishments which make the costs of such disobedience prohibitively high. Or, those subject to power can be deprived of any insight into the possibility of a state other than the one they are in, thus again making action aimed at changing things extremely unlikely because the contingent, or humanly fabricated, nature of power is not seen clearly. The other side's freedom of action can be curtailed directly. They can be made to carry out only routine actions and so their capacity for the exercise of choice is sapped and withers through non-use. The upshot of all these devices is that the other side ceases to be a source of uncertainty. Its decisions do not figure in the equation. It can be effectively discounted as an actor, and hence as a player in the current game. As Bauman puts it, 'one could disregard [the other side] as a source of action and, consequently, as a factor in calculating the results' (1982: 95).

This idea lies behind Bauman's acceptance and use (in *Memories of Class*, 1982) of Foucault's generalized notion of disciplinary power. Bentham's Panopticon is the central image: the inmates' actions become thoroughly transparent to the guardian who has a full view of all inmates at all times.[6] This is something distinctively modern. It develops with the centralization of power

219

in the absolute monarchies. Before this time, populations were not subject to the actions of states; rulers' interest in their subjects was intermittent and confined to creaming off the economic surplus. Power did not extend to people's minds and bodies. This conception is the pivot on which hinges Bauman's interpretation of the formation of class society (and its subsequent 'exhaustion'). Post-modernity enters the picture when *repression*, as he later calls the power complex of modernity, comes to be supplemented by the *seduction* of consumer society (although it should be noted that consumption is in no sense 'power free' – it is about the struggle for self and group identity). For the moment, however, it will be enough to remark on the various empirical contexts in which Bauman uses his conception of power.

Take, for example, the situation of factory labour in the early phase of the industrial revolution. Factory discipline, he says, was 'forced down the throats of recalcitrant workers with the help of finicky and intrusive rules' (1982: 63). Between them, these stipulations tended to regulate every moment of a worker's time on duty. A long list of such requirements was collected by the Hammonds, for example, and it testifies to the relentless ingenuity of the early factory owners. The Hammonds show how, at Tyldesley Mill, one case among many, the door was locked throughout the working day; a spinner found dirty was fined a shilling, the same fine was levied on one found washing; or heard whistling, or with an opened window. Bauman comments that the remarkable feature of such rules was their manifest irrelevance to whether or not labour was performed efficiently. Factory rules often could not be complied with, because one would contradict another. The object of the rules was to force the labourers into a total and unquestioning submission. What the rules expressed was the drive to control absolutely and in every detail the bodily movements of the workers. And thereby, too, presumably, their spiritual existence also. The 'battle' was for 'full domination over workers' bodies' (ibid.: 63).

Actors are here hemmed in by rules; the rule-makers enjoy the freedom of rule-setters (or uncertainty-generators). The same idea can be found in Bauman's stress on the repressed condition of the beneficiaries of state-support in the consumer society: those who are deemed incapable of fending for themselves, i.e. behaving as consumers. He quotes numerous instances of how such people's lives are subject to an intense scrutiny by others, who are not themselves scrutinized in return. 'Means testing' is the classic ground of such ordering activity on the part of the state and its officials (1987a: ch. 11).

The most poignant of Bauman's analyses is, however, undoubtedly that of the plight of the Jews during the Holocaust and earlier, in the years of the assimilatory drive, particularly in Germany. The role of the relatively powerless here falls under the microscope. This makes the analysis of the power relationship fully two-way. And it produces a deeply insightful reading which succeeds in dispelling a central puzzle of the Holocaust, namely why there was so little resistance. It is a sociological truism since Simmel that freedom is always involved in action: there is no such thing as the truly powerless actor. Still, the role of the victims' freedom, and with it the deployment of those actors' rationality, in securing the outcome – mass destruction of European Jewry – has not been more clearly examined or more trenchantly stated than in Bauman's chapter in *Modernity and the Holocaust* (1989) on 'soliciting the co-operation of the victims'.

Bauman points out that in part the Holocaust was possible because the victims co-operated with their tormentors and executioners. The diabolical nature of the Holocaust lay in the fact that everything the victims did contributed to the Hitlerian design. Choice situations were so structured at each stage that the rational decisions of the victims were harnessed to the genocidal purpose. The greater freedom of manoeuvre – the capacity for unpredictability – of those who controlled the social machinery of extermination was used to create situations for the Jews in which they could not avoid believing – or could only with the utmost difficulty – that their best chance lay in trying to save what could be saved and thereby preferring the 'least-worst' option. Their compliance – tragically – only made the end more certain.

Bauman's point is that this is the means whereby bureaucratic oppression normally works, even in less extreme situations. He says of the Jews: 'the doomed population had apparently a range of options to choose from. Co-operation with their sworn enemies and future killers was not without its own measure of rationality' (ibid.: 122). They assisted, while rationally seeking to survive. Like bureaucratically controlled populations in general, the Jews were 'captive', sealed off: their help could then be enlisted. The victims had to behave logically because survival apparently depended on such behaviour: their captors found in an unplanned way that they could manipulate this for their own purposes.

The Nazis stumbled gradually upon the realization that their victims' behaviour could be made predictable; and by the same token, manipulable and controllable. And that to achieve this they had to induce their victims to behave rationally. This, in turn, could be accomplished by getting the victims to believe that if they responded positively, something could in fact be saved; and that making such a response was a matter of following certain agreed principles. There must be 'something to save' and 'clear rules as to how one should go about saving it' (ibid.: 130). The victims had to be convinced that the group as a whole would not be treated the same: each individual would be treated on merit. Their individual conduct must be seen to matter. What was involved in this setting was the tacit acceptance by many of the Jewish leaders themselves of the principle that some persons deserve their fate, and the objective differences between people that this implies. This, in turn, was prompted by the rational 'save what you can' strategy. Survival chances seemed manipulable, using one's own resources.

This belief arose from the (externally) manipulated situation in which the Jewish communities were placed by their enemies. In effect, Bauman shows, the communal authorities became part, in fact the lowest rung, of the Nazi machine – the system of social organization that led to their immolation. Consistent with his view of power as unpredictable, in this case unthinkable, Bauman declares that '[i]t was because the ultimate objective of the Holocaust operation defied all rational calculation that its success could be built out of the rational actions of its prospective victims' (ibid.: 137). The objective was so monstrous that the victims could not imagine it. '[T]he *rationality of the ruled*', Bauman remarks, '*is always the weapon of the rulers*' (ibid.: 142; italics in original).

The moral implications are stark indeed: under these conditions self-preservation becomes an absolute imperative. Revealed in the Holocaust, Bauman comments, is the possibility of a sharp antinomy between psychological rationality and objective rationality, understood as an action's *consequences*. Where some are relatively powerless and others have very great power, the rationality of the actor – the psychological kind – can turn into a suicidal weapon because it does not chime in, and finds no alignment, with the actor's situation. Then, rational considerations push the actor to forget his or her moral qualms; and the action so guided ends in defeating its own purpose. In the end, nothing is saved. 'Under sharply asymmetrical power conditions rationality of the ruled is ... a mixed blessing' (ibid.: 149; italicized in original).

This asymmetrical power structure is also found in the context of the Jewish drive towards assimilation in the nineteenth and twentieth centuries. The Jews, it seemed, had to be tested by the group to which they aspired to assimilate. But there was no way that the Jews could pass this test. 'The "anti-Semites" ', Bauman writes, 'wrote the scenario for Jewish self-constructing and self-enabling efforts.' They did so by listing the traits for which the Jews were to be rejected. 'They had all the initiative ... from writing the scenario to the critique of the production and the ultimate sanction of firing the cast.' That is, actions of the Jews took their meaning from others' evaluations of them. The preju-diced among the German population were both judges and accusers. The accused had not only to show that the charges were untrue, but also to convince others that they could not apply in the future also. Clearly, the task was impossible. For 'the same people who brought forth the charges would pronounce on the cogency of the proofs' (1991: 115).

The Jews, Bauman writes, were the victims not just of the Nazis but of modernity, as are other groups also who 'sit astride the barricades' (a favourite metaphor). Jews were ambiguous. They were the foreigners 'inside'. As the boundary-drawing urge of modernity grew, so did hatred of the Jews. 'The conceptual Jew was a semantically overloaded entity, comprising and blending meanings which ought to be kept apart, and for this reason a natural adversary of any force concerned with drawing border-lines and keeping them watertight' (1989: 39).[7] As the pre-modern status order collapsed, so regulation, keeping things apart that should be so kept, became an immense undertaking. '[T]here was hardly a single door slammed on the road to modernity in which the Jews did not put their fingers. ... They were the opacity of the world fighting for clarity, the ambiguity of the world lusting for certainty' (ibid.: 56; second sentence, italicized in original). While we will return to this highly significant theme later, we merely note here that culture and power – ordering and controlling uncertainty – are linked in a more fundamental way in Bauman's writings than might appear at first sight. They form the primary drive to structure the world according to a rational design.

MODERNITY AND POST-MODERNITY

In *Culture as Praxis* Bauman says that he would prefer to see culture as the making of taboos to 'keep things apart'. (This is in contrast to what he sees as the Durkheimian view in which society creates the sacred, which has the function, among other things, of moralizing its members.) Marginality then arises as a topic. There is a 'we–them' border. (See also Bauman 1990a: ch. 2.) Ambiguity must be resolved. Culture strives towards unambiguous borders and boundaries. Marginality, however, involves not just borders, but rather 'falls on everybody who dares to question the "natural", supra-human, once-and-for-all character of the order imposed on and by the common praxis' (1973a: 131). Interestingly, as early as 1973, in his English-language writings at any rate, Bauman considers the possibility of the slackening within Western societies of this drive to 'establish the borders'. He sees the glimmerings of a counter-tendency to the one on which culture is based. 'The tendency in question', he wrote,

> denies the very need of the struggle ... it denies the sliminess of the slimy [i.e. the ambiguous or marginal – *'le visqueux'*]. ... What seems to be emerging slowly ... is a new level of tolerance toward sliminess, and, indeed, toward trespassing of vital functions of meaning. ... If the chance materializes, human culture will face a revolution unmatched by the most drastic upheavals of the past.
>
> (ibid.: 156–7)

The features of this tendency are, furthermore, 'not located on the left–right axis' (ibid.). Post-modernity is foreshadowed here.

Already, in *Memories of Class* (1982) it is clear that for Bauman the *modern* (cultural) order is a *legislative* one. Time and again in Bauman's books he comes back to the documented eighteenth-century experience of 'masterless men'. With the collapse of the protective system of the pre-industrial order, the number of beggars, vagrants and other displaced people multiplied. This was accompanied by state action designed to avert this threat to social 'order'. Legislative action aimed at containing and confining these displaced people was 'fervent, at times panic-stricken'. Legislators, manufacturers, doctors and psychiatrists 'co-operated in using enclosure as a main method of separating order from disorder, the speakable from the unspeakable, the visible from the unseen' (ibid.: 8).

In *Legislators and Interpreters* (1987a) Bauman was to argue that this 'legislative bustle' on the part of the modern state was the source of the characteristically modern conception of culture as a cultivating kind of activity (the German *Bildung* expresses it well). Education in the widest sense and the activity of intellectuals, as suppliers of blueprints and as teachers or instructors of the public, attended this development. This situation of intellectual activity defined the modern intellectual role as a legislating one. Reason was the touchstone, the guiding principle in the name of which this cultivating, educating activity was carried on. And because it was a programme involving Foucault's disciplinary power, it is quite clear that knowledge and power are indissolubly linked. Science had always had a social role – it has even been turned to genocidal purposes in the twentieth century. Culture is here firmly identified with the modern project of conquering nature and producing the perfect society. It makes no difference whether it is the society of sovereign individuals of capitalism or of the communists' 'social regulation of needs'.

This development in Bauman's vision is foreshadowed in *Memories of Class*, where he sketches for the first time the supersession of the old sovereign power, the erosion of the protective institutions of the old 'wild culture' and, accompanying these changes, the mounting repression of popular and folk culture by powers bent on moral regulation over the totality of the life process through surveillance. '[I]diosyncrasy... is stigmatized, criminalized, medicalized or psychiatrized' (1982: 41). As social control is extended in this manner, so one can witness the emergence of the modern notion of the duality of human nature. For the modern person, reason will triumph over animality, and must be made to. The prominent division becomes one between enlighteners and enlightened. The cultural crusade or the civilizing mission thus become possible, as they are inherent in the new disciplinary power.

In this book, protest directed at this disciplinary effort, particularly by skilled craftspeople[8] who could remember an era of personal independence, is the key element in the making of class society – a particular kind of society which Bauman now regards as receding. Two processes were at work. On the one hand, the disciplinary power bears down on all the uprooted, making them into a single class. On the other hand, the skilled artisans resist being treated along with all the others as subject to discipline; they remember the guild system and aim to avoid disciplinary power within the factory. This gave rise to distinctively class forms of organization. Disciplinary power does eventually triumph in the factory as the conflict is 'economized', but the workers fight back through the struggle over wages, or distribution. Since distribution is not normatively controlled, the contest over rewards is an open-ended one,[9] though it is always one in which power is involved. In this kind of conflict, power struggle is defused or, the state having become drawn into the process, the consequences off-loaded on to distributional quarrels.

Like many writers in the 1970s and 1980s (Habermas, Offe, O'Connor), Bauman believed that the system had run up against certain limits, principally the production limitations of the capitalist economy and the capacity of the system to cope with the attendant demands on it. He, like them, detected a deep-seated fault-line in the capitalist arrangement of power in the Western democracies and became convinced that a crisis was afoot (Bauman 1982: 32, 150, 191ff).[10] But, for Bauman, this became not the crisis of capitalism, but that of *modernity*.[11] In analysing this crisis he attributed a greatly enhanced significance to consumption, consumers and consumerism. Here we have the key to the political economy, so to speak, of post-modernity. The consumer orientation is first developed as a 'by-product ... of the industrial pattern of control'. It has now been 'prised from its original stem and transformed into a self-sustained and self-perpetuating pattern of life. A new type of power is called for, one that cannot be seen as the opposition between reason and passion, prudence and self-indulgence, work and idleness'. The spread of the new powers typical of consumer society is a 'de-civilizing process'. 'Passions, self-indulgence, entertainment are cleansed of disgrace. ... The new powers are articulated in terms of self-identity, authenticity, fullness of life, etc.' (ibid.: 180). Bourdieu's idea of 'seduction', later used by Bauman extensively, here makes its first appearance. So, too, does the idea of the victims of post-modernity: the repressed. 'The field of the most drastic inequalities, conflicts and unresolved problems has shifted ... towards the deprived sectors of social life' (ibid.: 191).[12]

226

THE ROAD TO THE POST-MODERN CONDITION

Bauman has always been intensely preoccupied with the role of intellectuals, their social function and the situation of intellectual activity. There are traces of these concerns throughout his writings. The problem of the function of intellectuals is a concern of *Socialism: The Active Utopia* (1976b). Intellectuals are culture creators and therefore *ipso facto* power contenders. In modern times intellectuals have claimed to be guided by reason. Apparently, this was what made socialism superior. But the role of socialist intellectuals as guides and leaders of the masses raises fundamental ethical and political questions; Bauman showed in his chapter on the Soviet experiment that he was acutely conscious of these. One suspects that he sought to escape from them through the idea of socialism as a utopia or counter-culture of capitalism, that is, a horizon of hope,[13] from which the present reality could be criticized.[14] However, this avoided the issue rather than confronting it.

Bauman's unease, as we can see in retrospect, was indicated at the point where he identifies as a feature of utopian thought, changing people through education, expressed classically by Rousseau as '[o]n façonne des plantes par la culture et les hommes par l'éducation' (quoted by Bauman 1976b: 23). Bauman observes that there is an élitist component in European culture: there are educators and there are the educated. There are 'the benevolent despot; the Legislator; the Philosopher; [and] the Scientist' (ibid.: 24). They all claim in their own ways esoteric knowledge and superior insight.

> This answer is still very much with us, deep down in the commonsense of the twentieth century, manifesting its presence in whatever has been left of our almost uncritical faith in the ability of science and the scientists to pave the way to a better and more congenial future.
>
> (ibid.)

The same is true on the Left. Here the reality is seen as changing spontaneously. But it needs a midwife – the social scientist or the 'guides': both of these figures make up for the weakness of the individual who cannot see properly. The utopian attitude involves the idea that 'people must be led into a better life, either by force, or by being shown the pattern they otherwise would not construct for themselves' (ibid.). Only the intellectual élite can reconstruct themselves; only they can be trusted to learn independently. There is an affinity between this deeply engrained attitude and modern science: the latter involves the 'substitution of a human-made and human-desired order for the natural one, which obviously was not cut to the measure of human needs' (ibid.: 29). And the same thing holds for liberalism, whose adherents held that what already obtains is basically sound, but it needs re-arranging. For the revolutionary socialists, once modernity was entered upon, a perversion of the good society resulted; it all has to be swept aside, and a fresh start made.

There is a second worry, barely articulated in *Socialism*, but none the less implied in it. If socialism is the counter-culture of capitalism, then perhaps its fate is ultimately bound up with it, in a way other than the dialectics of transcendence articulated in classical Marxism. Perhaps if capitalism, or industrial society as Bauman called it in the 1970s, runs into insoluble difficulties as a type of social system, socialism will somehow be implicated in that transformation, at least to the point that the family resemblance will become more than merely an oft-remarked paradox. Perhaps a deeper similarity (their common root in modernity) will come to be evident. A hint of this – Bauman's later view – is expressed in *Socialism*. A counter-culture, he says, 'contains a dialectical and conflict-ridden unity of continuity and rejection' (ibid.: 47).

> To be a counter-culture, a system of beliefs and postulates must engage in a significant polemic with the dominant culture, must question it, so to speak, in its own words, and to do so must speak essentially the same language.
>
> (ibid.)

Was there more to this 'same language' than met the eye? We are facing, Bauman wrote, a loss of utopian horizon. 'The socialist utopia has brought contemporary society as far as possible while acting within the framework circumscribed by what has come to be known as industrial society' (ibid.: 108). 'The advanced socialist thought of today is breaking new horizons, reaching beyond the historical limits fixed by the industrial epoch *for both bourgeois culture and its traditional socialist counter-culture*' (ibid.: 111; italics added). But was it just traditional socialism that was implicated or perhaps socialism *tout court*?[15]

In *Legislators and Interpreters* (1987a) the answer is clear. The full implications of the thesis emerging but not yet fully proposed in *Socialism* are accepted. And they are profound ones: the situation of the intellectual has fundamentally changed, and with it, the relationship of the intellectual to power, and its concentrated embodiment in modern times, the state. Intellectual practice as it has been known until recently[16] was, he says, conducted within assumptions framed by intellectuals' collective memory of the Enlightenment. This is modernity. Power and knowledge conjoin to produce a syndrome, in which, loosely, the state has the ambition and, to a considerable extent, the capacity to administer society according to a blueprint. There emerges, concurrently, a type of discourse capable of supplying this blueprint and the attendant practices of administration. Post-modernity, again loosely, is understood as the disengagement of the two halves of this modern conjuncture. The state goes in one direction; intellectual practice, its erstwhile servant and inspiration, goes in another: each sphere undergoes an inner transformation that makes the separation complete, and sets the partners off on different roads. Bauman implies that in the future this separation will more and more be the case.

Following Phillipson, he likens modernity to a vessel at sea: 'the ship [modernity] has passed by; its passage roughened the waters, left a turbulence so that all sailors would have to rework the course of their boats' (1991: 271). From our vantage point in its wake we can gain a perspective we never had when we were on the ship (inside modernity). We can see modernity, in other words, as a *project* – with all its flaws as well as its grandeur – something that was never possible for its prophets.[17] Stated thus, the idea of post-modernity as an awareness of limits is unobjectionable.

Perhaps more striking is Bauman's notion of the impossibility of modernity: an awareness perhaps that the ship could *never* reach its destination. The idea is explored in *Modernity and Ambivalence* (1991), where post-modernity is described as 'modernity coming to terms with its own impossibility' (ibid.: 272). Previously stated theses are re-stated; this ground has already been thoroughly trodden earlier. 'Civilizing' is a power process; it is repressive. Culture is still at the heart of the analysis. The eighteenth-century period of the early industrial revolution, now termed the onset of modernity, was marked by a cultural crusade.

Reflecting Bauman's unrelenting interest in power, absolutism –
the rise of centralized monarchies in Europe and their successors
– involved a new type of power: it is now termed legislative
power. The accompanying civilizing mission is seen as a bid for
a share in this power. Those who defined it were its prophets and
executors, the men of letters – *les philosophes.*

The rise to power of the absolute state was accompanied by
the destruction of popular culture. Masterless people arose. Intellectuals supplied an 'order' – as teachers. The power–knowledge
complex formed. Culture came to be seen as cultivation.[18] A
certain modern vision arose from Marx to Simmel. But now, in
the contemporary period, all the modern hierarchies are broken
(as is the power configuration sustaining them). There has been
a collapse of Matthew Arnold's sense of culture because there
are now no common values: aesthetic, moral or cognitive
(Bauman 1991: 156). Culture moves away from its former function of systemic integration. There are no integrating values, and
models of the social system founded on this assumption – including the counter-models which are built on the denial of this –
become untenable. Now at the level of social integration, there
is only the market.

The post-war debate over the significance of mass culture, in
which protagonists were either for or against the phenomenon,
now shows its age, since the debate still reflected the assumptions
and concerns of those who would be legislators. Intellectuals were
here concerned with culture, the masses and the binding and
elevating effect of the former upon the latter. Now, however,
life's needs are met through consumption. To be precise, the
alternatives seem to be either communist-style 'dictatorship over
needs' (Féher et al. 1983) or the market for consumer goods,
unassisted in the case of the majority by the state. By and large
the state retreats. Within the non-communist states, power is
deployed through the *seduction* of the majority in the shape of
the offering of consumer goods, and for those who cannot qualify
as consumers, through *repression.*[19] By and large, Bauman
observes, the state 'engages' people not as producers principally,
but as consumers. Accompanying this, the intellectuals lose their
former role as legislators. They were not needed in a justificatory
role in the communist states, which articulated values on their
own, without the intellectuals' assistance. In the West, however,
the market effectively determines values, again unassisted.

A significant shift has thus occurred in Bauman's views. He now no longer claims to detect a socialist utopian horizon as a potential social reality. He is able to account for the retreat of the state from active social engagement in the 1980s in several of the major Western countries. And he has struck out on his own with a model of social-systemic integration that has departed substantially from his earlier somewhat derivative ideas on the systemic crisis of capitalism (although he had called it industrial society). He is now operating on the plane of the modern and post-modern, and couching his analysis in terms of vantage points and 'intellectual situation', rather than purely concrete socio-economic analysis. The continuity lies in his retaining the idea that reality is interpreted and understood; and it is that element of 'memory' or consciousness that matters in cultural and political terms. Intellectuals, freed from their legislative role, unwanted by the contemporary state, have a chance – an opportunity – to develop their discourses unhindered by power considerations of the type that formerly held them in thrall. They can become interpreters. They can simply offer up their ideas to whoever will listen, so to speak, without strings.

THE HOLOCAUST AS A MODERN PHENOMENON

The fresh look that Bauman urges we take at modernity from the post-modern standpoint is exemplified in *Modernity and the Holocaust* (1989). Rationality and efficiency – both products of the civilizing mission, implemented progressively by the 'gardening state' – were, Bauman says, necessary conditions of genocide. The Holocaust as a modern programme is inconceivable without bureaucracy and technocracy. The modern mentality stresses control and the engineering of solutions to 'technical' problems. To achieve this, discipline – the idea of duty – and the following of orders are necessary. Furthermore, modern solutions are implemented at a distance from the perceived problem sources. Long chains of command are involved. Order-givers do not execute their decisions themselves, but do so rather through a chain of intermediaries. These mediating links in the chain, as Weber observed long ago, have pre-set, finite, technical tasks to fulfil. In the course of fulfilling them, the overall effect of the operation becomes invisible. This is the normal, modern way of doing things and in this respect the Holocaust was normal too.

Civilization did not 'fail'. On the contrary, one important dimension of civilization made the Holocaust possible. Like other engineering efforts, it was planned, rational and scientifically informed. It employed experts, was increasingly efficiently managed, using the rational co-operation of the victims. And it was co-ordinated. It brought together a complex of modern technologies from transport to the techniques of extermination themselves.

Genocide throws a different light on the social functions of utopia and on the achievements of modern society, of which all utopias are a part. It was seen as a means to an end: the perfect society. It was a form of social engineering, part of an overall plan. As such it partook – in its holism, in its ambitiousness – of modernity. The whole of society was to be re-made on a scientific basis through the elimination of 'undesirable' minorities. Reality was to be improved, to be made objectively better, aesthetically more pleasing.

In this perspective, the crimes of Hitler and Stalin are not to be seen as aberrations, as departures from the upward curve of the path of civilization. Nazism and communism are the same in this perspective. They are products of the garden culture and of the civilizing drive to re-make the world. De-humanization is possible under modern conditions to the degree that the passions are disciplined, moral questions removed from the field of vision and human behaviour made through an extreme 'instrumentalization' to go 'in any direction', the 'good' or the natural part of human nature being overlaid by institutions that make it almost infinitely flexible. The Hobbesian picture of an untamed human nature requiring discipline to become 'good' is thus turned upside down. Furthermore, modern power is centralized, concentrated power: power as potential, and therefore capable of issuing in a degree of violence not feasible in pre-modern societies.

The machinery of the Holocaust was bureaucratic. To reiterate, it employed means that are routinely used in modern societies. The victims were isolated from the surrounding population, who could not see them. As captives their help could be enlisted. Actions were systematically encouraged that contributed to the overall plan, without their authors being aware of it. In the co-operating, many of the victims came tacitly to accept the racist logic of their tormentors: that some are less worthy than others, some should be sacrificed before others who were 'more deserving' and should be spared. Like those who worked within the machine, the community leaders who were co-opted on to the lowest rungs could hardly help but concentrate on the immediate, practical tasks at hand. They, too, could easily avoid confronting what lay at the end of the line down which the machine was being propelled by the planners and the experts. This is not a far cry from experiences common to the point of ordinariness in advanced industrial societies and the large-scale organizations through which all major public undertakings are administered in the twentieth century.

Essentially, the modern project is doomed to failure, says Bauman, because it can never be completed. The irrationality concealed in the worship of reason is that it is purposeless, merely technical and therefore unbounded by any finite, achievable results. This much has been said before, notably by Horkheimer and Adorno, whose views Bauman endorses: 'Enlightenment is mythic fear turned radical. . . . Nothing at all may remain outside because the mere idea of outsideness is the very source of fear' (Horkheimer and Adorno 1944: 16). Enlightenment involves the domination of people and nature. It has extinguished its own self-consciousness. It is effective, but in the end self-destructive. Bauman adds sociological flesh to these philosophical bones. The drive to produce order cannot but extrude, as a by-product, ambiguity, in the shape of things that fit neither category – insider or outsider, belonging or not belonging, native or foreign, strange or familiar. Modern practice sustains and produces both order and ambivalence, as Bauman terms it, equally. Thus, ambivalence cannot ever be defeated. Perhaps his most fruitful application of this idea is his analysis of the contradictions of the Jewish assimilation drive in Europe.

Liberalism, he argues, contains a deception. Assimilation to a dominant culture – like all acts of individual mobility or migration – requires that the superiority of the rulers and their way of life and ideas be conceded. This is the price of admission. Liberalism holds out the promise of assimilation to all. Yet this offer is not, in a sense, meant to be taken up by everyone. If it was acted upon successfully by all those outside the culture in question, inevitably the values enshrined in that culture would in the process be eclipsed. So, the offer is made confidently, because it is known – in advance as it were – that few will take it up. The values of the culture can appear invitingly universal because the power that sustains them remains invisible; and this hidden quality is possible because the masses do not successfully take up the assimilatory offer. The sustaining power is not needed by the culture except as a background factor. The culture is instead sustained by an ever-shifting series of discriminations that ensure that assimilation remains an ambition rather than a reality for the individuals aspiring to it.

The analysis of the doomed assimilatory drive – a case study in order and its ambivalence-generating 'progress' – proceeds in parallel to that of nationalism. The modern state aims to unify the population, particularly culturally: for the state, cultural diversity within its borders is a problem – state power sustains the national culture, so that political citizenship and cultural belonging tend to become synonymous. It was to the former – citizenship – that the Jews in Europe, but particularly German Jews, aspired, but to achieve it they had to acculturate themselves.

> The drive to acculturation put the ostensible identity of politics and culture to the test, and exposed the ambivalence with which the fusion was inescapably burdened and which in the long run proved responsible for the ultimate failure of the assimilatory programme.
>
> (1991: 142)

In this situation, where not all proceeded to assimilate at the same rate, those in the vanguard could not win. They remained identified with those, more 'backward', i.e. relatively unassimilated, than themselves.

Yet the difficulty was more fundamental still, for cultural identity can never be acquired; it cannot be allowed to seem what it actually is: '[T]he community, though itself a product of culture, could sustain its modality as a nation only through emphatic denial of a "merely cultural", i.e. artificial, foundation' (ibid.: 143). The would-be assimilants were therefore trapped in their in-between position. Wanting to assimilate, the aspirants tended to stress what was universal about them, rather than most parochial and therefore suspiciously 'backward'. But in doing this, they succeeded only in proving their eternal unfitness for acceptance into the particular, unique culture they aspired to share. It was this situation, Bauman argues, that underlay the first creative insights of people like Kafka and Simmel into the nature of modernity itself.

AN INTERIM REPORT

Even at this interim stage of Bauman's exploration of sociological problem areas opened up by the adoption of the post-modern vantage point, it is possible to see that for him power and culture are still the central concerns. Their interrelationship is what concerns him, as it did at the start of his inquiries. Two preliminary conclusions to the present attempt to trace the continuities in Bauman's work suggest themselves.

Firstly, the European 'civilizing process' has been understood by Norbert Elias (1939) as the long-term result of shifting *multi-polar* power balances between interdependent groups. Bauman, on the other hand, has developed, particularly in his book on the Holocaust, a contrasting *polarized*, 'élite–masses' interpretation. He asserts that the state-directed 'civilizing' drive was a two-pronged, sharply differentiated one. The work of the French social historian Robert Muchembled is quoted most recently in support of this (Bauman 1992b: 100–1). Civilizing was not, according to that writer, a matter of the 'trickling down' of behavioural standards first adopted in the upper class.

For Bauman, too, the active end of the modern character-formation process, visible among élites, involves the preoccupation with self-formation, self-drilling and self-improvement. There is also a receiving end, manifest in the tendency to biologize, medicalize, criminalize and increasingly police the masses, judged to be brutal, dirty and incapable of holding their passions in check. The most profound changes in sensibility are therefore seen as being limited to a narrow élite. This leads to a self-distancing and a vantage point from which the élite is able to see the masses as vulgar and, at first, uncivilizable. They have to be confined, policed and subjected to surveillance. Bauman comments: 'The civilizing process is best understood as the "recomposition" of the new structure of control and domination once the pre-modern institutions of social integration have proven inadequate and were gradually decomposed' (1992b: 101). Under conditions of the post-modern power configuration, this surveillance can now be lifted from part of the population. This section Bauman calls the seduced, contrasted with the repressed.

To repeat, modernity is essentially an active ordering of reality. In this respect it has an affinity to the disease metaphor through its connection to science. Having broken down the caste-like

divisions of the pre-modern world, modernity produces the challenge of 'foreigners in our midst', strangers, and so forth. It also
offers the solution, albeit an irredeemably imperfect or incomplete one, in the form of a re-drawing of the boundaries – forcibly
and through the appeal to blood. Racism and its genocidal potential is therefore, while appearing archaic and pre-modern, on the
contrary, thoroughly modern. Moreover, it has employed in
the twentieth century the full force of state power and modern
technology to accomplish its ends. These are ever-present tendencies of modern society. But the balance may be shifting away
from the 'ordering' pattern.

The second principal conclusion Bauman offers is an emerging
model of society that incorporates his culture-inspired, though
not culture-dependent, post-modern diagnosis. The post-modern
mentality fits the emerging pattern of social relations of the consumer society for two reasons. Firstly, in a consumer society, what
are principally at stake are symbols rather than finite resources.
Consumerism has the remarkable feature of undoing certain key
antinomies which bound the industrial-type of society. The power
contest need not any longer be strictly zero-sum, one party necessarily losing as the other gains. As in Weber's vision of status
competition, there is the freedom to re-define oneself anew
through new symbolic means on another occasion. Something of
the old constraint of the power contest is lost. And, in addition,
the consumer can avoid the older 'costs' of freedom in the form of
isolation and loss of social conferment of selfhood, i.e. alienation,
because consumers can feel their choices applauded and shared
by others in a consumer culture.

Secondly, and more profoundly, the deployment of state power
in a consumer society is such that the post-modern proliferation
of ideas can be 'afforded', since such a flourishing of opinion
poses no threat to the position of the government. Power no
longer depends on a ruling ideology. Therefore, challenges to
ideology lose their force. Ideological legitimacy is not there to be
challenged. This is for the reason that social and system integration – as well as individual identity – are constructed for the
majority through the consumer market. The state has lost its role
because it is no longer needed to underwrite production. The
latter has ceased to be central, since the axis of power has shifted
to the sphere of consumption. This happens as the emancipatory

impulse shifts, or is displaced from production into consumption, where it is politically defused.

The contrast with the former communist states is striking. Communism, in a sense, embodied modernity more profoundly than its capitalist competitor. State power – disciplinary, surveilling – was developed to the ultimate degree – to the extent, in fact, 'of limiting the individual choice to the point of near-extinction' (1988: 86). Bureaucratic domination was exercised over the majority of the citizens. Such a system could not compete with a Western alternative, in which such surveillance was coming to be applied only to a minority. The majority in the West were becoming seduced consumers. In communist societies, voices raised in dissent, to even an apparently small degree, did have consequences for the cohesion of the entire system. And they were accordingly repressed.

This was a patronage state, one that manages the satisfaction of needs, as well as their definition, so it inevitably collectivized grievances. It is to the state that messages of dissatisfaction are eventually addressed. The post-modern sensibility flourishes in the West, because Western society systematically encourages it as a new form of social control substantially different from the older repressive form. This latter is now reserved for the few who lack the wherewithal to consume and are seen by intellectuals to have little or no political significance.

> Under post-modern conditions, when the exhilarating experience of ever new needs rather than the satisfaction of the extant ones becomes the main measure of a happy life (and thus the production of new enticements turns out to be the major vehicle of social integration and peaceful co-existence) the patronage state, adjusted to the task of defining and circumscribing the needs of its subjects, cannot stand competition with systems operated by the consumer market.
>
> (1991: 278)

The search for consumer goods and higher and different standards of consumption makes contemporary society 'work'. And insofar as it does, 'the coercive pressure of political bureaucracies may be relieved, the past political explosiveness of ideas and cultural practices defused, and the plurality of opinions, life-styles, beliefs, moral values or aesthetic views may develop undisturbed' (1988: 88).

The outlines of the emerging configuration – of culture, politics and society, no less than ethics, epistemology and aesthetics – are, Bauman concludes, by no means clear. What is certain is that a divide has been crossed, in the sense that some quite new conditions are appearing that throw into question the inherited assumptions of social and political theory, which were forged in the previous 'modern' era. The nature and function of sociology itself will, therefore, need to be re-thought. Entirely new areas of research, formerly masked by 'industrial society' assumptions, are thus coming into prominence. For Bauman himself, the most important of these is undoubtedly the question of morality, about which he first learned from his teacher Julian Hochfeld (Kilminster and Varcoe 1992: 208), but to which he had not returned until very recently.

The movement of Bauman's interest in this direction can be followed from the analysis he made in *Modernity and the Holocaust* (1989). There he wrote, following John Lachs, of the mediation of action (ibid.: 24–5), meaning that the consequences of an action are hidden from the actor because other people are involved in its implementation, often through a minutely specialized division of labour. The actor does not experience the action's consequences directly. The result is that it is always 'others' who carry out the purposes of whichever actor happens to stand above those others at each step in the chain of command – with the result that no one may feel responsible for the consequences of their action. Bauman calls this the flotation of responsibility (1993: 127). Each action both mediates, and is in turn mediated by, the next person in the chain. And so the part each actor plays in accomplishing the whole, collective task cannot be calculated. Its moral relevance is therefore effaced, because its causal role in producing the outcome cannot be assessed.

The counterpart of the flotation of responsibility on the level of individual action is the condition in which each actor is merely an agent of someone else's authoritative command, a tool or instrument, separated at once from the commander's purpose and those 'further down the line' who carry this actor's purpose forward for him or her, who are its executors, themselves in a similarly tool-like, or agentic (Milgram), state.

Additional mechanisms having a similar effect are identified in

Postmodern Ethics (1993). But we need only note how the problem of *flotation* identified in *Modernity and the Holocaust* provides the ground for the central thesis advanced in *Postmodern
Ethics*. This thesis is an extension of the moral predicament of
modernity and in a sense a response to it, though not a solution.
Post-modern society – if the modern condition has been eclipsed
– provides an opportunity morally, though it may not be grasped.
Something of the discipline of modern society may have been
relaxed, associated as we have seen in our discussion of the
political economy of post-modern society with the state having
'let go'. But now, more fundamentally, we have the chance to see
what we could not see before. Morality may not be a social
product. It may rather be pre-social.

In *Modernity and the Holocaust* Bauman wrote of 'moral pressures exerted by the existential mode, by the sheer fact of "being
with others" ' (1989: 174). He raised the question: has such a
'pre-social' moral awareness been crushed by the modern state,
at the same time that our consciousness of its possibility has been
obscured by modern 'legislating' intellectual practice as exemplified by a figure like Durkheim? '[S]ociety', he wrote, 'may ... on
occasion, act as a "morality-silencing" force' (ibid.: 174; italicized
in original).

This idea of 'pre-social grounds of moral behaviour' (ibid.:
177), as he puts it, requires that we revise radically our inherited
notions of the (social) sources of moral norms and their obligator-
iness. The argument is *a priori*. The experience of an immoral
society such as Nazi Germany teaches us that the ability to tell
right from wrong is an exception. But it is one which does not
follow any recognizable sociological pattern, all the conventional
'indicators' of such patterning of behaviour failing in the case of
those who defied the regime.[20] Such exceptional conduct *must be*
grounded in something other than the *conscience collective* of
society. Lévinas's importance lies in his being the philosopher
of the primal experience of 'being with others'. Bauman's concern
in *Postmodern Ethics* is to investigate the ways in which this can
be made sociologically relevant.

At this point, Bauman is not so far from his starting point in
utopia as a horizon of hope. Social theory inspired by liberalism
paints the 'other' in the dyadic relation as a source of uncertainty.
In other words, it builds a version of competitive individualism
into the way it presents the 'double contingency' (Parsons) of

interaction as precluding solidarity with the Other. Moral considerations are in effect squeezed out of the dyad in this paradigm. Bauman wants to recover the utopian moment[21] in 'being with the other' (1989: 182) ('being for the other'[22]), the key motif in which is an unconditional responsibility for the other. Responsibility comes with the proximity that bureaucracies, in particular, tend to destroy.

CONCLUSION

Lying behind this development in Bauman's thought is a central empirical observation from his study of the Holocaust: namely 'the amazing, logic-defying separation in the consciousness of most Germans between the images of Jew as such', that is, as 'a category', and the 'Jewish neighbour, the "Jew next door" ' (1993: 173n). This can only be explained by the 'moral saturation' of the personal image as distinct from the abstract stereotype. The 'proximity-cum-responsibility context within which personal images are formed surrounds them with a thick wall virtually impenetrable to "merely abstract" arguments'. The stereotype 'stops . . . where the sphere of personal intercourse begins. "The other" as an *abstract category* . . . does not communicate with "the other" I know'.

This second 'other' is the clue to Bauman's thinking in *Postmodern Ethics*. The passage from it to the abstract category is accomplished whenever the modern predisposition to genocide is realized – through a process of exclusion from the universe of moral proximity and responsibility. Saying farewell to this exclusionary possibility and recognizing its alternative is the challenge of post-modernity.

It marks a continuation of the same concerns, though not the same themes, which informed earlier books such as *Culture as Praxis* (1973a) and *Socialism: The Active Utopia* (1976b). However, a number of sociologists with socialist leanings, including Bauman, have in recent years employed this 'modernity gambit', as it may be termed, in response to the events and developments in Eastern and Western Europe. In this view, socialism and capitalism are simply two sides of the same modern coin. They thus share many basic assumptions. According to this argument, variants of which are offered, the problem is not capitalism, with socialism the solution, but rather modernity itself. Moreover, modernity has always been the problem. Hence, one is justified in rejecting the excesses of both the communist experiments and the old enemy, capitalism. On this view, both are more or less pathological versions of the same underlying disease. Until now, this condition has not been fully visible.

In our view, this argument depends heavily on the usefulness of the term 'modernity'. This general category is asked to do an enormous amount of explanatory work. Furthermore, in Bauman's recent writings in particular, it is used extensively and perhaps excessively, in a reified manner, in forms such as modernity 'is coming of age' and is now 'consciously abandoning what . . . it was unconsciously doing' (1990b: 23). It could be argued that such usages, whilst in some respects illuminating, do not lend themselves well to empirical application. Empirical grounding generally is not the thesis's strong point.

Consistently with our suggestion that the post-modern idea fills a gap, left by the departure of Marxism in particular, it is interesting to note that classical Marxian themes seem to have been recast by Bauman in a new key for a post-industrial, post-modern world. And yet, the 'emancipatory' edge of the original has been retained. A Marxist identification means, he says, looking for a class which will take up the 'redemptive struggles' of our time. This search is inherently problematic because

> [l]ike the factory workers of the early nineteenth century [today's] undifferentiated mass of sufferers cast out by the dissolving industrial society waits to be forged, through struggle, into a new power strong enough to focus upon itself the redemptive aspirations of our times.
>
> (1987b: 8)

Here, the older 'standpoint of the proletariat' has effectively been transformed. And yet, as the more diffuse identification with *any* underprivileged group, the 'horizon of hope' which it expressed, is retained: 'What does depend on socialists . . . is whether the criterion they and only they can promote and force into action . . . will figure as centrally in the coming history of post-modernity as it did in the past history of the modern era.' The application of this standard involves 'judging society by the *care it takes of its weakest member*'. And: 'when judged by this criterion the post-modern practice looks as flawed as its predecessor' (1990b: 23).

For Bauman and others, the post-modern world-view offers a fundamental critique of Marxism, understood as a 'metanarrative'

(Lyotard) or philosophy of history in the traditional sense. This is music to the ears of former critics of the versions of Marxism which were used by communist élites in Eastern Europe to buttress their power. On the other hand, post-modernism is widely understood as also being associated with political conservatism, relativism and nihilism. These are decidely unacceptable. It can be surmised that, for Bauman, a way must be found to reconcile these tensions. His strategy appears to be the one of solving this contradiction by adopting the post-modern vantage point as a way of opening up *sociological* issues. That is, as a way of looking at old questions in a new way.

Here we do find something of a contrast between him and the many writers in the present period who have rejected the 'one world-story' of Marxism, but have then apparently, equally zealously, gone over to another world-story, i.e. the post-modern insistence that *there is no* one world-story. However, the post-modern standpoint is only an imperative for those in our time who have believed, but no longer do, in a metanarrative – whether this be ethnic or racial destiny, the march of Reason in history, geographical determinism, evolutionary inevitability or the universal standpoint of women, though most commonly it is Marxism in one form or another. Bauman, however, unlike these authors, is steeped in the sociological tradition and he remains passionately attached to it. And from this point of view, the question of historical inevitability and the problem of a theory of society have been raised time and again. Consequently Bauman is like other sociologists. Very few indeed of them have ever believed in one world-story in the first place. Since at least Simmel and Weber, the fallacies of such a view have been widely known and discussed. It is not therefore a return to the untenable which is central to Bauman's project, but rather an exploration of his original theme of the human way of being-in-the-world, practised under what he sees as new conditions of cultural and moral fragmentation.

Bauman sits astride – to use his own metaphor – the socialist and the sociological. Both sets of concerns motivate him intellectually. His position, or rather perhaps his tireless mapping out of problems, is a highly sophisticated one. We would not agree with all of this. But it has not been part of our intention to offer a critical analysis. That task must be undertaken elsewhere, and by others. However, it is to be hoped that the ensuing debate will benefit from the signposts we have offered to a rich body of sociological insights and from the kind of broad scholarship of which Bauman himself is such an exemplar. Through his intellectual brilliance and familiarity with the tradition of sociology, he has helped both to extend that tradition and to ensure its continuing vitality in the face of our rapidly changing, always challenging times.

NOTES

1 'Gramsci's well-known view of organized action as the only available way of "verifying" social predictions fits this attribute of utopia very well' (1976b: 17).
2 This reflects the fact that culture is both given, accomplished, 'already there' *and*, on the other hand, something that is 'made' via the offering of a creative challenge to what is established and 'real' – socialism, of course, stresses, or should be about stressing, the second. 'Culture [too] ... is a daring dash for freedom *from* necessity and freedom to create' (1973a: 172).
3 Or something given, fixed, sedimented (for that would be a restricted view of culture), only one side of the coin, the other side of which is activity. Culture is a concept

ascertainable not in the relation to an accomplished, inflexible and ... stabilized entity, but in relation to a process, to the endless and open-ended chain of human activity ... [T]he function of cultural patterns consists in creating order *and* orientation; or, rather, in the two-pronged process of ordering societal environment and human-behaviour-in-this-environment. Neither of the two reciprocally constitutive sides of human praxis claims priority over the opposite side.

(1973a: 81–2)

By the same token, it is misleading to see 'social relations themselves' as somehow frozen. 'The social structure exists through the ever-continuing process of the social praxis; and this particular kind of existence is rendered possible by the fact that the praxis is patterned by a limited amount of cultural models' (ibid.: 105). Culture here is indeed Marx's *praxis* understood as the objective embodiment of activity which then once externalized constrains the active human subject. Bauman's point seems to be that culture will reveal the rules or grammar by which this process unfolds.
4 Bauman had seen that social structure versus culture was a dualism; and that it stood for the unhelpful opposition between structure and agency, as well as other philosophical dualisms of long standing.
5 Such a view is alien to the British and American anthropological traditions, as Bauman was only too aware. It is doubtful whether his conception was fully successful in re-orientating the theoretical

outlooks of sociologists, principally because the argument was advanced together with, and in the context of, a strong plea for the importance of structuralism as a research programme offering to fulfil the promise of the structured/structuring view of the human predicament. In its reception, one may surmise, it tended to share the same fate as its preferred vehicle. Without speaking of the grounds of objection to this vehicle, structuralism did not receive a wide endorsement among Anglo-American social scientists.

6 Bauman puts this rather well in *Freedom*:

It is the difference, not similarity, which integrates Bentham's system. The perfectly co-ordinated mini-society is held together by a strictly observed division of power. The division of power, in its turn, consists of nothing more than the distinction between a choice unrestrained and a choice reduced to the bare existential minimum; the distinction between freedom and unfreedom. Those who rule are free; those who are free, rule. Those who are ruled, are unfree; those who are unfree are ruled.

(1988: 21–2)

Later he says, 'those who are free to choose limit the choice of those who are placed at the receiving end'. The source of this insight is Michel Crozier. Power is linked to

control over the sources of uncertainty; those closest to the seats of uncertainty (those whose conduct *is* the source of uncertainty in the situation of others), rule. Action may generate uncertainty in so far as it is free from normative (legal or customary) regulation; the absence or paucity of norms renders conduct poorly predictable, and hence those affected by the conduct in question are exposed to the vagaries of will of those who may choose freely. On the other hand, people may disregard the behaviour of those ... who are normatively bound and hence behave routinely, in an easily anticipated way: repetitive, monotonous behaviour does not constitute the 'unknown' value in the situational equation.

(ibid.: 23; see also Bauman 1976b: 92)

7 'The conceptual Jew was ... slimy ... – an image construed as compromising and defying the order of things, as the very epitome and embodiment of such defiance' (1989: 39).

8 This is discussed and documented in *Between Class and Élite* (1972c; original Polish edition, 1960).

9 One cannot help being reminded of Durkheim at this point.

10 The basic arguments are (1) that the classes are schizoid about the state, for all depend on it to some degree and this impedes consistent state action; (2) that because the state 'divides up the cake', this process is removed from the classes pure and simple and exploitation is no longer simply a product of class society; and (3) that the economy cannot continue to support the consumerist 'buy off' because the demands are just too great.

11 After all, disciplinary power did not originate in the factory but was

extended to it. He did not at first use this terminology, preferring to speak of the crisis of industrial society as such; as the characteristic form of disciplinary power pervaded the production sphere, so consumption was opened up to struggle, and this he sees as being concerned with the symbolization of group identity.

12 These groups have no future in power terms. They are fragmented, 'voiceless', or their deprivation is 'mediated'. They have no adversary groups. Above all, they have no economic strength.

The argument at this point is that the economization of social conflicts, particularly manifest in the 1970s, is a substitute for a lack of power at work. Self-fulfilment as a task is displaced into the consumption sphere. The problem would appear to be the disciplinary power. This generates the maximizing spiral that threatens social integration. But what is the source of disciplinary power itself?

13 '[S]ocialism shares ... the unpleasant quality of retaining its fertility only in so far as it resides in the realm of the possible. The moment it is proclaimed as accomplished, as empirical reality, it loses its creative power' (1976b: 36).

14 Bauman sees socialism as 'a constantly active critical leaven within the texture of present society' (1976b: 51). Socialism (as it was for Gramsci) is culture fighting the bourgeois culture (hegemony) with a new philosophy, or concept of reality and human potentialities and social relations. It is not about institutions, or managing the economy.

> The power of socialism ... consisted in its status as the counter-culture of capitalism, and in its role as a thoroughly critical utopia, exposing the historical relativity of capitalist values, laying bare their historical limitations, and thereby preventing them from freezing into an horizon-less commonsense.
>
> (ibid.: 99)

Here the interrelations between socialism and culture are particularly apparent. Socialism is counter-*culture*; and its thrust is against the *culture* of capitalism. Referring to the ideas of Gramsci, Bauman says:

> The stability of capitalism acquired a cultural foundation. This means that the ideals of a good life, accepted ends of action, wants perceived as a reflection of needs, cognitive schemata which organize world perception, and above all the way in which the borderline between the 'realistic' and the 'utopian' has been drawn, sustain and perpetuate the totality of capitalist relations with little or no interference by the political state.
>
> (ibid.: 103)

Equally, change at the level of the state will not get rid of capitalism – a cultural shift is needed for socialism.

There are constant echoes here of Bauman's argument about culture as praxis. To see culture merely as what is learned is an implicitly conservative view. Utopia, by contrast, is a matter of imagined futures, fresh values that enter into action in the present and make the future 'open' (in a more than merely subjective sense). 'Utopias share with the totality of culture the quality – to paraphrase Santayana – of a knife with the edge pressed against the future' (ibid.: 12). Utopia is an image of the future that can only be tested in *practice*. We cannot know if it will work or not, in advance.

Possibility is itself a factor in any situation: whether a utopia is realistic or not can only be decided in the course of action. It cannot be decided by reference to a conservative realism, and to the measure of what is and has been. The full range of options must be considered in any situation; and this includes that which is desired, or hoped for, as a goal of action. What is *projected* is essential to human life itself.

15 In this book Bauman still believed in the mission of intellectuals enough to give them the historic mission not just as 'interpreters' but as makers of experience, of leading people to an 'alternative society' (1976b: 118).

16 And still today, since, Bauman insists, we are not speaking of self-contained, successive stages.

17 The idea of post-modernity as a *vantage point* has implications not just for our view of modernity but also for our perception of *its* judgements:

[T]his 'insider' experience of modernity ... supplies the frame of reference for the perception of non-modern forms of life. At the same time ... no outside vantage point was available as a frame of reference for the perception of modernity itself ... modernity was ... self-referential and self-validating.

(1991: 116)

So, as much as anything else, it is the mood that has changed:

What has happened in recent years could be articulated as the appearance of a vantage point which allows the view of modernity itself as an enclosed object, an essentially complete product, an episode of history with an end as much as a beginning.

(ibid.: 166)

At least, it may be instructive to think so.

Postmodernist discourse looks back at its immediate past as a closed episode, as a movement in a direction unlikely to be followed, as perhaps even an aberration, the pursuit of a false track, an historical error now to be rectified.

(ibid.: 177)

18 Culture *emerged*: 'The conditions had been created for culture to become conscious of itself as an object of its own practice' (1987a: 67).

19 Bauman has some interesting things to say about the working class. In *Memories of Class*, he says:

[T]he historically created institutions of organized labour ... are hardly adequate to the kind of action one would expect of a 'historical class', which cannot defend its own interests without fighting deprivation in all its forms.

(1982: 169)

Even more caustically:

The trade unionist form of labour organization ... is structurally committed to the defence of work ethics, the performance principle and welfare derived from the contribution to market exchange. It is ill fitted to face the challenge arising from the failure of the market to provide for an ever-growing part of the population.

(ibid.: 171)

On the fascination of intellectuals with the proletariat, since Marx, he is yet more trenchant still. The latter were seen as heroes by intellectuals, because they would usher in the rational society. This was a mistaken perception. Bauman's own researches convinced him of this. We know, he says, that 'their [the workers'] militancy reached its peak in the vain attempt to arrest "the progress of Reason", that is, the substitution of factory confinement for what memory held alive as the freedom of the petty producer' (ibid.: 174). However, 'at the time ... no such wisdom was available and it was easy to naturalize the historically occasioned militancy and impute to the restless, backward-looking factory hands the interests they did not possess' (ibid.).

20 There is a notable

absence of any correlation between the assumption of supreme moral responsibility [by those who did in respect to the Jews] and all the 'objective' or objectifiable factors which are believed to be the 'social determinants' of behaviour.... [M]orally induced conduct appears to be totally unpredictable, and thus ... uncontrollable.

(1993: 167)

21 He says (1993: 76) that in looking for morality before moral selves we are not exactly *founding* the moral self – morality cannot come before being. But it is the searching that counts: this is a utopian moment. He stresses the difference in this connection between a mere idle and abstract utopian fantasy and 'an *active utopia*' (italics ours), 'a utopia capable (*just capable*) of generating moral action' (ibid.). Note that there is the same promise of universality that was present in *Socialism* (1976b). Relativity is precisely not a feature of the ' "uncodified" moral condition' (but it is of power-driven – i.e. modern – ethics). We can now see 'the common moral condition that precedes all diversifying effects of the social administration of moral capacity' (1993: 14).

22 Actually, for Lévinas morality comes before ontology (being). Being *for* is before being *with*. We are moral selves before we are social selves (Bauman 1993: 13, 14, 72, 75).

BIBLIOGRAPHY OF THE WORKS OF ZYGMUNT BAUMAN

BOOKS

Zagadnienia centralizmu demokratycznego w pracach Lenina, Warsaw: Książka i Wiedza, 1957.

Socjalizm brytyjski: Źródła, filozofia, doctryna polityczna, Warsaw: Państwowe Wydawnictwo Naukowe, 1959.

Klasa-ruch-elita: Studium socjologiczne dziejów angielskiego ruchu robotniczego (Studia socjologiczno-polityczne 5), Warsaw: Państwowe Wydawnictwo Naukowe, 1960.

Z dziejów demokratycznego ideału (Biblioteka uniwersytetów robotniczych), Warsaw: Iskry, 1960.

Kariera: Cztery szkice socjologiczne (Wiedza, kultura, społeczeństwo; biblioteka uniwersytetów robotniczych), Warsaw: Iskry, 1960.

Z zagadnień współczesnej socjologii amerykańskiej, Warsaw: Książka i Wiedza, 1961.

Bauman, Zygmunt, et al., *Systemy partyjne współczesnego kapitalizmu*, Warsaw: Książka i Wiedza, 1962.

Sotsyologyah shel yahase enosh ['Robotnik; z dziejów stereotypu' (Hebr.)], Merhavya, 1962.

Społeczeństwo, którym żyjemy, Warsaw: Książka i Wiedza, 1962.

Zarys socjologii: Zagadnienia i pojęcia, Warsaw: Państwowe Wydawnictwo Naukowe, 1962.

The Limitations of 'Perfect Planning' (CAG occasional papers), Bloomington, Ind.: American Society for Public Administration, 1964.

Wizje ludzkiego świata: Studia nad społeczną genezą i funkcją socjologii, Warsaw: Książka i Wiedza, 1964.

Socjologia na co dzień (Seria 'Co to jest?'), Warsaw: Iskry, 1964.

Zarys marksistowskiej teorii społeczeństwa, Warsaw: Państwowe Wydawnictwo Naukowe, 1964.

Kariera: Cztery szkice socjołogiczńe (Seria 'Co to jest?'), Warsaw: Iskry, 1965.

Sociologie pro každý den [*Socjologia na co dzień* (Czech.)], Prague: Mlada Fronta, 1965.

Sociologie [*Socjologia na co dzień* (Czech.)], Prague: Orbis, 1966.

Kultura a spoleczeństwo: Preliminaria, Warsaw: Państwowe Wydawnictwo Naukowe, 1966.

Zarys marksistowskiej teorii spoleczeństwa, Warsaw: Państwowe Wydawnictwo Naukowe, 1966.

Kariéra: Sociologické črty [*Kariera* (Czech.)], Prague: Mlada Fronta, 1967.

Vizie l'udskeho svetga: Studia o spolocenskej geneze a funkcii sociologie [*Wizje ludzkiego świata* (Czech.)], Bratislava: Obzor, 1967.

Marksitička teorija društva [*Zarys marksistowskiej teorii spoleczeństwa* (Serb.)], Belgrade: Rad, 1969.

Lineamenti di una sociolgia marxista [*Zarys marksistowskiej teorii spoleczeństwa* (Ital.)] (Nuova biblioteca di cultura 101), Rome: Editori riuniti, 1971.

Between Class and Élite: The Evolution of the British Labour Movement: A Sociological Study, trans. S. Patterson, Manchester: Manchester University Press, 1972.

Culture as Praxis, London: Routledge & Kegan Paul, 1973.

Cultura come prassi [*Culture as Praxis* (Ital.)], Bologna: Mulino, 1976.

Socialism: The Active Utopia, London: George Allen & Unwin, 1976.

Socialism: The Active Utopia, New York: Holmes & Meier Publishers, 1976.

Towards a Critical Sociology: An Essay on Common-Sense and Emancipation, London: Routledge & Kegan Paul, 1976.

Bauman, Z. and Janos, A. C. (eds) *Authoritarian Politics in Communist Europe: Uniformity and Diversity in One-party States* (Research series/Institute of International Studies, University of California 28), Berkeley: Institute of International Studies, University of California, 1976.

Por uma sociologia critica: Un ensaio sobre senso comum e emancipação [*Towards a Critical Sociology* (Brazil.)], Rio de Janeiro: Zahar, 1977.

Hermeneutics and Social Science: Approaches to Understanding, London: Hutchinson, 1978.

Hermeneutics and Social Science, New York: Columbia University Press, 1978.

Critica del senso commune: Verso una nuova sociologia [*Towards a Critical Sociology* (Ital.)], Rome: Editori riuniti, 1982.

Memories of Class: The Pre-History and After-Life of Class, London: Routledge & Kegan Paul, 1982.

Memorie di classe: Preistoria e sopravvivenza di un concetto [*Memories of Class* (Ital.)], Turin: G. Einaudi, 1982.

Kultura i društvo [*Culture as Praxis* (Serb.)], Belgrade: Prosveta, 1984.

Memorie di classe: Preistoria e sopravvivenza di un concetto [*Memories of Class* (Ital.)] (Einaudi paperbacks 177), Turin: G. Einaudi, 1987.

Legislators and Interpreters: On Modernity, Postmodernity and Intellectuals, Cambridge: Polity Press, 1987.

Legislators and Interpreters: On Modernity, Postmodernity and Intellectuals, Ithaca, NY: Cornell University Press, 1987.

Freedom, Milton Keynes: Open University Press, 1988.

Freedom, Minneapolis: University of Minnesota Press, 1988.

Modernity and the Holocaust, Cambridge: Polity Press, 1989.

249

Modernity and the Holocaust, Ithaca, NY: Cornell University Press, 1989.
Auschwitz och det moderna samhället [*Modernity and the Holocaust* (Swed.)], Gothenburg: Daidalos, 1989.
Thinking Sociologically, Oxford: Basil Blackwell, 1990.
Paradoxes of Assimilation, New Brunswick, NJ: Transaction Publishers, 1990.
Modernity and Ambivalence, Cambridge: Polity Press, 1991.
Modernity and Ambivalence, Ithaca, NY: Cornell University Press, 1991.
Nowoczesność i zagłada [*Modernity and Ambivalence* (Pol.)], Warsaw: Masada, 1991.
Modernity and the Holocaust, Ithaca, NY: Cornell University Press, 1992.
Modernità e olocausto [*Modernity and the Holocaust* (Ital.)], Bologna: Mulino, 1992.
Mortality, Immortality and Other Life Strategies, Cambridge: Polity Press, 1992.
Döden och odödligheten i det moderna samhället [*Mortality, Immortality and Other Life Strategies* (Swed.)], Gothenburg: Daidalos, 1992.
Dialektik der Ordnung: Die Moderne und der Holocaust [*Modernity and the Holocaust* (Ger.)], Hamburg: Europ. Verl.-Anst., 1992.
Intimations of Postmodernity, London: Routledge, 1992.
Att tänka sociologiskt [*Thinking Sociologically* (Swed.)], Gothenburg: Korpen, 1992.
La decadenza degli intellectuali: Da legislatori a interpreti [*Legislators and Interpreters* (Ital.)], Turin: Bollati Boringhieri, 1992.
Moderne und Ambivalenz: Das Ende der Eindeutigkeit [*Modernity and Ambivalence* (Ger.)], Hamburg: Junius, 1992.
Postmodern Ethics, Oxford: Basil Blackwell, 1993.
Modernitet og Holocaust [*Modernity and the Holocaust* (Dan.)], Copenhagen: Hans Reitzels, 1994.
Tod, Unsterblichkeit und andere Lebenstrategien [*Mortality, Immortality and Other Life Strategies* (Ger.)], Frankfurt: Fischer, 1994.
Pensando sociologicamente [*Thinking Sociologically* (Brazil)], Buenos Aires: Nueva Vision, 1994.
Moderne und Ambivalenz: Das Ende der Eindeutigkeit [*Modernity and Ambivalence* (Ger.)], Frankfurt: Fischer, 1995.
Wieloznaczność nowoczesna, nowoczesność wieloznaczna [*Modernity and Ambivalence* (Pol.)], Warsaw: PWN, 1995.
Life in Fragments: Essays in Postmodern Morality, Oxford: Basil Blackwell, 1995.

ARTICLES AND PAMPHLETS

'Problem nacjonalizacji przemysłu w programie i w polityce brytyjskiej Partii Pracy', *Nowe Drogi* 10 (1956), 5: 77–89.
'Kilka uwag teoretycznych o zasadzie centralizmu demokratycznego', *Nowe Drogi* 11 (1957), 3: 91–101.

BIBLIOGRAPHY OF THE WORKS OF ZYGMUNT BAUMAN

Bauman, Z. and Wiatr, J. J., 'Marksizm a socjologia współczesna', *Myśl Filozoficzna* 27 (1957), 1: 3–23.

'Ewucja elity angielskiego ruchu robotniczego', *Studia Socjologiczno-Polityczne* 1 (1958): 25–122.

'O zawodzie socjologa', *Kultura i Społeczeństwo* 4 (1960), 3: 163–76.

'Robotnik; z dziejów stereotypu', *Studia Filozoficzne* 4 (1960), 2–8 (17–18).

'Z zagadnień politycznego mechanizmu demokracji burzuazyjnej', *Nowe Drogi* 15 (1961), 1: 129–41.

'Wzory sukcesu warszawskiej młodzieży', *Studia Socjologiczne* 1(1961), 3: 103–28.

'Values and Standards of Success of the Warsaw Youth', *The Polish Sociological Bulletin* 2 (1962), 1–2 (3–4): 77–90.

'Wariacje na tematy socjologiczne', *Kultura i Społeczeństwo* 6 (1962), 2: 47–64.

'Social Structure of the Party Organization in Industrial Works', *The Polish Sociological Bulletin* 2 (1962), 3–4 (5–6): 50–64.

'Członkowie partii i aktyw partyjny w zakładzie produkcyjnym', *Kultura i Społeczeństwo* 6 (1962), 4: 55–70.

'Tendencje i szkoły w socjologii współczesnej: Próba typologii', *Studia Socjologiczne* 2 (1962), 4: 5–41.

'Struktura władzy społeczności lokalnej', *Studia Socjologiczno-Polityczne* (1962), 12: 7–30.

'O pojęciu władzy', *Studia Socjologiczno-Polityczne* (1962), 13: 7–28

'Parsonsa teoria czynności i teoria systemu u społecznego', *Studia Socjologiczne* 2 (1962), 7: 71–94.

'Studium o brytyjskim kapitalizmie', *Nowe Drogi* 17 (1963), 9: 123–7.

'Antonio Gramsci – czyli socjologia w działaniu', *Kultura i Społeczeństwo* 7 (1963), 1: 19–34.

'Metodologiczne zagadnienia badań nad kulturą robotniczą', *Studia Socjologiczne* 1 (1964), 12: 19–34.

'W sprawie urbanizacji wsi', *Kultura i Społeczeństwo* 8 (1964), 3: 51–70.

'Economic Growth, Social Structure, Elite Formation: The Case of Poland', *International Social Science Journal* 16 (1964), 2: 203–16.

'Bieguny analizy kulturowej', *Studia Socjologiczne* 4 (1964), 14: 51–92.

'Social Structure and Innovational Personality', *The Polish Sociological Bulletin* 5 (1965), 1 (11): 54–9.

'Dwie notatki na marginesie kultury masowej', *Kultura i Społeczeństwo* 9 (1965), 1: 35–50.

'Three Remarks on Contemporary Educational Problems', *The Polish Sociological Bulletin* 6 (1966), 1 (13): 77–89.

'Kultura i społeczeństwo: Związki semantyczne i genetyczne', *Kultura i Społeczeństwo* 10 (1966), 1: 71–98.

'The Limitations of Perfect Planning', *Co-existence* 3 (1966), 2: 145–62.

'Möglichkeiten und methodologische Klippen soziologischer Forschungen', *Deutsche Zeitschrift für Philosophie* 14 (1966), 1: 32–44.

'Two Notes on Mass Culture', *The Polish Sociological Bulletin* 6 (1966), 1 (14): 58–74.

'Znak, struktura, kultura', *Kultura i Społeczeństwo* 11 (1967), 3: 69–95.

'Les membres et les activistes du parti dans l'entreprise de production', *L'Homme et la Société* 2 (1967), 5: 127–39.

'Człowiek i znak', *Studia Socjologiczne* 7 (1967), 26: 49–82.

'Image of Man in Modern Sociology', *The Polish Sociological Bulletin* 7 (1967), 1 (15): 12–21.

' "Kulturologija" i dihotomicnost ljudskogsveta', *Sociologija* 9 (1967), 1: 61–75.

'Some Problems in Contemporary Education', *International Social Science Journal* 19 (1967), 3: 325–37.

'Modern Times, Modern Marxism', *Social Research* 34 (1967), 3: 399–415.

'Kultura licnost i drustvena struktura', *Sociologija* 9 (1967), 2: 25–50.

'Człowiek i historia w "Kapitale" Karola Marksa', *Nowe Drogi* 21(1967), 5: 34–45.

'Polish Youth and Politics', *Polish Round Table* 1 (1967): 69–77.

'Marx and the Contemporary Theory of Culture', *Social Science Information* 7 (1968), 3: 19–34.

'Semiotics and the Function of Culture', *Social Science Information* 7 (1968), 5: 69–80.

'Osnove marksistickog shvatanja sociologije saznanja', *Sociologija* 10 (1968), 2: 83–98.

'Image de l'homme dans la sociologie moderne: quelques remarques d'ordre méthodologique', *Revue de l'Institute de Sociologie (Bruxelles)* 41 (1968), 4: 637–50.

'Macrosociology and Social Research in Contemporary Poland', *The Social Sciences: Problems and Orientations, Selected Studies* (New Babylon. Studies in the behavioral sciences), The Hague and Paris: Mouton/UNESCO, 1968.

'Modern Times: Modern Marxism', in P. Berger (ed.) *Marxism and Sociology: Views from Eastern Europe*, New York: Appleton-Century-Crofts, 1969.

'Marxism and the Contemporary Theory of Culture', in *Marx and Contemporary Scientific Thought*, The Hague: Mouton, 1969.

'Essai d'une théorie marxiste de la société', *L'Homme et la Société* 5 (1970), 15: 3–26.

'Uses of Information: When Social Information Becomes Desired', *Annals of the American Academy of Political and Social Science* 393 (1971), 1: 20–31

'Social Dissent in the East European Political System', *Archives Européennes de Sociologie* 12 (1971), 1: 25–51.

'20 Years After: Crisis of Soviet-type Systems', *Problems of Communism* 20 (1971), 6: 45–53.

'The Second Generation Socialism: A Review of Socio-cultural Trends in Contemporary Polish Society', in L. B. Shapiro (ed.) *Opposition in One-Party States*, London: Macmillan, 1971.

'Culture, Values and Science of Society', *The University of Leeds Review* 15 (1972), 2: 185–203.

'Praxis: The Controversial Culture–Society Paradigm', in T. Shanin (ed.) *Rules of the Game: Cross-Disciplinary Essays in Scholarly Thought*, London: Tavistock, 1972.

BIBLIOGRAPHY OF THE WORKS OF ZYGMUNT BAUMAN

'The Structuralist Promise', *The British Journal of Sociology* 24 (1973), 1: 67–83.
'On the Philosophical Status of Ethnomethodology', *Sociological Review* 21 (1973), 1: 5–23.
'Between State and Society', *International Journal of Contemporary Sociology* 10 (1973), 1: 9–25.
'Drustvena previranja u istochno-evropskom politickom sistemu', *Socioloski Pregled* 8 (1974), 2–3: 329–50.
'Officialdom and Class: Bases of Inequality in Socialist Society', in F. Parkin (ed.) *The Social Analysis of Class Structure*, London: Tavistock, 1974.
'Theory and Society', *Sociology* 10 (1976), 3: 525–8.
'Stalin i rewolucja chłopska, studium dialektyki pana i niewolnika', in B. Rakowski, Z. Brzezinski and Z. Bauman *Wokół rewolucji rosyjskiej*, Warsaw: Niezależna Oficyna Wydawnicza, 1980.
'On the Maturation of Socialism', *Telos* (Spring 1981), 47: 48–54.
'Ideology and the "Weltanschauung" of the Intellectuals', *Canadian Journal of Political and Social Theory* 7 (1983), 1–2: 104–17.
'Industrialism, Consumerism and Power', *Theory, Culture & Society* 1 (1983), 3: 32–43.
'On the Origins of Civilisation: A Historical Note', *Theory, Culture & Society* 2 (1985), 3: 7–14.
'Stalin and the Peasant Revolution: A Case Study in the Dialectics of Master and Slave', *Leeds Occasional Papers in Sociology* 19 (1985).
'The Left as the Counter-Culture of Modernity', *Telos* (Winter 1986–7), 70: 81–93.
'The Importance of Being a Marxist', in W. Outhwaite and M. Mulkay (eds) *Social Theory and Social Criticism: Essays for Tom Bottomore*, Oxford: Basil Blackwell, 1987 (reprinted, Aldershot: Gregg Revivals, 1992).
'Intellectuals in East-Central Europe: Continuity and Change', *East European Politics and Societies* 1 (1987), 2: 162–86.
'On Immoral Reason and Illogical Morality', *Polin* 3 (1988): 294–301.
'Exit Visas and Entry Tickets: Paradoxes of Jewish Assimilation', *Telos* (Fall 1988), 77: 45–77.
'The Twisted Road to Perestroika', *The Jewish Quarterly* (Autumn 1988): 9–15.
'Strangers: The Social Construction of Universality and Particularity', *Telos* (Winter 1988–9), 78: 7–42.
'Postoji li postmodernisticka sociologija', *Revija za Sociologiju* 19 (1988), 3: 309–23.
'Sociology after the Holocaust', *The British Journal of Sociology* 39 (1988), 4: 469–97.
'Sociology and Postmodernity', *Sociological Review* 36 (1988), 4: 790–813.
'Britain's Exit from Politics', *New Statesman & Society* 1 (1988), 8: 34–8.
'Vänstern som modernitetens motkultur', *Ord & Bild* 2 (1988): 3–13.
'Is There a Postmodern Sociology?', *Theory, Culture & Society* 5 (1988), 2–3: 211–37.
'Poland: On Its Own', *Telos* (Spring 1989), 79: 47–68.

'Legislators and Interpreters: Culture as Ideology of Intellectuals', in H. Haferkamp (ed.) *Social Structure and Culture*, Berlin and New York: de Gruyter, 1989.

'Sociology and Postmodernity', *The Polish Sociological Bulletin* 29 (1989), 3–4 (87–8): 81–98.

'Sociological Responses to Postmodernity', *Thesis Eleven* (1989), 23: 35–63.

'Hermeneutics and Modern Social Theory', in D. Held and J. B. Thompson (eds) *Social Theory of Modern Societies: Giddens and His Critics*, Cambridge: Cambridge University Press, 1989.

'From Pillars to Post', *Marxism Today* (February 1990): 20–5.

'Effacing the Face: On The Social Management of Moral Proximity', *Theory, Culture & Society* 7 (1990), 1: 5–38.

'Assimilation and Enlightenment (in Reference to the Jewish Experience in Germany)', *Society* 27 (1990), 6 (188): 71–81.

'Gesetzgeber und Interpreten: Kultur als Ideologie von Intellektuellen', in H. Haferkamp (ed.) *Sozialstruktur und Kultur*, Frankfurt am Main: Suhrkamp, 1990.

'Philosophical Affinities of Postmodern Sociology', *Sociological Review* 38 (1990), 3: 441–4.

'Modernity and Ambivalence', *Theory, Culture & Society* 7 (1990), 2–3: 143–69.

'Communism: A Post-Mortem', *Praxis International* 10 (1990–1), 3–4: 185–92.

'The Social Manipulation of Morality Moralizing Actors, Adiaphorizing Action' (Amalfi-Preisrede, May 1990), *Theory, Culture & Society* 8 (1991), 1: 139–53.

'Postmodernizm a socjalizm', *Literatura na świecie* (June 1991): 268–79.

'Jacek Tarkowski: In Memoriam', *Telos* (1991), 89: 102.

'Suolo, sangue, identità', *Mondoperaio* (November 1991): 129–36.

'Moderne und Ambivalenz', in U. Bielefeld (ed.) *Das Eigene und das Fremde: Neuer Rassismus in der Alten Welt*, Hamburg: Junius, 1991.

Sociologia Postmodernizma, Moscow: Institut Molodezhi, 1991.

'A Sociological Theory of Postmodernity', *Thesis Eleven* (1991), 29: 33–46.

'Living without an Alternative', *Political Quarterly* 62 (1991), 1: 35–44.

'Ideology and the "Weltanschauung" of the Intellectuals', *Canadian Journal of Political and Social Theory* 15 (1991), 1–3: 107–20.

'Survival as a Social Construct', *Theory, Culture & Society* 9 (1992), 1: 1–36.

'Simmel, ou l'éclosion de l'expérience postmoderne', *Sociétés* 35 (1992): 3–16.

'Moderne und Ambivalenz (Vorabdruck aus der gleichnamigen Übersetzung von "Modernity and Ambivalence")', *Mittelweg* 36. 1 (1992), 3: 9–17.

'Om postmodernitet og sociologi' (interview with Poul Poder Pedersen and Timo Cantell), *Tendens* (October 1992): 9–18.

'Soil, Blood and Identity', *Sociological Review* 40 (1992), 4: 675–701.

Bauman, Z., Kilminster, R. and Varcoe, I., 'Sociology, Postmodernity

and Exile: An Interview with Zygmunt Bauman', in Z. Bauman, *Intimations of Postmodernity*, London and New York: Routledge, 1992.
'Love in Adversity: On the State and the Intellectuals, and the State of the Intellectuals', *Thesis Eleven* (1992), 31: 81–104.
'Auf der Suche nach der postkommunistischen Gesellschaft – das Beispiel Polen', *Soziale Welt* 44 (1993), 2: 157–76.
'Biologie und das Projekt der Moderne', *Mittelweg* 36.2 (1993), 4: 3–16.
'Europe of the Tribes: On Regional Identities and the Fear of Difference – Europa der Stämme: über regionale Identitäten und den Schrecken der Uneindeutigkeit', *Perspektiven* (1993), 15: 3–8.
'Filosofia i postmodernistkaia sociologia', *Voprosy Filosofii* (1993), 3: 46–61.
'Die Gewalt und die Verwaltung der Differenz: Zur Diskussion um kollektives, gewaltsames Handeln', *Perspektiven* (1993), 16: 33–5.
'A Postmodern Revolution?', in J. Frentzel-Zagórska (ed.) *From a One-Party State to Democracy: Transition in Eastern Europe* (Poznań Studies in the Philosophy of the Sciences and Humanities 32), Amsterdam/Atlanta: Editions Rodopi, 1993.
'Dismantling a Patronage State', in J. Frentzel-Zagórska (ed.) *From a One-Party State to Democracy: Transition in Eastern Europe* (Poznań Studies in the Philosophy of the Sciences and Humanities 32), Amsterdam/Atlanta: Editions Rodopi, 1993.
'Europe of the Tribes', in B. Schäfers (ed.) *Lebensverhältnisse und Soziale Konflikte im neuen Europa: Verhandlungen des 26. Deutschen Soziologentages in Düsseldorf 1992*, Frankfurt am Main: Campus, 1993.
'Ponowoczesne wzory osobowe', *Studia Socjologiczne* (1993), 2 (129): 7–32.
'Benjamin the Intellectual', *New Formations* 20 (1993): 47–58.
'Racism, Anti-Racism and Moral Progress', *Arena* (1993), 1: 9–22.
'Hol az osztályérdek mostanában?', *2000* (August 1993): 9–16.
'Domen frän Nürnberg gäller inte längre', *Ord & Bild* 6 (1993): 24–34.
'Das Urteil von Nürnberg hat keinen Bestand', *Das Argument* (August 1993): 519–32.
'Van-e posztmodern szociológia?', *Replika* 9–10 (1993): 7–22.
'Walter Benjamin-intelektualista', in A. Zeidler-Janiszewska (ed.) *"drobne rysy w ciągłej katastrofie . . .": Obecność Benjamina w kulturze współczesnej*, Warsaw: Instytut Kultury, 1993.
'Przedstawienie na pustyni', in A. Zeidler-Janiszewska (ed.) *"drobne rysy w ciągłej katastrofie . . .": Obecność Benjamina w kulturze współczesnej*, Warsaw: Instytut Kultury, 1993.
'Narrating Modernity', in J. Burnheim (ed.) *The Social Philosophy of Agnes Heller* (Poznań Studies in the Philosophy of the Sciences and Humanities 37), Amsterdam/Atlanta: Editions Rodopi, 1994.
'Das Jahrhundert der Lager', *Die neue Gesellschaft Frankfurter Hefte* (January 1994): 28–37.
'Parvenu und Paria – Held und Opfer der Moderne', *Merkur* (March 1994): 237–48.
'Moralne obowiązki, etyczne zasady', *Etyka* 27 (1994): 9–28.
'Spor o postmodernismie', *Sociologicheski Zhurnal* (1994), 4: 69–80.

BIBLIOGRAPHY OF THE WORKS OF ZYGMUNT BAUMAN

'After the Patronage State: A Model in Search of Class Interests', in C. G. A. Bryant and E. Mokrzycki (eds) *The New Great Transformation? Change and Continuity in East-Central Europe*, London: Routledge, 1994.

'Nogmaals de Vreemdeling', *Nexuz* 10 (1994): 95–104.

'Frän pilgrim till turist', *Moderna Tider* (September 1994): 20–5.

Bauman, Z. and Israel, J., 'Politik, identitet och valfrihet', *Ord & Bild* 6 (1994): 11–17.

Bauman, Z. and Signorelli, A., 'Questa esistenza cosi disagiata', *Prometeo* (June 1994): 123–37.

'Intellectuelen in de postmoderne weld', *Streven* (October 1994): 771–81.

'A Revolution in the Theory of Revolution?', *International Political Science Review* 15 (1994), 1: 15–24.

Dwa szkice o moralności ponowoczesnej, Warsaw: Instytut Kultury, 1994.

Alone Again: Ethics after Certainty, London: Demos, 1994.

'Vom Pilger zum Touristen – Postmoderne Identitätsprojekte', in H. Keupp (ed.) *Lust an der Erkenntnis: Der Mensch als Soziales Wesen*, Munich: Piper, 1995.

'Van pelgrim tot toerist', *Tijdschrift voor Sociologie* 19 (1995), 1: 31–50.

'A jeśli etyki zabraknie...', *Kultura Współczesna* (1995), 1–2: 145–59.

BOOK REVIEWS

Images of Society: Essays on the Sociological Theories of Tocqueville, Marx and Durkheim, by G. Poggi, *Times Higher Education Supplement* (1973), 13 April: 29.

Soviet and American Society: A Comparison, by P. Hollander, *American Political Science Review* 68 (1974), 4: 1811–12.

Individualism, by S. Lukes, *Sociological Review* 22 (1974), 1:157.

Social Groups in Polish Society, by D. Lane and G. Kolankiewicz, *Slavonic and East European Review* 52 (1974), 127: 306–9.

Legitimation Crisis, by J. Habermas, *New Society* 38 (1976), 733:147–8.

The Civilizing Process, Vol. 1: The History of Manners, by N. Elias; *What is Sociology?*, by N. Elias; *Human Figurations: Essays for Norbert Elias* (ed.) J. Goudsblom; *Sociology in the Balance: A Critical Essay*, by J. Goudsblom, *Sociology* 13 (1979), 1: 117–25.

Meaning and Change: Explorations in the Cultural Sociology of Modern Societies, by R. Robertson, *The British Journal of Sociology* 30 (1979), 3: 376–7.

Sozializmus in Theorie und Praxis: Festschrift für Richard Löwenthal, by H. Horn, A. Schwan and T. Weingartner, *Political Studies* 28 (1980), 1: 178.

Max Weber, by F. Parkin, *Times Literary Supplement* (1982), 4135: 715.

In Search of the Spirit of Capitalism: An Essay on Max Weber's Protestant Ethic Thesis, by G. Marshall, *Times Literary Supplement* (1982), 4135: 715.

Making Sense of Reification, by A. Schütz; *Constructionist Theory*, by B. Thomason, *Times Literary Supplement* (1982), 4155: 1283.

BIBLIOGRAPHY OF THE WORKS OF ZYGMUNT BAUMAN

Life Forms and Meaning Structure, by A. Schütz, *Times Literary Supplement* (1982), 4155: 1283.

Authority, by R. Sennett, *Theory, Culture & Society* 1 (1982), 2: 128–30.

The Foundations of Structuralism: A Critique of Lévi-Strauss and the Structuralist Movement, by S. Clarke, *Sociology* 16 (1982), 3: 451–3.

Concept Formation in Social Science, by W. Outhwaite, *Times Literary Supplement* (1983), 4178: 441.

Anti-Nuclear Protest: The Opposition to Nuclear Energy in France, by A. Touraine, Z. Hegedus, F. Dubet, M. Wieviorka and *Solidarité; Analyse d'un mouvement social: Pologne: 1980–1981*, by A. Touraine, F. Dubet, M. Wieviorka and J. Strzelecki, *Sociology* 17 (1983), 4: 596–8.

The Politics of Social Theory: Habermas, Freud and the Critique of Positivism, by R. Keat, *The British Journal of Sociology* 34 (1983), 1: 154–6.

Bauman, Z. (in part), Symposium: *Dictatorship Over Needs*, by F. Fehér, A. Heller and G. Markus; *The Neo-Stalinist State: Class, Ethnicity and Consensus in Soviet Society*, by V. Zaslavsky, *Telos* (Summer 1984), 60: 173–8 (the whole 155–91).

The Idea of Natural Inequality and Other Essays, by A. Béteille, *Sociology* 18 (1984), 4: 601.

Alfred Schütz: An Intellectual Biography, by H. R. Wagner, *Times Literary Supplement* (1984), 4235: 621.

The Content of Social Explanation, by S. James, *Times Literary Supplement* (1985), 22 February: 211.

Ideology in a Socialist State: Poland 1956–1983, by R.Taras, *Soviet Studies* 37 (1985), 4: 577–8.

Bauman, Z. (in part), Symposium: *Soviet Peasants*, by L. Timofeev, *Telos* (1986), 68: 124–7 (the whole 109–27).

False Consciousness and Ideology in Marxist Theory, by R. Eyerman, *Sociology* 20 (1986), 3: 467–8.

Hermeneutics and the Sociology of Knowledge, by S. J. Hekman, *Theory, Culture & Society* 4 (1987), 1: 172–6.

'The Philosopher in the Age of Noise: A Reading of Richard J. Bernstein's "Philosophical Profiles" ', *Theory, Culture & Society* 4 (1987), 1: 157–65.

Autonomy and Solidarity, (ed.) P. Dews, *Times Literary Supplement* (1987), 13 February: 155.

The Making of Modern Society, by R. Nisbet, *Contemporary Sociology* 16 (1987), 6: 902–3.

Max Weber, Rationality and Modernity, (eds) S. Whimster and S. Lash, *The International Journal of Sociology and Social Policy* 8 (1988), 6: 76–9.

Culture, Identity and Politics, by E. Gellner, *Times Literary Supplement* (1988), 1 January: 4.

The Philosophical Discourse of Modernity, by J. Habermas, *Sociology* 22 (1988), 3: 473–5

La gauche divine; Les strategies fatales, by J. Baudrillard, *Theory, Culture & Society* 5 (1988), 4: 738–43.

257

America, by J. Baudrillard, *Times Literary Supplement* (1988), 16 December: 1391.

Selected Writings – *Jean Baudrillard*, (ed.) M. Poster, *Times Literary Supplement* (1988), 16 December: 1391.

A Social Analysis of Postwar Polish Jewry, by I. Hurwic-Nowakowska, *Polin* 3 (1988): 438–42.

Love as Passion: The Codification of Intimacy, by N. Luhmann, *American Journal of Sociology* 93 (1988), 5: 1240–3.

Culture and Agency: The Place of Culture in Society, by M. S. Archer, *History of the Human Sciences* 2 (1989), 2: 260–5.

Kontynuacje, by J. Strzelecki, *Times Literary Supplement* (1989), 3 February: 103.

Legitymacja – *klasyczne teorie i Polskie doświadczenia*, (eds) A. Rychard and A. Sulek, *Times Literary Supplement* (1989), 24 November: 1295.

Osobowość, orientacje moralne i postawy polityczne, (ed.) A. Jasińska-Kania, *Times Literary Supplement* (1989), 24 November: 1295.

Fragments of Modernity: Theories of Modernity in the Work of Simmel, Kracauer and Benjamin, by D. Frisby, *The British Journal of Sociology* 40 (1989), 4: 701–2.

Minorities in the Open Society: Prisoners of Ambivalence, by G. Dench, *The British Journal of Sociology* 40 (1989), 4: 709–11.

Polska dziecięca, (ed.) B. Szacka, *Times Literary Supplement* (1989), 24 November: 1295.

Die marxistische Bewegung und die Polenfrage, by J. Jaroslawski, *Times Literary Supplement* (1989), 22 December: 1406.

The Condition of Postmodernity, by D. Harvey, *Times Literary Supplement* (1990), 11 May: 501.

Metropolis, by E. Jones, *Times Literary Supplement* (1990), 11 May: 501.

The Roots of Evil, by E. Straub, *Times Literary Supplement* (1990), 6 July: 722.

'The Twilight of the New Politics', review of *Beyond Glasnost: The Post-Totalitarian Mind*, by J. C. Goldfarb, *Canadian Journal of Political and Social Theory* 14 (1990), 1–3: 230–2.

Studia nad ładem społecznym, (eds) W. Nieciuński and T. Żukowski, *Times Literary Supplement* (1990), 12 October: 1095.

Postmodern Conditions, (eds) A. Milner, P. Thomas and C. Worth, *Thesis Eleven* (1990), 25: 173–8.

The Generation: The Rise and Fall of the Generation of Jewish Communists of Poland, by J. Schatz, *Acta Sociologica* 33 (1990), 2: 175–6.

Jean Baudrillard: From Marxism to Postmodernism and Beyond, by D. Kellner, *Sociology* 24 (1990), 4: 697–9.

Totalitarizm kak istoricheskii fenomen, (eds) A. A. Klara-Murza and A. K. Voskresensky, *Times Literary Supplement* (1990), 12 October: 1095.

Norbert Elias: Civilization and the Human Self-Image, by S. Mennell, *Sociological Review* 38 (1990), 2: 366–9.

Domination and the Arts of Resistance, by J. C. Scott, *Times Literary Supplement* (1991), 11 January: 7.

Why did the Heavens Not Darken?: The 'Final Solution' in History, by A. J. Mayer, *Social History* 16 (1991), 3: 391–4.

Confessions of a Reluctant Theorist, by W. G. Runciman, *Times Literary Supplement* (1991), 24 May: 28.

Under Technology's Thumb, by W. Leiss, *Canadian Journal of Sociology* 16 (1991), 1: 107–9.

O Loma!: Constituting a Self (1977–84), by K. H. Wolff, *Sociological Review* 39 (1991), 2: 411–12.

Face à l'extrême, by T. Todorov, *Times Literary Supplement* (1991), 14 June: 13.

Plausible Worlds, by G. Hawthorn, *Times Literary Supplement* (1991), 11 October: 26.

A Critical Dictionary of Sociology, by R. Boudon and F. Bourricaud, *The British Journal of Sociology* 42 (1991), 2: 295–7.

Social Forms/Human Capacities: Essays in Authority and Differences, by P. Corrigan, *Sociological Review* 40 (1992), 1: 168–70.

The Revolutionary Reign of Terror: The Role of Violence in Political Change, by R. H. O'Kane; *The Legitimation of Power*, by D. Beetham, *Sociology* 26 (1992), 3: 551–4.

Reading Rorty: Critical Responses to 'Philosophy and the Mirror of Nature', by A. Malachowski, *History of the Human Sciences* 5 (1992), 3: 57–63.

Modern Conditions, Postmodern Controversies, by B. Smart; *Transition to Modernity: Essays on Power, Wealth and Belief*, (eds) J. A. Hall and I. C. Jarvie, *Political Studies* 40 (1992), 2: 365–6.

'The Solution as Problem', review of *Risk Society: Towards a New Modernity*, by U. Beck, *Times Higher Education Supplement* (1992), 13 November: 25.

Democracy and Complexity: A Realist Approach, by D. Zolo, *Times Literary Supplement* (1992), 4671: 11.

Political Theory and Postmodernism, by S. K. White, *Political Studies* 40 (1992), 2: 365–6.

Philosophical Papers, Vol. 1: Objectivity, Relativism, and Truth, by R. Rorty, *History of the Human Sciences* 5 (1992), 3: 57–63.

Media, State and Nation: Political Violence and Collective Identities, by P. Schlesinger, *Media, Culture & Society* 14 (1992), 3: 489–92.

The Persistence of Modernity: Essays on Aesthetics, Ethics and Postmodernism, by A. Wellmer, *Sociology* 26 (1992), 1: 173–5.

Democracy: The Unfinished Journey, 508 BC to AD 1993, (ed.) J. Dunn, *Times Literary Supplement* (1992), 4671: 11.

Justice by Lottery, by B. Goodwin, *Times Literary Supplement* (1993), 4693: 23.

The Broken Middle: Out of Our Ancient Society, by G. Rose, *Economy and Society* 22 (1993), 1: 114–22.

Crime Control as Industry: Towards Gulag, Western Style?, by N. Christie, *Sociology* 27 (1993), 3: 555–6.

The Transformation of Intimacy: Sexuality, Love and Eroticism in Modern Societies, by A. Giddens, *Sociological Review* 41 (1993), 2: 363–8.

The Society of Individuals, by N. Elias, *Sociological Review* 41(1993), 3: 585–9.

Arendt, Camus, and Modern Revolution, by J. C. Isaac, *Sociology* 28 (1994), 1: 317–18.

Genocide: A Sociological Perspective, by H. Fein, *Sociology* 28 (1994), 2: 613–14.

Knowledge and Passion: Essays in Honour of John Rex, (ed.) H. Martins, *Sociology* 28 (1994), 2: 629–31.

Judaism and Modernity: Philosophical Essays, by G. Rose, *Sociological Review* 42 (1994), 3: 572–6.

REFERENCES

Abrams, P. (1981) 'The Collapse of British Sociology?', in P. Abrams, R. Deem, J. Finch and P. Rock (eds) *Practice and Progress: British Sociology, 1950–1980*, London: George Allen & Unwin.

Ackerman, B. (1988) 'Neo-Federalism', in J. Elster and R. Slagstad (eds) *Constitutionalism and Democracy*, Cambridge: Cambridge University Press.

Acton, Lord (1906) *Lectures on Modern History*, London: Fontana, 1960.

Akin, W. E. (1977) *Technocracy and the American Dream: The Technocratic Movement, 1900–1941*, Berkeley and Los Angeles: University of California Press.

Anderson, P. (1968) 'Components of the National Culture', *New Left Review* 50, July–August: 3–57.

Arato, A. (1990) 'Revolution, Civil Society and Democracy', *Praxis International* 10: 24–38.

—— (1994) 'Revolution and Restoration: On the Origins of Right-Wing Radical Ideology in Hungary', in C. G. A. Bryant and E. Mokrzycki (eds) *The New Great Transformation? Change and Continuity in East-Central Europe*, London: Routledge.

Arendt, H. (1963) *On Revolution*, London: Faber & Faber.

Aron, R. (1969) *Progress and Disillusion*, London: Pall Mall Press.

Avineri, S. (1991) 'Reflections on Eastern Europe', *Partisan Review* 3, Summer: 442–8.

Baechler, J. (1979) 'Preface' to Cochin 1979.

Bailes, K. E. (1977) 'Alexei Gastev and the Soviet Controversy over Taylorism, 1918–24', *Soviet Studies* 29, 3: 373–94.

—— (1978) *Technology and Society under Lenin and Stalin: Origins of the Soviet Technical Intelligentsia*, Princeton, NJ: Princeton University Press.

Bailyn, B. and Fleming, D. (eds) (1969) *The Intellectual Migration: Europe and America, 1930–1960*, Cambridge, Mass.: Belknap Press of Harvard University Press.

Balcerowicz, L. (1992) *800 dni. Szok kontrolowany*, Warsaw: BGW.

Banac, I. (ed.) (1992) *Eastern Europe in Revolution*, Ithaca, NY: Cornell University Press.

261

Banks, O. (1968) *The Sociology of Education*, London: B. T. Batsford Ltd (reprinted 1970).

Bauman, Z. (1972a) 'Praxis: The Controversial Culture–Society Paradigm', in T. Shanin (ed.) *Rules of the Game: Cross-Disciplinary Essays in Scholarly Thought*, London: Tavistock Publications.

—— (1972b) 'Culture, Values and Science of Society', *The University of Leeds Review* 15, 2: 185–203.

—— (1972c) *Between Class and Élite: The Evolution of the British Labour Movement: A Sociological Study*, trans. S. Patterson, Manchester: Manchester University Press.

—— (1973a) *Culture as Praxis*, London: Routledge & Kegan Paul.

—— (1973b) 'On the Philosophical Status of Ethnomethodology', *Sociological Review* 21, 1: 5–23.

—— (1976a) *Towards a Critical Sociology: An Essay on Commonsense and Emancipation*, London: Routledge & Kegan Paul.

—— (1976b) *Socialism: The Active Utopia*, London: George Allen & Unwin.

—— (1982) *Memories of Class: The Pre-History and After-Life of Class*, London: Routledge & Kegan Paul.

—— (1987a) *Legislators and Interpreters: On Modernity, Postmodernity and Intellectuals*, Cambridge: Polity Press.

—— (1987b) 'The Importance of Being a Marxist', in W. Outhwaite and M. Mulkay (eds) *Social Theory and Social Criticism: Essays for Tom Bottomore*, Oxford: Basil Blackwell (reprinted, Aldershot: Gregg Revivals, 1992).

—— (1987c) 'Intellectuals in East-Central Europe: Continuity and Change', *East European Politics and Societies* 1, 2: 162–86.

—— (1988) *Freedom*, Milton Keynes: Open University Press.

—— (1989) *Modernity and the Holocaust*, Cambridge: Polity Press.

—— (1990a) *Thinking Sociologically*, Oxford: Basil Blackwell.

—— (1990b) 'From Pillars to Post', *Marxism Today*, February: 20–5.

—— (1991) *Modernity and Ambivalence*, Cambridge: Polity Press.

—— (1992a) *Intimations of Postmodernity*, London: Routledge.

—— (1992b) *Mortality, Immortality and Other Life Strategies*, Cambridge: Polity Press.

—— (1993) *Postmodern Ethics*, Oxford: Basil Blackwell.

Beard, C. A. (1947) *The Rise of American Civilization*, 2 vols, New York: Macmillan.

Bell, D. (1967) 'Toward the Year 2000: Work in Progress', *Daedalus*, Summer: 639–994.

—— (1974) *The Coming of Post-industrial Society: A Venture in Social Forecasting*, London: Heinemann.

Ben-David, J. (1968) *Fundamental Research and the Universities: Some Comments on International Differences*, Paris: OECD.

Benjamin, W. (1930) 'Theorien des deutschen Faschismus', in *Gesammelte Schriften*, 3, Frankfurt: Suhrkamp (1977); also available in translation as 'Theories of German Fascism', trans. J. Wikoff, *New German Critique* 17 (Spring 1979): 120–8.

—— (1940) 'Theses on the Philosophy of History', trans. H. Zohn, in *Illuminations*, New York: Harcourt Brace Jovanovich, 1968.

Béracha, S. (1930) *Rationalisation et révolution*, Paris: Valois.

Berlin, I. (1990) 'The State of Europe: Christmas Eve, 1989', *Granta* 30: 148–50.

Bernal, J. D. (1939) *The Social Function of Science*, London: Routledge & Kegan Paul.

Bernal, M. (1987) *Black Athena: African and Asian Roots of Classical Civilization*, London: Free Press Association.

Bernhard, G. (1923) *Wirtschaftsparlament*, Vienna: C. Barth.

Bettelheim, C. (1949) 'Discussion', in G. Gurvitch (ed.) *Industrialisation et technocratie*, Paris: Librairie Armand Colin.

Blackburn, R. (1991) 'Fin de Siècle: Socialism after the Crash', in R. Blackburn (ed.) *After the Fall: The Failure of Communism and the Future of Socialism*, London: Verso.

Blumenberg, H. (1983) *The Legitimacy of the Modern Age*, trans. R. M. Wallace, Cambridge, Mass.: MIT Press.

Bobbio, N. (1984) *Il futuro della democrazia*, Turin: Guilio Einaudi Editore.

—— (1986) 'Postfazione', in *Profilo ideologico del novecento italiano*, Turin: Guilio Einaudi.

Boden, D. (1992) 'Reinventing the Global Village: Communication and the Revolutions of 1989', in A. Giddens (ed.) *Human Societies: A Reader*, Cambridge: Polity Press.

Bon, F. and Burnier, M.-A. (1971) *Les Nouveaux Intellectuels*, Paris: Éditions du Seuil.

Bondanella, P. and Musa, M. (eds) (1979) *The Portable Machiavelli*, New York: Penguin Books.

Bottomore, T. (1990) *The Socialist Economy: Theory and Practice*, New York: Guilford Press.

Bottomore, T. and Goode, P. (1978) *Austro-Marxism*, Oxford: Clarendon Press.

Boudon, R. (1989) 'La teoria della conoscenza nella *Filosofia del denaro* di Simmel', *Rassegna Italiana di Sociologia* 30, 4, Oct./Dec.: 473–501.

Bouglé, C. (1931) 'Le Bilan de Saint-Simonisme', *Annales de l'Université de Paris*, Sept.–Oct.: 446–63; and Nov.–Dec.: 540–56.

Bouglé, C. and Halévy, E. (1924) *Doctrine de Saint-Simon*, Paris: douzième séance.

Bourbonnais, M. (1923) *Le néo-Saint-Simonisme dans la vie sociale d'aujourd'hui*, Paris: Presses Universitaires.

Bourricaud, F. (1949) 'Discussion', in G. Gurvitch (ed.) *Industrialisation et technocratie*, Paris: Librairie Armand Colin.

Bova, R. (1991) 'Political Dynamics of the Post-Communist Transition', *World Politics* 44, 1: 113–38.

Bowen, R. (1947) *German Theories of the Corporative State: With Special Reference to the Period 1870–1919*, New York: Russell & Russell.

Bozóki, A. (1992) 'The Hungarian Transition in Comparative Perspective', in A. Bozóki, A. Körösènyi and J. Schöpflin (eds) *Post-Com-*

munist Tradition: Emerging Pluralism in Hungary, London: Pinter Publishers.

Brinton, C. (1965) *The Anatomy of Revolution*, revised and expanded edition, New York: Vintage Books.

Brus, W. and Laski, K. (1989) *From Marx to the Market: Socialism in Search of an Economic System*, Oxford: Clarendon Press.

Bryant, C. G. A. (1990) 'Tales of Innocence and Experience: Developments in Sociological Theory since 1950', in C. G. A. Bryant and H. Becker (eds) *What Has Sociology Achieved?*, London: Macmillan.

Burnham, J. (1962) *The Managerial Revolution*, Harmondsworth: Penguin Books.

Burnheim, J. (ed.) (1994) *The Social Philosophy of Agnes Heller* (Poznań Studies in the Philosophy of the Sciences and Humanities 37), Amsterdam/Atlanta: Editions Rodopi.

Callinicos, A. (1991) *The Revenge of History: Marxism and the East European Revolutions*, Cambridge: Polity Press.

Caputo, J. D. (1987) *Radical Hermeneutics*, Bloomington and Indianapolis: Indiana University Press.

Carr, E. H. (1952) *The Bolshevik Revolution, 1917–23*, Vol. 2, London: Macmillan.

Cavalli, A. and Perucchi, L. (1986) 'Introduction' to G. Simmel, *Filosofia del denaro*, Turin: UTET.

CBOS (1992) Raport 'Pieniądze na co dzień' (Money for every day), Report, Warsaw: August.

Chase, S. (1933) *Technocracy: An Interpretation* (John Day pamphlets no. 19), New York: John Day Company.

Chirot, D. (1991a) 'Introduction' to D. Chirot (ed.) *The Crisis of Leninism and the Decline of the Left: The Revolutions of 1989*, Seattle: University of Washington Press.

—— (1991b) 'What Happened in Eastern Europe in 1989?', in D. Chirot (ed.) *The Crisis of Leninism and the Decline of the Left: The Revolutions of 1989*, Seattle: University of Washington Press.

Cochin, A. (1924) *La Révolution et la libre pensée*, Paris: Plon Nourrit.

—— (1979) *L'Ésprit du jacobinisme*, Paris: Universitaires de France.

Cohen, I. B. (1980) 'The Fear and Distrust of Science in Historical Perspective: Some First Thoughts', in A. S. Markovits and K. W. Deutsch (eds) *Fear of Science – Trust in Science: Conditions for Change in the Climate of Opinion*, publication of the Science Centre, Berlin, Vol. 19, Cambridge, Mass. and Königsten/Ts.: Oelgeschlager, Gunn and Hain, Publishers, Inc. and Verlag Anton Hain.

Cohen, J. and Arato, A. (1992) *Civil Society and Political Theory*, Cambridge, Mass.: MIT Press.

Comisso, E. (1991) 'Political Coalitions, Economic Choices', in G. Szoboszlai (ed.) *Democracy and Political Transformation: Theories and East-Central European Realities*, Budapest: Hungarian Political Science Association.

Cournot, A. (1875) *Matérialisme, vitalisme, rationalisme: Études sur l'emploi des données de la science et philosophie*, Paris: Hachette.

Cumings, B. (1991) 'Illusion, Critique and Responsibility: The Revolution of '89 in West and East', in D. Chirot (ed.) *The Crisis of Leninism and the Decline of the Left: The Revolutions of 1989*, Seattle: University of Washington Press.

Dahrendorf, R. (1990) *Reflections on the Revolution in Europe*, London: Chatto & Windus.

Darnton, R. (1991) 'Runes of the New Revolutions', *Times Higher Education Supplement*, 6 September: 16–17.

Davies, J. C. (1962) 'Toward a Theory of Revolution', *American Sociological Review* 27: 5–18.

Deák, I. (1992) 'Survivors', *New York Review of Books*, 5 March: 43–51; 28 May: 56–7 (letter by G. Ross, reply by I. Deák); 16 July: 53–4 (letter by R. J. Bogdan, reply by I. Deák).

Derrida, J. (1974) *Of Grammatology*, trans. G. Spivak, Baltimore: Johns Hopkins University Press.

—— (1982) *Margins of Philosophy*, trans. with notes by A. Bass, Chicago: University of Chicago Press.

—— (1987) *Post-Card: From Socrates to Freud and Beyond*, trans. A. Bass, Chicago: University of Chicago Press.

Devinat, P. (1927) *Scientific Management in Europe*, International Labour Office, Studies and Reports, series B, no. 17, Geneva: ILO.

Diamond, L. (1990) 'Democracy as Paradox', paper prepared for the Conference on 'Israeli Democracy Under Stress', Stanford, Calif.: Hoover Institution.

di Palma, G. (1991) 'Legitimation from the Top to Civil Society', *World Politics* 44, 1: 49–80.

Domański, H. (1991) 'Structural Constraints on the Formation of the Middle Class', *Sisyphus* VII: 59–64.

—— (n.d.) 'Nowe mechanizmy stratyfikacyjne i nowe klasy' (New stratification mechanisms and new classes), unpublished typescript.

Dunn, J. (1978) *Rethinking Modern Political Theory*, Cambridge: Cambridge University Press.

—— (1984) *Locke*, Oxford: Oxford University Press.

Durbin, E. F. M. (1949) *Problems of Economic Planning*, London: Routledge & Kegan Paul.

Durkheim, É. (1928) *Socialism and Saint-Simon*, trans. C. Sattler, Yellow Springs, Ohio: Antioch Press, 1958.

Eberle, J. (1990) 'Understanding the Revolutions in Eastern Europe', in Prins 1990.

Edwards, E. G. (1982) *Higher Education For All*, London: Spokesman Press.

Eisenstadt, S. N. (ed.) (1972) *Post-Traditional Societies*, New York: W. W. Norton.

—— (1973) *Tradition, Change and Modernity*, New York: Wiley.

—— (ed.) (1991) *Democracy and Modernity: International Colloquium on the Centenary of David Ben-Gurion*, Leiden: E. J. Brill.

—— (1992) 'The Breakdown of Communist Regimes and the Vicissitudes of Modernity', *Daedalus*, Spring: 21–42.

Ekiert, G. (1991) 'Democratization Processes in East-Central Europe: A

Theoretical Consideration', *British Journal of Political Science* 21, 3: 285–313.

Elias, N. (1939) *The Civilizing Process*, 2 vols, Vol. I, *The History of Manners* (1978); Vol. II, *State Formation and Civilization* (1982), trans. E. Jephcott, Oxford: Basil Blackwell. [Also published as one volume, Oxford: Basil Blackwell, 1994.]

—— (1987) 'The Retreat of Sociologists into the Present', *Theory, Culture & Society* 4, 2–3: 223–47.

Elsner, H. (1967) *The Technocrats: Prophets of Automation*, Syracuse, NY: Syracuse University Press.

Engelberg, S. (1990) 'Poland's Jewish Uproar, But No Jews', *New York Times*, 17 September.

Enzensberger, H. (1991) 'Ways of Walking: A Postscript to Utopia', in R. Blackburn (ed.) *After the Fall: The Failure of Communism and the Future of Socialism*, London: Verso.

Féher, F., Heller, A. and Markus, G. (1983) *Dictatorship over Needs*, Oxford: Oxford University Press.

Filmer, P., Phillipson, M. and Silverman, D. (eds) (1972) *New Directions in Sociological Theory*, London: Collier-Macmillan.

Finer, H. (1923) *Representative Government and a Parliament of Industry: A Study of the German Federal Economic Council*, London: George Allen & Unwin.

Floud, J. E. (1971) 'A Critique of Bell', *Survey* 17, 1: 25–37.

Frank, A. G. (1990) 'Revolution in Eastern Europe: Lessons for Democratic Social Movements (and Socialists?)', *Third World Quarterly* 12: 36–52.

Frankel, E. (1990) *Deutschland und die Westlichen Demokratien*, Frankfurt: Suhrkamp.

Frederick, J. G. (ed.) (1933) *For and Against Technocracy*, New York: Business Bourse.

Frisby, D. (1981) *Sociological Impressionism*, London: Heinemann.

—— (1990) 'Georg Simmel's Concept of Society', in M. Kaern, B. Phillips and R. Cohen (eds) *Georg Simmel and Contemporary Sociology*, Dordrecht: Kluwer Academic Publishers.

Frisby, D. and Sayer, G. (1986) *Society*, New York: Ellis Horwood Ltd.

Fukuyama, F. (1992) *The End of History and the Last Man*, New York: Free Press.

Furet, F. (1981) *Interpreting the French Revolution*, trans. E. Forster, Cambridge: Cambridge University Press.

—— (1982) *Rethinking the French Revolution*, trans. J. Mandelbaum, Chicago: University of Chicago Press.

—— (1990) 'From 1789 to 1917 and 1989', *Encounter*, September: 3–7.

Gadamer, H. G. (1975) *Truth and Method*, trans. G. Barden and J. Cumming, New York: Seabury Press.

—— (1976) *Philosophical Hermeneutics*, trans. and ed. D. E. Linge, Berkeley: University of California Press.

—— (1988) 'On the Circle of Understanding', in *Hermeneutics versus Science?*, trans., ed. and introduced by J. M. Connolly and T. Keutner, Notre Dame, Ind.: University of Notre Dame Press.

Garton Ash, T. (1989) *The Uses of Adversity: Essays on the Fate of Central Europe*, Cambridge: Granta Books/Penguin Books.

—— (1990) *We, the People: The Revolution of '89*, Cambridge: Granta Books/Penguin Books.

Gay, P. (1969) *Weimar Culture: The Outsider as Insider*, Harmondsworth: Penguin Books.

Gellner, E. (1968) 'The New Idealism', in I. Lakatos and A. Musgrave (eds) *Problems in the Philosophy of Science*, Amsterdam: Van Nostrand.

Geremek, B. (1990) 'Between Hope and Despair', *Daedalus*, Winter: 91–109.

Gouldner, A. (1979) *The Future of the Intellectuals and the Rise of the New Class*, New York: Seabury Press.

Grebing, H. (1969) *Linksradikalismus gleich Rechtsradikalismus: Eine Falsche Gleichung*, Stuttgart: Athenaeum/Droste.

Grilli di Cortona, P. (1991) 'From Communism to Democracy: Re-thinking Regime Change in Hungary and Czechoslovakia', *International Social Science Journal* 128: 315–30.

Grove, J. W. (1980) 'Science as Technology: Aspects of a Potent Myth', *Minerva* 8, 2: 293–312.

Gurvitch, G. (1949) 'La Technocratie: est-elle inévitable?', in G. Gurvitch (ed.) *Industrialisation et technocratie*, Paris: Librairie Armand Colin.

Habermas, J. (1971) 'Technology and Science as "Ideology" ', in *Toward a Rational Society: Student Protest, Science and Politics*, trans. J. J. Shapiro, London: Heinemann.

—— (1974) *Theory and Practice*, trans. J. Viertel, London: Heinemann.

—— (1976) 'The Analytical Theory of Science and Dialectics', in T. W. Adorno, H. Albert, R. Dahrendorf, J. Habermas, H. Pilot and K. Popper, *The Positivist Dispute in German Sociology*, trans. G. Adey and D. Frisby, London: Heinemann.

—— (1984) *Theory of Communicative Action*, trans. T. McCarthy, Vol. I, Boston: Beacon Press.

—— (1987a) *Theory of Communicative Action*, trans. T. McCarthy, Vol. II, Boston: Beacon Press.

—— (1987b) *The Philosophical Discourse of Modernity*, trans. F. Lawrence, Cambridge, Mass.: MIT Press.

—— (1991) 'What Does Socialism Mean Today? The Revolutions of Recuperation and the Need for New Thinking', in R. Blackburn (ed.) *After the Fall: The Failure of Communisim and the Future of Socialism*, London: Verso.

Halliday, F. (1990) 'The Ends of Cold War', *New Left Review* 180: 5–23.

Halsey, A. H., Floud, J. and Anderson, C. A. (eds) (1961) *Education, Economy and Society*, Glencoe, Ill.: Free Press.

Hawthorn, G. (1976) *Enlightenment and Despair: A History of Sociology*, Cambridge: Cambridge University Press.

Heidegger, M. (1927) *Being and Time*, trans. J. Macquarrie and E. Robinson, New York: Harper & Row, 1977.

Held, D. (ed.) (1993) *Prospects for Democracy: North, South, East, West*, Cambridge: Polity Press.

Heller, A. (1990) 'Hermeneutics as a Social Science', in *Can Modernity Survive?*, Cambridge: Polity Press.

Herf, J. (1984) *Reactionary Modernism: Technology, Culture and Politics in Weimar and the Third Reich*, Cambridge: Cambridge University Press.

Hessen, B. (1931) 'The Social and Economic Roots of Newton's *Principia*', in N. I. Bukharin, B. Hessen, A. F. Joffe, M. Rubinstein, B. Zavadovsky, E. Colman, N. I. Vavilov and W. T. Mitkewich, *Science at the Cross-Roads*, London: Frank Cass, 1971.

Hill, R. G. (1992) 'Revolutions Waiting to Happen? An Analysis of the Revolutions of 1989', paper presented to the annual conference of the British Sociological Association, University of Kent, Canterbury, April.

Hirschfeld, G. (ed.) (1984) *Exile in Britain: Refugees from Hitler's Germany*, Leamington Spa: Berg Publishers (for the German Historical Institute, London).

Hirschman, A. O. (1970) *Exit, Voice and Loyalty*, Cambridge, Mass.: Harvard University Press.

Hirst, P. (1991) 'The State, Civil Society and the Collapse of Soviet Communism', *Economy and Society* 20: 217–42.

Hoch, P. K. (1985) 'No Utopia: Refugee Scholars in Britain', *History Today*, November: 53–6.

Holmes, L. (1993) *The End of Communist Power: Anti-Corruption Campaigns and Legitimation Crisis*, Cambridge: Polity Press.

Horkheimer, M. and Adorno, T. (1944) *Dialectic of Enlightenment*, trans. J. Cumming, New York: Herder & Herder, 1972.

Howard, M. (1990) 'Impressions from a Journey in Central Europe', *London Review of Books*, 25 October: 3–6.

Hughes, H. S. (1959) *Consciousness and Society: The Reorientation of European Social Thought, 1890–1930*, New York: Knopf.

—— (1975) *The Sea Change: The Migration of Social Thought, 1930–65*, New York: McGraw-Hill.

Huntington, S., Crozier, M. and Watanuki, J. (1975) *The Crisis of Democracy*, New York: New York University Press.

Jackson, J. O. (1992) 'Can This Marriage Be Saved?', *Time*, 6 July.

Janos, A. C. (1991) 'Social Science, Communism and the Dynamics of Political Change', *World Politics* 44, 1: 81–112.

Jerschina, J. and Górniak, J. (1992) 'Social Consciousness and the Transformation of Post-Communism in Poland', unpublished typescript.

Jowitt, K. (1991) 'The Leninist Extinction', in D. Chirot (ed.) *The Crisis of Leninism and the Decline of the Left: The Revolutions of 1989*, Seattle: University of Washington Press.

—— (1992a) 'The Leninist Legacy', in Banac 1992.

—— (1992b) *New World Disorder: The Leninist Extinction*, Berkeley and Los Angeles: University of California Press.

Judt, T., et al. (1990) 'Post-Communist Eastern Europe: A Survey of Opinion', *East European Politics and Societies* 4, 2: 153–207.

Kant, I. (1787) *Critique of Pure Reason*, trans. N. K. Smith, New York: Macmillan, 1973.

REFERENCES

—— (1788) *Critique of Practical Reason*, trans. L. W. Beck, New York: Macmillan, 1985.

—— (1790) *The Critique of Judgement*, trans. J. Creed Meredith, Oxford: Clarendon Press, 1952.

Karl, T. L. and Schmitter, P. C. (1991) 'Modes of Transition in Latin America, Southern and Eastern Europe', *International Social Science Journal* 128: 269–84.

Kautsky, K. (1902) *The Social Revolution*, trans. A. M. and M. W. Simons, Chicago: Charles H. Kerr.

Keane, J. (1988a) *Democracy and Civil Society*, London: Verso.

—— (ed.) (1988b) *Civil Society and the State: New European Perspectives*, London: Verso.

Kilminster, R. (1992) 'Theory', in M. Haralambos (ed.) *Developments in Sociology*, Ormskirk: Causeway Press.

Kilminster, R. and Varcoe, I. (1992) 'Sociology, Postmodernity and Exile: An Interview with Zygmunt Bauman', in Bauman 1992a.

King, M. D. (1968) 'Science and the Professional Dilemma', in J. Gould (ed.) *Penguin Survey of the Social Sciences*, Harmondsworth: Penguin Books.

Kołakowski, L. (1992) 'Amidst Moving Ruins', *Daedalus*, Spring: 43–56.

Kolerska-Bobińska, L. (1988) 'Social Interests, Egalitarian Attitudes, and the Change of Economic Interests', *Social Research* 55: 111–39.

—— (n.d.) 'Social Interests and Their Political Representation: Poland during Transition', photocopy.

Konrád, G. and Szelényi, I. (1979) *The Intellectuals on the Road to Class Power: A Sociological Study of the Role of the Intelligentsia*, New York: Harcourt Brace Jovanovich.

Korzeniowski, K. (1992) 'Szanse idei społeczeństwa otwartego', *Nowa Europa*, 24–6 July.

Kovacheva, S. (1992) *The Student Movement in Post-Communist Bulgaria*, unpublished MA sociology dissertation, Central European University, Prague.

Kraemer, E. (1933) *Was ist Technokratie?*, Berlin: K. Wolff.

Kuisel, R. F. (1967) *Ernest Mercier: French Technocrat*, Berkeley and Los Angeles: University of California Press.

—— (1973) 'Technocrats and Public Economic Policy: From the Third to the Fourth Republic', *Journal of European Economic History* 5: 53–9.

—— (1981) *Capitalism and the State in Modern France: Renovation and Economic Management in the Twentieth Century*, Cambridge: Cambridge University Press.

Kumar, K. (1988) 'Twentieth-Century Revolutions in Historical Perspective', in *The Rise of Modern Society*, Oxford: Basil Blackwell.

—— (1992a) 'The Revolutions of 1989: Socialism, Capitalism and Democracy', *Theory and Society* 21: 309–56.

—— (1992b) 'The 1989 Revolutions and the Idea of Europe', *Political Studies* 40: 439 61.

—— (1993) 'Civil Society: An Inquiry into the Usefulness of an Historical Term', *The British Journal of Sociology* 44, 4: 375–95.

Kuran, T. (1991) 'Now Out of Never: The Element of Surprise in the East European Revolution of 1989', *World Politics* 44: 7–48.

Kurczewska, J. (1992a) 'The Polish Intelligentsia: Retiring from the Stage', *The Polish Sociological Bulletin* 32, 2 (98): 149–58.

—— (1992b) 'The Polish Middle Class at the Close of the Eighties', *The Polish Sociological Bulletin* 32, 3–4 (98): 298–302.

Lasswell, H. D. (1972) *On Political Sociology*, ed. with introduction by D. Marwick, Chicago: University of Chicago Press.

Lavigne, M. (ed.) (1992) *The Soviet Union and Eastern Europe in the Global Economy*, Cambridge: Cambridge University Press.

Layton, E. T. (1971) *The Revolt of the Engineers: Social Responsibility and the American Engineering Profession*, Cleveland: Case Western Reserve University Press.

Lefebvre, H. (1967) *Positions: Contre les technocrates*, Paris: Gouthier.

Leibniz, G. W. von (1840) *Monadology*, trans. with notes by R. Latta, London: Oxford University Press, 1968.

Lenin, V. I. (1918) 'The Immediate Tasks of the Soviet Government', *Izvestia*, 28 April, trans. in V. I. Lenin, *Selected Works*, 11, Moscow: Foreign Languages Publishing House, 1947.

Lévinas, E. (1989) 'Ethics as First Philosophy', in S. Hand (ed.) *The Lévinas Reader*, Oxford and Cambridge, Mass.: Basil Blackwell.

Levine, D. (1967) 'Introduction' to *Georg Simmel on Individuality and Social Forms*, trans. and ed. D. Levine, Chicago: University of Chicago Press.

—— (1991) 'Simmel as Educator', *Theory, Culture & Society* [special issue on Simmel] 8, 3: 99–117.

Lewin, K. (1921) *Die Sozialisierung des Taylorsystems*, Berlin: Klemm.

Lewin, M. (1989) *The Gorbachev Phenomenon: An Historical Interpretation*, London: Hutchinson Radius.

Lewis, B. (1975) *History Remembered, Recovered, Invented*, Princeton, NJ: Princeton University Press.

Lijphart, A. (1991) 'Presidentialism and Majoritarian Democracy: Theoretical Observation', in G. Szoboszlai (ed.) *Democracy and Political Transformation. Theories and East-Central European Realities*, Budapest: Hungarian Political Science Association: 75–93.

Linz, J. J. (1990a) 'The Perils of Presidentialism', *Journal of Democracy* 1, 1: 51–69.

—— (1990b) 'The Virtues of Parliamentarism', *Journal of Democracy* 1, 4: 84–91.

Linz, J. J. and Stephan, A. (1992) 'Political Identities and Electoral Sequences: Spain, the Soviet Union and Yugoslavia', *Daedalus*, Spring: 123–39.

Lubbe, H. (1991) *Freiheit statt Emanzipationszwang: Die Liberalen Traditionen und das Ende der Marxistischen Illusionen*, Zurich: Edition Interfrom.

Lysis [E. Letailleur] (1919) *Vers la démocratie nouvelle*, Paris: Payot.

Maier, C. S. (1970) 'Between Taylorism and Technocracy: European Ideologies and the Vision of Industrial Productivity in the 1920s', *Journal of Contemporary History* 5: 27–61.

—— (1975) *Re-casting Bourgeois Europe: Stablization in France, Germany and Italy in the Decade after World War I*, Princeton, NJ: Princeton University Press.

—— (ed.) (1987) *Changing Boundaries of the Political*, Cambridge: Cambridge University Press.

Mann, M. (1986) *The Sources of Social Power*, Vol. 1, *A history of power from the beginning to A.D. 1760*, Cambridge: Cambridge University Press.

Mann, T. (1947) 'Deutschland und die Deutschen', in H. Kunzke (ed.) *Thomas Mann: Essays*, Band 2, *Politik*, Frankfurt: Fischer, 1977.

Mannheim, K. (1940) *Man and Society in an Age of Reconstruction*, London: Routledge & Kegan Paul, 1980.

Marcuse, H. (1941) 'Some Implications of Modern Technology', *Studies in Philosophy and Social Science* 9: 414–39. (Also in A. Arato and E. Gebhardt (eds) *The Essential Frankfurt School Reader*, New York: Urizen Books, 1978.)

—— (1966) *One-Dimensional Man*, Boston: Beacon Press.

Martin, D. and Irvine, J. (1986) *An International Comparison of Government Funding of Academically Related Research*, Falmer: Science Policy Research Unit.

Marx, K. (1867) *Capital*, Vol. I, trans. E and C. Paul, London: George Allen & Unwin, 1938.

—— (1894) *Capital*, Vol. III, trans. S. Moore and E. Aveling, London: Lawrence & Wishart, 1972.

Marx, K. and Engels, F. (1848) *The Communist Manifesto*, Chicago: Charles H. Kerr, 1888.

Mason, E. S. (1931) 'Saint-Simonianism and the Rationalization of Industry', *Quarterly Journal of Economics* 45: 640–83.

Matteucci, N. (1983) 'Democrazia e autocrazia nel pensiero di Norberto Bobbio', in *Per una teoria generale della politica – Scritti dedicatti a Norberto Bobbio*, Florence: Passigli Editori.

Millar, P. (1994) 'Exit Pole?', *Sunday Times Magazine*, 13 November: 56–64.

Miłosz, C. (1990) 'The State of Europe: Christmas Eve, 1989', *Granta* 30: 164–5.

Misztal, B. (1992) 'Must Eastern Europe Follow the Latin American Way?', *European Journal of Sociology* 33: 151–79.

Moellendorff, W. (1932) *Konservativer Sozialismus*, Hamburg: Hanseatische Verlaganstalt.

Mokrzycki, E. (1990) 'The Legacy of Real Socialism: Group Interests and the Search for a New Utopia', paper presented at the VIIth Conference of Polish Sociology, Toruń.

—— (1992) 'The Legacy of Real Socialism: Group Interests and the Search for a New Utopia', in W. C. Connors and P. Płoszajski (eds) *Escape from Socialism: The Polish Route*, Warsaw: IFiS Publishers.

Montesquieu, C. (1748) *The Spirit of the Laws*, trans. T. Nugent, Cambridge: Cambridge University Press, 1989.

Moore, Jr., B. (1966) *Social Origins of Dictatorship and Democracy:*

Lord and Peasant in the Making of the Modern World, Boston: Beacon Press.

—— (1972) *Reflections on the Causes of Human Misery*, London: Allen Lane, Penguin Press.

Müller, K. (1992) ' "Modernizing" Eastern Europe: Theoretical Problems and Political Dilemmas', *European Journal of Sociology* 33: 109–50.

Needham, J. (1937) *Integrative Levels: A Revaluation of the Idea of Progress* (The Herbert Spencer Lecture), Oxford: Clarendon Press.

Neumann, S. (1949) 'The International Civil War', *World Politics* 1: 333–50.

Nichols, T. (1969) *Ownership, Control and Ideology: An Enquiry into Certain Aspects of Modern Business Ideology*, London: George Allen & Unwin.

Nietzsche, F. (1895) *Thus Spake Zarathustra*, trans. with Introduction by R. J. Hollindale, Harmondsworth: Penguin Books, 1972.

Nove, A. (1983) *The Economics of Feasible Socialism*, London: George Allen & Unwin.

O'Donnell, G., Schmitter, P. C. and Whitehead, L. (eds) (1986) *Transitions from Authoritarian Rule*, 4 vols, Baltimore: Johns Hopkins University Press.

OECD (1981) *Science and Technology Policy for the 1980s*, Paris: OECD.

—— (1984) *Science and Technology Indicators. Basic Statistical Series. Recent Results. Selected Science and Technology Indicators 1979–84*, Paris: OECD.

—— (1987) *Universities Under Scrutiny*, Paris: OECD.

—— (1988) *Science and Technology Policy Outlook*, Paris: OECD.

—— (1991) *Technology and a Changing World*, Paris: OECD.

—— (1992) *Technology and the Economy: The Key Relationships*, Paris: OECD.

Ogburn, W. F. (1932) *Social Change*, New York: Viking Press.

Osiatyński, W. (1991) 'Revolutions in Eastern Europe', *University of Chicago Law Review* 58: 823–58.

Palmer, R. R. (1970) *The Age of the Democratic Revolution*, 2 vols, Princeton, NJ: Princeton University Press.

Panitch, L. and Miliband, R. (1992) 'The New World Order and the Socialist Agenda', in R. Miliband and L. Panitch (eds) *The Socialist Register 1992: New World Order?*, London: Merlin Press.

Pelz, W. (1974) *The Scope of Understanding in Sociology: Towards a More Radical Reorientation in the Social Humanistic Sciences*, London: Routledge & Kegan Paul.

Pizzorno, A. (1980) *I soggetti del pluralismo*, Bologna: Il Mulino.

Poggi, G. (1993) *Money and the Modern Mind: Georg Simmel's Philosophy of Money*, Berkeley and Los Angeles: University of California Press.

Polanyi, M. (1951) *The Logic of Liberty*, London: Routledge & Kegan Paul.

—— (1962) 'The Republic of Science: Its Political and Economic Theory', *Minerva* 1, 1: 54–74.

Price, D. K. (1958) *Government and Science*, New York: New York University Press.

—— (1965) *The Scientific Estate*, Cambridge, Mass.: Belknap Press of Harvard University Press.

Prins, G. (ed.) (1990) *Spring in Winter: The 1989 Revolutions*, Manchester: Manchester University Press.

Przeworski, A. (1985) *Capitalism and Social Democracy*, Cambridge: Cambridge University Press.

—— (1986) 'Some Problems in the Study of the Transition to Democracy', in O'Donnell, Schmitter and Whitehead 1986, Vol. 3.

—— (1991a) 'The "East" Becomes the "South"? The "Autumn of the People" and the Future of Eastern Europe', *PS: Political Science and Politics* 24: 20–4.

—— (1991b) 'Eastern Europe: The Most Significant Event in Our Life Time?', *Sisyphus* VII: 9–17.

—— (1991c) *Democracy and the Market: Political and Economic Reforms in Eastern Europe and Latin America*, New York: Cambridge University Press.

—— (1991d) 'Economic Reforms in New Democracies: Poland in the Eastern European Perspective', *East South Systems Transformation, Working Paper no. 19*, Department of Political Science, University of Chicago: November.

Pye, L. (1990) 'Political Science and the Crisis of Authoritarianism', *American Political Science Review* 84: 5–19.

Rady, M. (1993) 'Rebels by Reputation', *Times Higher Education Supplement*, 5 March: 30.

Ramet, P. (1984) *Nationalism and Federalism in Yugoslavia, 1963–1983*, Bloomington: Indiana University Press.

Rathenau, W. (1916) *Von Kommenden Dingen*, in *Gesammelte Schriften*, III, Berlin: S. Fischer, 1918.

—— (1917) *Die Neue Wirtschaft*, in *Gesammelte Schriften*, V, Berlin: S. Fischer, 1918.

Raymond, A. (1933) *What is Technocracy?*, New York: Whittlesey House.

Resar, K. (1935) *Technokratie, Weltwirtschaftskrise und Ihre Endgültige Beseitung: Physikalische Quellenforschung und Zielsetzung der Technokratie*, Vienna: C. Barth.

Rice, E. E. (ed.) (1991) *Revolution and Counter-Revolution*, Oxford: Basil Blackwell.

Riggs, F. W. (1988) 'The Survival of Presidentialism in America: Para-Constitutional Practice', *International Political Science Review* 9, 4: 247–78.

Rorty, R. (1989) *Contingency, Irony and Solidarity*, Cambridge: Cambridge University Press.

Rousseau, J.-J. (1968) *The Social Contract and Discourses*, ed., trans. and introduced by G. D. H. Cole, New York: Dutton Everyman's Library.

Rustow, D. A. (1990) 'Democracy: A Global Revolution?', *Foreign Affairs* 69: 75–91.

Saint-Simon, C. H. de (1819–20) *L'Organisateur*, Paris: Éditions Anthropos, 2, 1966.

REFERENCES

—— (1821) *Du système industriel*, Paris: Éditions Anthropos, 3, 1966.

—— (1825) *De l'organisation sociale*, Paris: Éditions Anthropos, 5, 1966.

Sakwa, R. (1990) *Gorbachev and His Reforms, 1985–1990*, Hemel Hempstead: Philip Allan.

Schama, S. (1989) *Citizens: A Chronicle of the French Revolution*, London: Penguin Books.

Schmitt, C. B. (ed.) (1990) *The Cambridge History of Renaissance Philosophy*, Cambridge: Cambridge Universty Press.

Schmitter, P. C. (1991) 'The Consolidation of Democracy and the Choice of Institutions', *East South Systems Transformation, Working Paper no. 7*, Department of Political Science, University of Chicago: September.

Schopflin, G. (1990) 'The End of Communism in Eastern Europe', *International Affairs* 66: 3–16.

Schöpflin, G. (1991) 'Conservatism and Hungary's Transition', *Problems of Communism* XL, 1–2, January–April: 60–8.

Scott, H. et al. (1933) *Introduction to Technocracy*, New York: John Day Company.

Seligman, A. (1992) *The Idea of Civil Society*, New York: Free Press.

Seton-Watson, H. (1972) 'Revolution in Eastern Europe', in J. P. Vatikiotis (ed.) *Revolution in the Middle East and Other Case Studies*, London: George Allen & Unwin.

Shanin, T. (1990) 'The Question of Socialism: A Development Failure or an Ethical Defeat?', *History Workshop Journal* 30: 68–74.

Shils, E. (1972) *The Intellectuals and the Powers and Other Essays*, Chicago: University of Chicago Press.

—— (1975) 'Center and Periphery', in *Center and Periphery: Essays in Macrosociology*, Chicago: University of Chicago Press.

Shoup, P. (1968) *Communism and the Yugoslav National Question*, New York: Columbia University Press.

Simmel, G. (1900a) *Philosophie des Geldes*, Frankfurt: Suhrkamp, 1988.

—— (1900b) *Philosophy of Money*, trans. T. Bottomore and D. Frisby, London: Routledge & Kegan Paul, 1978.

—— (1908) 'The Problem of Style', trans. M. Ritter, *Theory, Culture & Society* 8, 3, 1991: 63–71.

—— (1911) 'Der Begriff und die Tragödie der Kultur', in *Das Individuelle Gesetz: Philosophische Excurse*, ed. M. Landmann, Frankfurt: Suhrkamp, 1968; also available in translation as 'On the Concept and the Tragedy of Culture', in G. Simmel, *The Conflict in Modern Culture and Other Essays*, ed. and trans. P. Etzkorn, New York: Teachers Press, 1968.

—— (1926) *Der Konflikt des Modernen Kultur*, Leipzig: Duncker & Humblot.

Skinner, Q. (1978) *The Foundations of Modern Political Thought*, Cambridge: Cambridge University Press.

—— (1981) *Machiavelli*, Oxford: Oxford University Press.

Skocpol, T. (1979) *States and Social Revolutions: A Comparative Analysis of France, Russia and China*, Cambridge: Cambridge University Press.

REFERENCES

Smelser, N. J. (1963) *Theory of Collective Behaviour*, New York: Free Press of Glencoe.
Sorel, A. (1885) *Europe and the French Revolution*, trans. and ed. A. Cobban and J. W. Hunt, London: Fontana, 1969.
Strauss, L. (1958) *Thoughts on Machiavelli*, New York: Free Press.
—— (1989) *The Rebirth of Classical Political Rationalism*, Chicago: University of Chicago Press.
Suleiman, E. N. (1977) 'The Myth of Technical Expertise: Selection, Organization and Leadership', *Comparative Politics* 10: 137–58.
Szemplińska, E. (1993) 'A Predatory Plankton', *Polityka*, 6 March.
Talmon, J. L. (1960) *The Origins of Totalitarian Democracy*, New York: Praeger.
Taylor, C. (1979) *Hegel and the Modern Society*, Cambridge: Cambridge University Press.
—— (1989) *Sources of the Self: The Making of the Learned Identity*, Cambridge, Mass.: Harvard University Press.
Taylor, F. W. (1920) 'Testimony before the Special Committee of the House of Representatives, January 1917', *Bulletin of the Taylor Society*, June–August: 102.
Thorns, D. C. (ed.) (1976) *New Directions in Sociology*, Newton Abbot: David & Charles (Publishers) Ltd.
Tinbergen, J. (1968) 'Planning, Economic (Western Europe)', in *International Encyclopaedia of the Social Sciences*, Vol. 12, New York: Macmillan and The Free Press.
Tocqueville, A. de (1835) *Democracy in America*, trans. H. Reeve, London: Oxford University Press, 1953.
—— (1959) *The European Revolution and Correspondence with Gobineau*, ed. and trans. John Lukács, New York: Doubleday Anchor.
Toulmin, S. (1972) 'The Historical Background to the Anti-Science Movement', *Civilization and Science: In Conflict or Collaboration?*, a CIBA foundation symposium, North-Holland: Elsevier: Excerpta Medica.
—— (1990) *Cosmopolis: The Hidden Agenda of Modernity*, New York: Free Press.
Trevor-Roper, H. (1989) 'Europe's New Order', *The Independent Magazine*, 30 December: 14.
Vaihinger, H. (1924) *The Philosophy of 'As If': A System of Theoretical, Practical and Religious Fictions of Mankind*, trans. C. K. Ogden, London: Kegan Paul.
Vanous, J. (1982) 'Eastern European Economic Slow-Down', *Problems of Communism*, July–August: 1–19.
Veblen, T. (1921) *The Engineers and the Price System*, New York: Viking Press, 1954.
Wallerstein, I. (1989) 'The French Revolution as a World-Historical Event', *Social Research* 56: 33–52.
Weigel, G. (1992) *The Final Revolution: The Resistance Church and the Collapse of Communism*, Oxford: Oxford University Press.
Weitman, S. (1992) 'Thinking the Revolutions of 1989', *The British Journal of Sociology* 43, 1: 11–24.

REFERENCES

Werskey, G. (1971) 'British Scientists and "Outsider" Politics, 1931–1945', *Science Studies* 1: 67–85.

—— (1978) *The Visible College: A Collective Biography of British Scientists and Socialists in the 1930s*, London: Allen Lane.

Wiatr, J. J. (1992) 'Will Democracy Win in East-Central Europe?', in *Four Essays on East European Democratic Transformation*, Warsaw: Scholar Agency.

Woldring, J. (1986) *Karl Mannheim: The Development of His Thought*, Assen/Maastricht: Van Gorcum.

Wolff, K. (ed.) (1950) *The Sociology of Georg Simmel*, Glencoe, Ill.: Free Press.

Wood, N. (1959) *Communism and British Intellectuals*, London: Gollancz.

Woodward, S. L. (1992) 'The Future of the Yugoslav States', in D. Clark (ed.) *United States Relationships with Central and Eastern Europe*, Queenstown: Aspen Institute.

Wutke, E. R. (1964) 'Technocracy: It Failed to Save the Nation', unpublished PhD thesis, University of Missouri.

Zagórski, K. (1991) 'Comments on Social Structure and Politics', *Sisyphus* VII: 73–8.

Zagórski, Z. (n.d.) 'Rodząca się klasa średnia w Polsce' (The Emerging Middle Class in Poland), unpublished typescript.

Ziółkowski, J. (1990) 'The Roots, Branches and Blossoms of Solidarnosc', in Prins 1990.

Žižek, S. (1990) 'Eastern Europe's Republics of Gilead', *New Left Review* 183: 50–62.

NAME INDEX

SUBJECT INDEX

SUBJECT INDEX

historical progress, modernity and 28
historicity 121, 122
Holocaust: Bauman on 221–3, 231–3, 240; as modern phenomenon 231–4
Hungary 155, 156, 189, 203, 207, 210

intellectualization of existence, money and 52–3
intellectuals: Eastern European, social role of 7–8, 18, 166–83; free-floating 166, 169; German 42, 45, 51, 79; migration and 10; modernity and 225, 229; post-modernity and 229, 231; refugees in Britain 5–8; retreat of authority and 107–8; revolution and 132, 141; socialist 227–8; technocracy and 69, 78–80, 90; Voice and Exit options 168, 177, 178, 180; *see also* intelligentsia, Polish
intelligentsia, Polish 173–4, 199; decline of 189–90, 191, 192, 194; middle class and 196–7
interpretation, modernity and 105–22; community of interpreters 108, 111, 120; *interpretanda* 105, 108–13, 116; moral 118, 119
'inverted J-curve' theory of revolution 133–4
Italian Fascists 92

Jacobin orientations 35, 37
Jews: assimilatory drive and 221, 223, 233–4; Holocaust and 221–3, 231–3, 240; Soviet intellectuals 177

knowledge: de-centring of 114, 115, 116, 119; modernity and relativity of 47–9, 50; as power 92–3, 225; sociology of 45
knowledge class: Eastern Europe 190, 197, 199
Kremlin watchers 175

Kultura (magazine) 173–4

'legislative bustle' modernity and 224–5
liberalism 195, 228, 233, 239
liberty and equality, modernity and tensions between 31, 35
logos and *mythos* 27–8
Lutheran clergy: East Germany 174

man, emancipation of 30
marginality 224
market socialism 155, 156, 159–60, 165
Marxism 3, 4, 8, 139, 171, 228, 241–2
mass action 140–1
mass media and 1989 revolutions 145–6
materialism, money and 56
means–ends rationality 86
means/goals chains, money and 52–3, 60, 61, 63
means testing 221
middle class, new: Eastern Europe 19, 184–200
modernity, aspects of, in Simmel's *Philosophie des Geldes* 12, 42–65; advanced money economy 52–8; as epiphany 45–51; prevalence of alienation 58–65
modernity, omnivorous 14–15, 102–23; choosing the moral self 113–18; conclusion 120–2; eclipse of time 103–5; interpretation 105–7; morality, culture and science 118–20; retreat of authority 107–8; world according to one person 108–13
modernity in Bauman's writings 215, 223, 235–6, 240–1; Holocaust as a modern phenomenon 231–4; post-modernity and 224–31; structuring and 217
modernity and democracy, cultural programme of 11, 25–41;

282

radical strategy of economic
reform 204–5
ratio/intellectus distinction 114–15
reality, modernity and de-
substantialization of 47, 49–50
Redressement Français 87
'refolution' 128
refugee intellectuals in Britain 5–8
religious authorities and dissent:
Eastern Europe 173–4
religious fundamentalism: Eastern
Europe 203, 209–10
repression 220, 226, 230
revolution(s): communist 131,
134–5, 138–9; of 1848 141–2;
German 87; Great *see* Great
Revolutions; great and little
traditions 137–8; 'slow' 162;
violence and 128, 144; *see also*
revolutions of 1989
revolutions of 1989 in East-
Central Europe 16–17, 127–53,
154; *annus mirabilis* 127–32;
continuity and discontinuity
145–51; revolutionary tradition
and 16–17, 137–45; theories of
revolution and 132–6
rights and majoritarian decisions,
tensions between 33, 35
Roman Catholic church: Poland
173–4, 209–10
Romania 141, 144
rule of law 33
Russia 164, 165, 201–2; Revolution
(1917) 131, 135, 138–9

science and technology 27, 28, 114;
eclipse of time and 103–4; faith
in 74–6; fear of, and strains of
technocratic culture 76–80;
morality, culture and 118–20;
'normal' 181; 'swing effect' and
80; technocracy and democratic
politics 12–14, 66–101
scientism 5, 81, 84–6, 89–90, 91, 93
scientists 76, 80, 83–4, 114, 177–8
secularization, money and 56–7
seduction, consumer society and
220, 226, 230

Silesia 207–8
'social mobilization' 36
'social question', revolution and
142–3
social theory, technocracy and 88
socialism 191; Bauman on 217–18,
227–8, 240–1; capitalism and
228, 240–1; with markets 155,
156, 159–60, 165; socialist
economy in Europe 154–65
sociation process 43, 44
society concept 9, 43–4
sociology in Britain 2–10
Soviet Union 78, 135, 136, 147–8,
177–8, 208; *see also* Russia
specialism and general cultivation,
conflict between 79
speculation, money and 63
state: civil society and 31, 35–7, 38,
39; post-modernity and retreat
of 230, 236–7; welfare 34, 39, 204
structuralism 2, 4, 7
structuring 216–17, 219
students: Eastern Europe 171–2
subject: interpretation and 108–13,
119; subject/object relationship,
modernity and 45–7, 51, 58–9

techniciens 71–2, 90
technocracy and democratic
politics 12–14, 66–101, 231;
conclusion 89–93; cultural
politics and 67–71; faith in
science 74–6; fear of science and
strains of technocratic culture
76–80; from philosopher-kings
to rule by managers 86–9;
scientism 84–6; technocratic
thinking and ideologies 80–4; are
technocrats a class? 71–2;
technocrats' ideology 72–4
technology *see* science and
technology
'tele-revolutions' 145
tempo of existence, money and
53–4
theoretical competition 3
time, modernity and eclipse of
103–5